Educational Folly

Educational Folly

Teacher Well-Being and the Chaos of American Schooling

Lisa M. Gonsalves

ROWMAN & LITTLEFIELD
Lanham • Boulder • New York • London

Published by Rowman & Littlefield
An imprint of The Rowman & Littlefield Publishing Group, Inc.
4501 Forbes Boulevard, Suite 200, Lanham, Maryland 20706
www.rowman.com

86-90 Paul Street, London EC2A 4NE, United Kingdom

Copyright © 2023 by Lisa M. Gonsalves

All rights reserved. No part of this book may be reproduced in any form or by any electronic or mechanical means, including information storage and retrieval systems, without written permission from the publisher, except by a reviewer who may quote passages in a review.

British Library Cataloguing in Publication Information Available

Library of Congress Cataloging-in-Publication Data

Names: Gonsalves, Lisa, author.
Title: Educational folly: teacher well-being and the chaos of American schooling / Lisa M. Gonsalves.
Description: Lanham: Rowman & Littlefield, [2023] | Includes bibliographical references. | Summary: "Gonsalves offers a long overdue and comprehensive examination of public education reform, specifically, its impact on high need schools"—Provided by publisher.
Identifiers: LCCN 2023009953 (print) | LCCN 2023009954 (ebook) | ISBN 9781475855814 (cloth) | ISBN 9781475855821 (paperback) | ISBN 9781475855838 (epub)
Subjects: LCSH: Teachers—Mental health—United States. | Teachers—Job stress—United States. | Educational change—United States. | Children with social disabilities—Education—United States. | Educational psychology—United States.
Classification: LCC LB2840 .G646 2023 (print) | LCC LB2840 (ebook) | DDC 370.973—dc23/eng/20230419
LC record available at https://lccn.loc.gov/2023009953
LC ebook record available at https://lccn.loc.gov/2023009954

To the courageous and committed teachers who have completed the Teach Next Year Teaching Residency Program. I have learned so much from their passion, their sense of responsibility, and their devotion to their students, their schools, and themselves.

Contents

Foreword	ix
Preface	xiii
Acknowledgments	xv
Introduction	xvii

PART I: CHALLENGING ASPECTS OF AMERICAN SCHOOLING	**1**
1 So, You Want to Teach in a High-Needs School?: Family, Friends, and the Media	3
2 The Impact of Accountability Systems on Teachers and School Culture	15
3 Students: The Impact of Social-Emotional Struggles, Trauma, and Learning Difficulties on Classroom Behavior	29
4 What Ails the Children?	
5 Cognitive Complexity and the Need for Competence	61

PART II: TEACHER HEALTH AND WELL-BEING	**81**
6 How Under-Resourced Schools Thwart Teachers' Basic Human Needs	85
7 Emotions and Cognitive Dissonance: The Psychological Pain of Teaching	101
8 Colleagues and the Need for Relatedness in Schools	119

| 9 | Teachers of Color and White Teachers' Experiences in Schools: Different Causes, Similar Pain | 137 |

PART III: REFORMING URBAN SCHOOLS FOR TEACHER AND STUDENT WELL-BEING — **155**

10	Teacher Preparation: What Education Can Learn from the Field of Nursing	159
11	School Culture and Environment: More Lessons from the Field of Nursing	173
12	Nurses, Teachers, and Clinical Microsystems	185

Bibliography — 201

Foreword

How can the teacher's selfhood become a legitimate topic in education and in our public dialogues about reform?—Parker J. Palmer

Democracy is a fragile thing. It rests on and is inextricably intertwined with the education of the governed. In the end, the democratic ideal is not uniformly seen in every community and, certainly, education itself varies in every community and for every person. Much is dependent on the quality of the teaching and learning in public schools.

One can argue that teachers play a crucial role in passing democracy from one generation to the next. I can offer my own professional experience as an example of the outcomes that Dr. Gonsalves focuses on in this book. In 1967 I was assigned to a second-grade classroom in the Chicago Public Schools (CPS) on the west side of the city. I taught in a mobile unit placed in the playground of a K–6 school. I had no teaching credentials and hadn't been in a second-grade classroom since I was a second grader in a Chicago school.

I was smart, well-educated, and wanted to teach. I also thought I could change the world, or at least, teach the students well. But I had no one to help me; no one to support me in dealing with the exhausting stress and my many early classroom failures. Within seven years I had earned my full teaching credentials, had taken several graduate reading classes, and been transferred twice, but I still quit. I never taught in K–8 again.

I left teaching with a burning desire to understand how to better prepare teachers for success and happiness in their jobs. This led me to earn my PhD in curriculum and to teach for fourteen years in a teacher preparation program at a Chicago university. I went on to be the Dean of the Mary Lou Fulton Teachers College at Arizona State University. In all that time, and in every school I have taught, I have seen public school teachers lose status, be hamstrung by rules and, to my great shock and horror, be vilified and ridiculed.

Dr. Lisa Gonsalves has chronicled these struggles and offers an informed view, over time, of the conditions that teachers continue to endure in public schools. She also provides deep, thoughtful, and perceptive analyses of the professional and personal impact reform policies have had on teachers. Refreshingly clear and focused, her writing is based upon an entire career of observing classrooms and collaborating with and listening to teachers.

It is difficult to imagine, and heartbreaking to realize, that all the seemingly common-sense reforms have stalled or failed since I was a teacher in Chicago, and as Dr. Gonsalves points out, the "current school structures and mandated educational policies are still crippling teachers." A needed and welcomed voice, Dr. Gonsalves, talks about the actual well-being of the teacher and the student. Her insight that school reform has eroded the position of the teacher as a professional educator is especially significant. Humanizing the thousands of people who teach reveals that many are stressed, demoralized, and disappointed. It is no secret that because of difficult working conditions and low pay, it has become almost impossible to recruit teachers. The *We Are Teachers Newsletter*[1] affirms what Dr. Gonsalves emphasizes:

1. 80 percent of educators say that burnout is a serious problem.
2. 55 percent of educators now indicate that they are ready to leave the profession earlier than planned.
3. 80 percent of educators admit they are taking on more work due to unfilled job openings within their own schools.
4. 78 percent of educators say they feel symptoms of stress and depression.
5. 76 percent of teachers emphasize that lack of respect from parents and the public is a problem.

All of this results in just 10% of teachers recommending that others join the field.

Interestingly, Dr. Gonsalves talks about the central importance of justice for students and teachers. As long as I have been in education, "justice" has been at the base of everything we do. Clearly, it is a worthy goal, but it is also hard to pin down. What does justice look like in the preparation of teachers and specifically, children's learning? So much of the current dialogue about "justice" is difficult to access and steeped in incomprehensible philosophical rhetoric.

However, this book unlocks the mystery of how schools might be more just. Dr. Gonsalves has spent years in the community, lots of time in the schools, and along with her research knowledge, has built authentic relationships with school communities based on mutual respect. She uses these experiences to paint a clear picture of what just schools might look like, and what they can achieve.

As Susan Moore Johnson (2019) reminds us, "public education is a thoroughly human enterprise" (16). Democracy is also a truly human enterprise which calls up the commitment to being knowledgeable, enacting justice and a deep caring for our fellow humans. Dr. Gonsalves reminds us that all of us, educators and citizens must do better at ensuring its sustainability.

—Dr. Mari Koerner
Professor Emeritus, Mary Lou Fulton Teachers College, Arizona State University

NOTE

1. We Are Teachers, "These 2022 Teacher Shortage Statistics Prove We Need to Fix This Profession" Newsletter, June 15, 2022, https://www.weareteachers.com/teacher-shortage-statistics.

Preface

This book is about how teaching in high-poverty, low-resourced schools, many of them in urban and rural communities, hurts teachers' emotional well-being and damages their physical and mental health. Many of the current school structures and mandated educational policies in practice today are literally crippling teachers. The experience of working in some of our nation's most troubled schools is so harmful to teachers particularly because of the special calling many of them experience to teach and serve children.

When teachers are hurting, it is more difficult for them to fulfill their passion for aiding student academic, social, and emotional development. When teachers are hurting, students can't get the full impact of their educational experience. This is neither the teachers' nor the students' fault. Rather, it is the fault of educational policies that continue to ignore the rich professional knowledge, skill, and passion that teachers bring to the profession.

I conceived of, and started writing, this book before the pandemic hit. Yes, school communities struggled mightily during the pandemic, but as teachers know, the pandemic only exacerbated educational issues that have been brewing for a very long time. It is because of this fact that I do not dwell on pandemic-induced educational struggles. Each and every struggle teachers experienced during the pandemic was present before the pandemic. If anything, the pandemic only called attention to the deep dysfunction in some of our nation's schools.

I come to this work through my twenty-five years of experience working with veteran teachers in urban school systems to help prepare new, highly qualified, diverse teachers for high-needs schools. I am the director of a teaching residency program that places the new teachers in an urban school where they teach under the guidance of a mentor teacher. I have seen the incredible struggles that new teachers endure in their attempts to learn their craft and educate children. I have seen the dedication, and exhaustion, of seasoned teachers as they work hours on end teaching their own students while also shepherding their novice colleagues and mentees into the profession.

Psychological research has demonstrated that the human mind engages in specific mental processes in an attempt to sustain a positive self-image. This is one of the most basic psychological human needs. The fact that teachers struggle to maintain a positive self-image while doing their life's work is beyond sad. This book explains how these psychological processes manifest in certain school environments and the impact this has both on teacher well-being and on the educational, social, and relational aspects of the school community.

First, let me acknowledge what anyone who has been involved in educational reform knows: improving low-resourced schools is very complex and fraught with failure. This book takes a psychological, an ecological, and a systemic approach to unpacking why some schools are so challenging, especially for the teachers and students who inhabit them every single day.

This book is certainly not the first, and it won't be the last to attempt to grapple with the issues that plague high-poverty, low-resourced urban and rural schools. However, of the many books I have read that deal with educational reform, I have not seen one that specifically outlines the psychological impact these school environments have on teachers. I have not found one that highlights how the systemic nature of the issues that plague these schools hurt teachers. In fact, the books that do focus on teacher well-being tend to take an individual rather than a systemic approach. Many books put the onus on the individual teacher to find the inner strength to change her focus or behavior so that she can individually find fulfilment and be happy and healthy in what will inevitably remain a troubled school environment.

This book ties teacher well-being to the overall ecological system of the school and to the systemic nature of problems that plague low-resourced schools. The book demonstrates how many of the local, state, and federal educational mandates have not met their goals because they ignore teacher input and experience. It demonstrates how current organizational structures and policies in schools trigger unconscious psychological defense mechanisms in teachers that ultimately hurt their well-being.

Finally, this book argues for educational reform policies that treat teachers as the professionals that they are. It argues for policies that draw upon the teachers' professional skills and unwavering commitment to the children that they serve. We must let teacher professionals lead the way on educational reform. We must allow the teacher to lead, both in the classroom and the entire school. Only then will we see true educational reform in this country.

Acknowledgments

Many people played a vital role in educating me about the experiences of new teachers and enabling me to do the work necessary to support them. I am so grateful to the teachers who have completed the TNY program since 2000. It is from them that I have learned everything I know about what teachers need and how we, as a society, can best support them. Each and every one of them is so important to me and holds a special place in my heart. I want to especially thank Lianne Hughes, Cyndy Etler, Olivia DiFranco, Jennifer Rogers, Abner Zorrilla, and James Louis for always being available, for inviting me into their classrooms, and for fully sharing their working lives with me.

I am also grateful to the mentor teachers and students from our partner schools who open their classrooms to the TNY residents year after year. These teachers spend an enormous amount of time serving as role models and guiding new teachers through the ups and downs of learning how to teach and how to fit into various school cultures.

I owe much gratitude to Alicia Savannah and to Miriam Niedergang, who have helped me to coordinate and manage the program. They both make the work of preparing the TNY residents possible. I truly could not do this work without them.

I thank my colleagues from the University of Massachusetts/Boston who have engaged in this important work with me. I so appreciate how we have always encouraged each other to do the best we can for the new teachers who have entrusted us with their preparation.

I am indebted to my editor, Amber Smith, who pushed me and helped make the book accessible to a wider audience. Finally, but foremost, I thank my family. My wife, Diane Pullen, whose support and confidence in me and this book sustained me throughout the writing process, and my children and grandchildren who continuously remind me why this work is so vital.

Introduction

In 2007, in a city that could have been anywhere in America, eight-year-old Liquarry Jefferson was fatally shot by his seven-year-old cousin. Liquarry was in the third grade and had fallen victim to several of society's most intractable failings. According to the local newspaper,[1] Liquarry's father was in prison when he was born. His mother, though older when she gave birth to Liquarry, had had her first two children while she was still a teenager. She was a victim of domestic abuse, which left her prone to violence herself.

Liquarry had four siblings: two sisters, ages three and eleven, and two brothers, ages thirteen and fifteen, all of whom frequently witnessed screaming and physical fights at home. Liquarry's family lived in an extremely poor and violent neighborhood; when the children were not witnessing violence at home, they were witnessing it among friends and neighbors on the street. As a third-grader, Liquarry attended an elementary school full of kids like himself, kids whose families suffered from extreme poverty. Unfortunately, rather than providing a refuge for the children, Liquarry's under-resourced, high-needs school only amplified their suffering.

Liquarry's school was much like the one where Quay Dorsey taught. Quay, profiled in an article for the *Washingtonian*[2] in 2018, is an African American man who, at the age of twenty-nine, became a grade-level chair and member of the academic leadership team at an urban elementary school. Most of the students attending Quay's school lived in public housing and dealt with poverty, homelessness, and community violence on a regular basis. Quay was very excited when he was hired at the school, which had been his top choice upon completion of his alternative teacher prep program.

Unlike the vast majority of new teachers in the United States, who are white and female, Quay had grown up in a poor, urban neighborhood himself.

He had struggled with some of the same issues as the students and was eager to give back. "I know what it's like to have a mom who works your whole life, but you're still poor," Quay stated. "I am convinced I can do a better job for the children." The first months were difficult and chaotic. Quay described "coming home sobbing twenty-six out of thirty nights" during his first month. Some of his frustration came as a result of the children's behavior, but the bulk of it was with the system.

Quay had experience with hands-on learning and had personally witnessed the transformative power of this approach with poor, urban children. He saw how excited the kids got when they used math to build something or when they wrote letters to the editor about community issues. He was eager to implement these methods in his own teaching, but the testing protocols used in his district discouraged that approach in subjects like reading and math. As a reading teacher, Quay found that this presented him with a dilemma.

Reading, according to state mandate, had to be taught at grade level, but Quay's students were reading several levels behind, on average. Quay was caught between the kids' needs and the requirements of the test-driven curriculum. Of that first year, Quay said, "I just remember wanting the year to be over and hoping to be alive at the end. It was so hard to get to that point—where I was satisfying the kids and satisfying the system at the same time."

Even though Quay found his principal to be supportive, it was nearly impossible to meet with her. She was under pressure to turn around a failing school in half the usual amount of time—which, according to research, is five years. Unfortunately, she didn't make it and was let go at the end of her first year.

Despite these challenges, Quay was successful with his third graders. Their passing scores on the Partnership for Assessment of Readiness for College and Careers (PARCC) slowly began to rise, and by the end of the year, Quay achieved a passing score on the district's teacher evaluation rubric. The consequences of this were enormous because turnaround schools in Quay's district are punished if students and teachers do not receive predetermined scores on either the PARCC or teacher evaluation rubrics.

Principals are let go, and teachers are either fired or not given their bonus pay. This creates tremendous personal and institutional pressure, especially for new teachers, who often don't find out until the end of the year if they will be fired, invited back with restrictions, or kept on for another year.

Quay lasted four years at his school and taught there between the ages of twenty-five and twenty-nine. Those years, however, took a toll on him. He was sleep-deprived, got insufficient exercise, and had spent over $5,000 of his own money on classroom supplies as well as clothing and food for his students and their families. Leaving took a psychological toll on Quay as well. He felt like a traitor, that he was leaving a community that really needed him to stay. The most poignant part of Quay's departure was the fact that as an African American male, he shared the experience of childhood poverty with his students.

If this one urban school could not keep Quay, what did that say about the prospects of the hundreds of young, idealistic women and men following in Quay's footsteps year after year?

This is a book about high-needs schools in America—and you can't tell a story about high-needs schools without telling the stories of Liquarry and Quay. Why? Because they represent the children and teachers who are the mainstays of urban and rural education. If we do not understand the experiences and individual contexts of the children and teachers who populate our high-needs schools, we will fail to understand how to educate the children, how to retain the teachers, and, ultimately, how to remedy the most vexing problems faced by our nation's low-resourced, high-needs schools. Those problems—low achievement, poor graduation rates, and high teacher turnover—will ultimately undermine our democracy.

The purpose of public education—and how to get schools back on track once they've lost sight of that purpose—must be re-examined. In the context of this book, the function of schooling is to educate children. How do we help high-needs schools accomplish this goal? What do schools need in order to best educate their students? This question has been asked and answered ad nauseam.

A better question might be: where do we begin in the quest to educate children in the best possible way? Do we start with the content we want them to learn? Do we start with the teachers who provide and facilitate education? Or do we start with the children and families themselves?

Before any of these questions can be answered, let's first acknowledge what anyone who has been involved in reforming high-needs schools already knows: improving high-needs schools is very complex, and often fraught with failure. This has been true since the 1980s, with the curricular and structural reforms recommended in "A Nation at Risk: The Imperative for Educational Reform"[3] and continued with No Child Left Behind (NCLB) legislation. Despite these efforts, there remains a class of high-needs schools that has proven resistant to reform. Almost every U.S. city has at least one, and our largest urban centers have several.

Their problems are familiar:

- a lack of teacher autonomy, leading to stand-offs between administrators and educators
- a laser focus on standards and test scores (including penalties for both teachers and schools failing to meet those standards), to the detriment of positive outcomes

- high principal and teacher turnover
- a lack of resources
- a lack of communication between schools and families
- bitter struggles with school district headquarters

Each of these issues puts systems within the educational bureaucracy in conflict with each other, that is, classroom versus administration, teachers versus families, school versus district, district versus state, and state versus federal government. These systems are complex in their own right, but when they have to work together, the difficulty is magnified. We often lose sight of the two constituencies that matter most: students, who too often suffer from the effects of poverty, and teachers, who are often young and inexperienced but driven to help their students succeed.

This point about teachers and students is crucial. All too often, we lose sight of the fact that education is a human endeavor; and, as a result, education reform must give equal, if not greater, weight to the human aspects of these complex ecosystems.

The teachers and students populating our most troubled high-needs schools are the focus of this book. This book provides an exploration of the ways in which teachers and students are impacted by the environments fostered by troubled high-needs schools. The study of psychology helps us to understand how human beings, in general, react to unhealthy and dysfunctional environments—and the high-needs schools at the center of this book are unhealthy and dysfunctional in very specific ways. Human beings react to these particular types of dysfunction by behaving predictably.

The first part of this book details the specific characteristics of high-needs schools that create unhealthy ecosystems for the humans inhabiting them every single day. These include the psychological, emotional, and mental mechanisms upon which all human beings unconsciously rely to maintain one of the most basic psychological human needs: the need to maintain a positive self-image.

Unfortunately, this need has become more and more of a struggle for teachers in the context of the high-needs school environment. The human mind engages in specific mental processes when attempting to sustain a positive self-image. The second part of this book explains these processes and their impact on the educational, social, and relational aspects of those who work in our nation's high-needs schools.

The final part of the book raises the question of reform by looking closely at the ways in which similar healthcare institutions—such as hospitals—tackle these challenges and provide new ways for us to think about how we might improve high-needs schools. This is particularly true in the field of nursing. The purpose of hospitals is to heal the sick and wounded, and nurses play an outsized role in this endeavor.

We can ask the same questions of hospitals that we ask of high-needs schools. What do they need in order to best heal their patients? Where do hospitals start in the quest for healing? Do they begin with the medications they have on hand, with the nurses who provide the care, or with the patients themselves? In the case of hospitals and healing in general, the answers seem obvious. Hospitals must start with the patient because with no knowledge of their symptoms, diagnoses, and the medications they are already taking, doctors and nurses would have no idea where to begin in recommending the best healing plan for each patient.

In the hospital setting, nurses work with patients and families to gather this information and prepare the patient for the next steps in his or her treatment. Nurses take an interdisciplinary approach to provide a coherent plan with each discipline offering a unique perspective on the patient.

Nursing practice tends to evoke the same types of emotions in nurses that teachers experience in the classroom. One of the reasons nurses do better under these types of working conditions is that many hospitals have adopted a *just culture* framework.

> Just culture refers to a values-supportive model of shared accountability. It's a culture that holds organizations accountable for the systems they design and for how they respond to staff behaviors fairly and justly. In turn, staff members are accountable for the quality of their choices and for the ways they communicate their struggles within the system.[4]

This practice gives nurses more autonomy over their work and prevents them from being continually held accountable for problems with systemic causes. Education can learn a great deal from nursing, especially when it comes to the ways teachers and nurses are trained to deal with the more challenging aspects of their professional workplaces and taught to approach working with both clients and colleagues.

One of the most promising new approaches in healthcare is *clinical microsystems*. The field of healthcare defines clinical microsystems as "small, functional, front-line units that provide most healthcare to most people. They are the essential building blocks of larger organizations, and of the health system."[5] We must take a similar approach to high-needs schools.

> An ecological systems approach to school reform focuses on optimal human development *at all age* levels. This means that in the context of the school, optimal growth and development would be the ultimate goal for both teachers and students. In this approach, all other reform efforts, i.e., the tightening of educational standards, the strengthening of school partnerships, the overhaul of curriculum, and the restructuring of school communities, would be in service toward this end.[6]

Thus, in our efforts to reform high-needs schools, we must focus on the clinical microsystem of the classroom as well as the needs of both teachers and students.

With regard to this type of focus, high-needs schools are much like hospitals. In fact, teaching in high-needs schools has shifted from being a job about *educating children* to being a job about *providing services* for children. Urban and rural teaching have moved from a primary focus on educational content to a primary focus on the services kids need in order to learn that content.

The two approaches represent very different motivations. It has become extremely difficult for teachers to provide the best education for children without knowing the context in which the children have developed socially, emotionally, and cognitively. We know so much more today about how a child's environment impacts his or her well being and abilities. This knowledge has made it abundantly clear that schools must begin with the child in order to best determine the content and how it should be delivered.

Unfortunately, the support, resources, and organizational structures that would enable teachers in high-needs schools to use their professional knowledge to successfully teach children have not been forthcoming. Instead, high-needs teachers have been held solely accountable when children fail to learn at the rate deemed appropriate by state and federal mandates. This has occurred without regard for established knowledge about what it takes to truly and effectively educate children in high-needs school environments.

Even though teachers in high-needs schools have the professional knowledge and skills to successfully teach children in their care, they are actually prevented from practicing this knowledge because the schools in which they teach every day are not optimally structured to allow them to meet the educational needs of their students. Deconstructing this old, faulty model is the first step in building a new and functional approach to education reform.

NOTES

1. Scott Allen and Maria Cramer, "Crime Consumed a Family, and an 8-Year-Old Is Lost," *The Boston Globe* (August 2007): A.1.

2. Sarah Stodder, "A Heartwrenching Story about why Teachers Are Leaving DC in Droves," *Washingtonian,* November, 2018, http://www.washingtonian.com/2018/11/04/a-heartwrenching-story-about-why-teachers-are-leaving-dc-in-droves

3. National Commission on Excellence in Education, "A Nation at Risk: The Imperative for Educational Reform," *The Elementary School Journal,* 84, no. 2 (November 1983): 113.

4. K Griffith, "Column: The Growth of a Just Culture," *The Joint Commission Perspectives on Patient Safety,* 9, no. 12 (2009): 8; Barbara Brunt, "Developing a Just Culture," *HealthLeaders Media* (May 2010): 1

5. Eugene Nelson et al., "Microsystems in Health Care: Part 1. Learning from High-Performing Front-Line Clinical Units," *The Joint Commission*, 28, no. 9 (September 2002): 474.

6. Lisa Gonsalves and Jack Leonard, *New Hope for Urban Schools: Cultural Reform, Moral Leadership and Community Partnership* (Westport, CT: Praeger, 2007): 140.

Part I

Challenging Aspects of American Schooling

Chapter 1

So, You Want to Teach in a High-Needs School?

Family, Friends, and the Media

This chapter focuses on the reactions that many young people face when they say they want to teach—particularly when they say they want to teach in high-needs schools. It also focuses on the media and societal criticisms of those in the teaching profession. A significant percentage of those who choose to teach face criticism and societal judgment from the beginning, which often has a significant impact on their first years on the job.

"SUPPORTIVE BUT ..."

This is how many new teachers describe the reactions of family and friends to their decision to pursue a career in teaching, particularly in high-needs schools. Nancy, an aspiring English teacher, is bewildered by her family's "reluctant" support.[1]

> While they are supportive of my becoming a teacher and encouraging me that it is something I will excel in, they do not understand why I need to be in an urban environment. I grew up in the suburbs and went to private Catholic schools. My parents are not ignorant of the plight of the inner city since they lived there for a time and at one time had little money. However, because they don't understand why I want to work in an urban school, they continue to nudge me to go to a suburban school. It is difficult to listen when they ask when I am going to look for a Catholic school position. They do not seem to want to accept that I like being in an urban school and do find working with my students rewarding. I hope they will understand eventually, but, for now, it is a challenge to not have the complete support and understanding of my family.

Cindy, an aspiring science teacher, also feels deeply impacted by the lack of family support. Unlike Nancy, Cindy has not fully told her family about her choice to be an urban teacher. Because of this, "it is hard to talk to them about my experiences at school, both good and bad. This causes me to become more introverted, affecting my self-esteem as well as my pride in my work. An unknowledgeable support system can only be so supportive, making it difficult for me to be completely sure of my choices. Without a consistently stable emotional base, it becomes hard for me to set goals and believe in myself to reach those goals."

Nancy is not the only aspiring teacher who has had to hide her full intentions from family. Ellie, another young science teacher, feels she has to constantly edit what she tells her family and friends about her new profession.

> I grew up in a suburban town and my entire family and most of my friends still live there. I grew up in a very safe neighborhood and my family worries extensively about my safety. Because of this, I have to be careful about what bits and pieces of my life I share with them. For example, some members of my family are not entirely sure where I teach every day. Some of my siblings still have the misconception that I work in a private school since the name of the school contains the word institute. I cannot tell them when fights break out in my classroom or about the gang shootings that have occurred just outside school grounds because they would be so worried that I would no longer be able to call and ask for help when brainstorming for lesson plans or when frustrated when too many students fail exams.

The inability to share the ups and downs of a new job with family and friends can be very discouraging to a young person. It is also isolating to have to maintain this type of silence with a respected parent. Darcy, a science teacher, explains that she "majored in biology as an undergrad because she loved science." Her father was proud of her choice and thought she would work in the medical field. Now that she has chosen to go into urban teaching, she says "my father does not support my decision to go into education at all."

> Once I told him that I was going to be an urban teacher, there was tension between us. He does not understand my reason for wanting to work in an urban school. He has a distorted perspective from stories that he has heard about urban schools. In order to still have a relationship with my father, I realized that I could just not talk about the topic. When we talk on the phone or in person, he does not ask me about the program or how it is going, and I do not share anything with him.

Fears about safety underscore the judgments many families make about their loved ones teaching in high-needs schools, but to the aspiring teacher, these fears can be suffocating and disheartening. Gillian, an aspiring history teacher, says that she

> resents the implication that as a woman, or as a white person, or as a young person, that I am too fragile to handle it. Several people have asked if I feel safe, and when I assure them that none of my eighth graders are threatening me with weapons, they seem skeptical. The fact that my family thinks I'm constantly in danger has definitely made it hard to bridge the gap between my personal life and my professional life.

Many of these fears are driven by the pervasive stereotypes held by much of American society about inner-city neighborhoods and the people who live in them. These stereotypes are fed by mainstream media, which shapes the viewer's perspective and has an outsized impacted on the ways in which many perceive Black and Brown students.

According to media portrayals, which often include the language of the "school to prison pipeline" and "mass-incarceration," working in a high-needs school means that one is choosing to work in a challenging environment, with difficult children, who are not well behaved, and incapable of learning—all stereotypes that are inherently racist, and not true about Black and Brown students. New teachers learn all to quickly, that for their family and friends, to work in high-needs schools is to work in an environment that is not career fulfilling and emotionally not safe.

Fran, a former accountant, talks about the reactions she gets from her core group of friends.

> Since I began preparing to be a teacher, I have been unable to devote as much time to my social life. Sometimes I am not able to see my closest friends for long stretches of time, so when I do get to see them, I look so forward to it. But every time we get together, they ask me a series of questions that never seem to change: "How is teaching in the ghetto going? Is it dangerous? Are the kids mean to you? Do you have any crazy stories? Anyone pull a knife on you?" Then they tell some off-putting jokes, and I end up defending myself while trying to change the subject. It discourages me that people I have respected and known for so long treat something that I am passionate about, and have devoted so much time to, as endless fodder for ridicule and their chance to hear stories that fulfill every myth they know about urban education. My disappointment in them is matched by their disappointment when I only have positive experiences to share with them.

As Fran's experience illustrates, new teachers not only have to deal with the fears of their family members; they also must contend with the outright judgments of their friends. Alice, another former accountant turned math teacher, says her friends often make her feel less than:

Me and most of my friends majored in accounting or finance and then moved to the city to get jobs. I had very few friends outside of the business school. When I moved to the city, I worked as an accountant so I always had something to talk about with my friends, but now that I teach, we have less in common. My friends work a lot of long hours. They ask politely how teaching and grad school are going, but they don't really want to hear any details about the school because they just think "oh, summers off" and think they work so much harder. I have wanted to be a teacher for a long time, and I really enjoy working with kids, and I want to tell them that teaching is not an easy job! I feel as if I am finally doing something I want to do, but I think many of them look at this as a step-down. I almost feel like some of them think they are better than me because I chose a different path, and they think that path is "easier."

These negative judgments are not only hurtful, but they can also cause new teachers to question their desire to teach. Another aspiring math teacher explains,

My friends and family do not understand why I am choosing to work with this population of students. They ask why I would want to work with them day in and day out, and what benefit teaching in the inner city can possibly provide to me. They tell me that working in the city is not worth it and that I should work in a "white" school. They even tell me that working in an urban school will make me a second-rate teacher and that I will not make a difference to any of the kids. The hard part is that on days that are stressful and difficult these people actually start to make sense to me, and I believe that I do not make any difference to my students. At times I start believing the negative statements that these people make about me.

William, who also left a lucrative job in finance to teach English in an urban school, says that both his family and friends have been "supportive, but they seem to think I am kind of crazy for doing this. This attitude causes me to be rather defensive about my profession and about the kids. It also makes me angry. I want to be bringing positive energy to my teaching, and their opinion can rub me the wrong way at times."

TEACHER BASHING

Negative attitudes about teaching are so pervasive that they haunt aspiring teachers right from the start. As these quotes reveal, the fears, stereotypes, and judgments of friends and loved ones are deeply hurtful to aspiring teachers. Not only do aspiring teachers have to contend with the misconceptions of their family members and friends, they also have to deal with half-truths about teaching that are perpetrated by the media daily.

Everyone knows the major themes of what has come to be known as "teacher bashing" in the media. "American children score the worst out of developed countries on international assessments"; "too many children fail state and national standardized tests." "Bad" teachers, who cannot be fired, are to blame for these failures, yet their unions continually fight for more taxpayer money.

While children fail, teachers enjoy the benefits of tenure, short workdays, early dismissals, and summers off. When not focusing on educational outcomes, the media tends to focus on the social dysfunction of high-needs schools, in particular, portraying them as violent and desolate institutions where the children are out of control and no learning takes place, unless there is a "hero" teacher, usually an outsider with no professional credentials, who comes in and miraculously engages the students.

These themes lead to both resentment and panic in the public at large. Many resent teachers because of the fiction that they have too much time off and a "job for life" that is protected by bloated unions. These people have no idea what happens in schools. Others feel panic for their loved ones who are interested in a career in teaching. This panic is reflected in the stories above.

Friends and relatives of teachers, overcome by their own fears of urban environments, are consumed with worry for their loved ones' on-the-job safety. They also worry about their ability to make a living on teacher pay and their reputation as intelligent, capable professionals in the eyes of others. This last worry stems from the all too common myth that "those who can, do; those who can't, teach," as if teaching was a last resort job for those who are not able to succeed in any other profession.

As an aspiring male math teacher once told me,

> As I personally develop as a teacher, I immediately think of our country's common opinion of educators "those who can't, teach." Even certain members of my own extended family have a low opinion of educators. The lack of societal respect is no small challenge.

How did we come to this? How did this country's attitudes toward teachers become so negative?

In an attempt to answer this question, I expected to trace the history of teachers and teaching back to a point in time when teachers were respected as professionals. From there, I planned to identify the turning point, the incident or incidents, that turned the tide against teachers from respected professionals to what we have today, a profession made up of mostly women who are attacked at every turn.

What I found instead was that there was no turning point, no specific incident. Many of the struggles we engage in over public education today were there from the very beginning. The underlying reason for this has to do with the main characters involved: women and the poor, minority, and immigrant children they teach in our nation's high-needs schools.

The truth is, the moment that this country proposed public schooling for all children, was the same moment that education as a profession was devalued.

The specific moves that led to the devaluation of public education happened in very deliberate ways and were influenced by the beliefs and mores of society at particular points in time. Each attempted improvement of public education, including the notion that we should have public education at all, has been opposed by the same group of individuals from the very start—those with business and corporate interests.

Three struggles, in particular, can be connected to the establishment of nationwide public schooling: first, the alignment of the business community and conservative politicians to control the curriculum and thus the purposes of public education; second, the quality of teacher preparation and third, the fight over equal pay for teachers. Dana Goldstein's book, *The Teacher Wars: A History of America's Most Embattled Profession,* which traces the history of the teaching profession, confirms these connections.

Struggle Number One: The Business Community, Conservatives, and the Curriculum

According to Goldstein, in the early 1800s, there were two main advocates for nationwide public education, Catherine Beecher and Horace Mann. Beecher was a wealthy woman from the Northeast and one of the first to advocate for nationwide public schooling. Beecher made three major contributions to the establishment of public schools. At a time when most teachers were male, Beecher argued that women would make better teachers than men for two reasons. According to Goldstein,

> In her famous 1846 lecture, "The Evils Suffered by American Women and American Children" she enthusiastically cited a New York State report on local schools that called male teachers "incompetent" and "intemperate . . . coarse, hard, unfeeling men, too lazy or stupid" to be entrusted with the care of children. "Would it not be better to put the thousands of men who are keeping school for young children into the mills, and employ the women to train the children?"[2]

Beecher's second argument was that hiring female teachers would save money.

Beecher openly pitched hiring female teachers as a potential money-saving strategy for state and local governments launching compulsory schooling for the first time. "A woman needs to support only herself" while "a man requires support for himself and a family," she wrote, appealing to the stereotype that women with families did not do wage-earning work.[3]

Part of Beecher's agenda, as an educated, well-off, unmarried, white woman, was to create opportunities for fulfillment for women like herself. These women were not able to attend college, work as professionals, or become business owners or even preachers. Beecher came to believe that "teaching was the one profession in which a woman could gain 'influence, respectability and independence' without venturing outside 'the prescribed boundaries of feminine modesty.'"[4]

To help women realize this type of freedom, Beecher created what Goldstein calls the first "Teach for America prototype" the "Board of National Popular Education." The Board prepared "well-bred, evangelical young women from the Northeast" to go west to work as teachers. Beecher thought of them as "missionary teachers, migrating west to educate the two million 'ignorant and neglected American children' of the frontier, whose parents presumably lacked the educational commitment of the New England elite."[5]

It is clear from this quote that in Beecher's view the purpose of public schooling was to educate poor and immigrant children to be obedient, moral citizens of "good character" rather than provide them with an academic education.

Beecher was good friends with politician Horace Mann, who saw Beecher's argument for hiring female teachers as a means to one of his political ends. Mann was elected to the Massachusetts Senate in 1834 as a member of the Whig Party, a party that was fiscally conservative but socially liberal.

At the time, Massachusetts legislators were debating a bill that would impose regulations designed to encourage business owners to pay higher wages among other reforms, and that would raise taxes in order to improve the living conditions of the poor citizens. Mann, however, believed that schooling could be just as effective in improving the lot of the poor as regulations and taxes and used his clout in the Senate to require that all children attend school and that all schools be overseen by a state board of education. Thus, Massachusetts became the first state in the nation that required that all children attend public school.

Mann then became the education secretary for the State, where, borrowing from Beecher, he made the case that public education should focus more on building character and morality, and less on rigorous academics, and that women were more suited to be teachers than men because of their more nurturing dispositions. He also adopted her argument that women could be paid far less and thus would not overburden taxpayers.

Business leaders and politicians supported this approach as an alternative method for improving society (as opposed to regulation) and as a way to keep a lid on taxes. They also appreciated the idea of educating the masses to be obedient and moral citizens, who would then go on to be industrious workers and consistent voters.

Here we see the birth of struggle number one, how business and corporate interests aligned with no taxes politicians to prevent the State's attempt to legislate for the benefit of children and workers. In the fight to establish public schools for all, the business community and conservative politicians used the argument that schools, and female teachers, could do a better job than regulation and increased funding to improve society for poor children. In the mid-1800s, they argued that children would learn better and be better equipped to join civil society if they were taught by women using a curriculum focused on character and moral behavior.

The business community is still at it today; framing their arguments as being in the best interest of poor, minority, and immigrant children. Today they have substituted standards-based education for character education, neither of which help kids, especially Black and Brown kids, think critically. They are still trying to control the curriculum by working with politicians on federal mandates which they argue will help more kids learn.

Struggle Number Two: Teacher Preparation

To make his vision a reality, Mann created what were called "Normal Schools" to train the growing corps of teachers, but *only females could* apply because once they became teachers it would cost the state less to hire them. The Normal Schools ensured a steady supply of lower-paid, female teachers for the state's schools. This vision of teacher preparation spread throughout the country between 1840 and 1870, when half of the states had normal schools. Goldstein explains:

> An 1842 manual for local schools . . . was unapologetic about promoting female teachers as the corner stone of "a cheap system" positing that the most talented women would be willing to work for half of what men of the "poorest capacity" would demand. The authors [also] made sure to add that "women have a native tact in the management of very young minds which is rarely possessed by men . . . they have a peculiar power of awakening the sympathies of children, and inspiring them with a desire to excel."[6]

In some states, Normal Schools became substitutes for high school, allowing girls as young as fourteen to enroll, meaning that many teachers did not even have a high school diploma by the time they started teaching. Others were seen as alternatives to college, but with lower academic standards thus they gained the reputation of being less academically rigorous. These developments led critics to believe that female teachers, the vast majority educated through normal schools, were not well prepared to offer a high-quality education.

By the late 1800s, the tide started to turn with calls to hire more college-educated, male teachers, who had been pushed out of the profession in droves. According to Goldstein, by 1890, only 30 percent of teachers nationwide and 10 percent in Massachusetts were male. Goldstein points out that this "feminization of teaching carried an enormous cost: Teaching became understood less as a career, than as a philanthropic vocation or a romantic calling,"[7] providing another reason why states could pay teachers less.

Critics also began to attack the curricular focus on character versus academics arguing that it was anti-intellectual and lowered America's educational standing among other European countries. Even though calls for these reforms came from many different directions, the reformers could not overcome America's overwhelming bias against women and the poor, minority, and immigrant children they taught.

State legislatures simply refused to raise taxes to pay teachers an equal wage. The reformers' solutions went unheeded as more and more women became teachers. By this time, teaching was no longer dominated by upper- and-middle class women. Now women of all backgrounds, working class, Catholic, and minorities, were becoming teachers. As the criticisms of teacher quality and rigor continued to mount, respect for the field of teaching began to diminish, pushing even more men away from the field, and emboldening female teachers to protect what was still the only profession open to them.

It is clear from this history that teacher preparation was established as a less rigorous and nonacademic educational track from the beginning. When Normal schools were created, women were still not allowed to enroll in college, so states created a two-tiered system. Normal schools for females, whose only professional option was to become teachers, and college for males, who could choose any profession.

Ironically, between 1910 and 1930, many of the Normal schools were converted to state colleges, which in many states are still known as teacher's colleges and as being less rigorous than universities. It only took thirty years as nationwide public schooling took root with the support of female teachers before the attacks began. This legacy of a less rigorous education for women and disadvantaged children has followed teacher education into the twenty-first century.

The quality of teacher preparation is still under attack today, over 100 years later. From Michele Rhee[8] sweeping bad teachers out of the classroom on the cover of *Time* magazine to the "We must fire bad teachers" written across the chalkboard on the cover of *Newsweek*, the quality of teaching has been used as an excuse for educational reforms, such as charter schools and merit pay, that keep power out of teacher's hands and money out of their pockets.

The situation we have today is a direct result of states' lack of investment in female professionals and poor, minority, and immigrant children.

Struggle Number Three: Equal Pay

Since the early 1800s, large numbers of upper- and middle-class women were encouraged to take a new path. Rather than living with their parents and waiting for a husband that might never come, they were encouraged to attend Normal Schools, as they were not allowed to enroll in college, and to work outside the home in the only profession available to them—teaching. Many came to relish their newfound freedoms, yet they also grew frustrated at the unequal pay they received for doing the same work as men.

For example, according to Goldstein, in 1850, nearly 9,000 out of NYC's 11,000 teachers were women, yet the 2,200 male teachers earned twice as much as the females. There were reformers who fought to improve public education, but they could not overcome America's overwhelming bias against women and the poor, working class, and immigrant children they taught. State legislatures simply refused to raise taxes to pay women an equal wage. By 1850, the teachers were getting fed up. In cities like New York and Chicago, they were teaching mostly immigrant children who spoke little English in overcrowded classrooms.

Their frustration coincided with the growth of the women's suffrage movement. The sense of independence women gained from teaching allowed them to imagine other roles they could play in society, causing many of them to join the women's movement in their fight for equal pay and wider opportunities.

The last straw that pushed the female teaching force to finally organize happened in Chicago in 1896 when business leaders and college presidents won control of the school curriculum, taking that control away from teachers and politicians. In Chicago, the majority of teachers were from Catholic and working-class backgrounds. As Goldstein points out, these women grew up with fathers and brothers who were union members. They knew about the power of unions.

These relationships led teachers to form the Chicago Teacher's Federation in 1897. The CTF operated as a labor union, not a professional union. The decision to align with labor has been greatly criticized to this day, but we cannot lose sight of why teachers did this.

Female teachers paired up with male labor unions because they knew that the opposition from the business community and state legislators to acknowledge that women were professional equals to men, and should receive equal pay, would never happen. Sexism was the norm during these times. The only chance teachers believed they had at getting equal pay was to argue that they be paid *for equal time spent on the job, like a laborer, not for their expertise as teachers*. Thus, teaching, even though it is a professional job, became forever compensated based on labor principles.

Interestingly enough, the biggest items on the bargaining list for the new teacher's union were higher pay, control over the curriculum, and control over disciplinary practices. The union also had the goal of countering negative media images of teachers. This was in 1899, and here we are 120 years later, and the still mostly female teaching force is fighting for the same things.

Today, teachers in communities across America are going on strike for these *very same reasons*! Equal pay that is commensurate with their educational background and professional skills is still an issue.

Discipline in the classroom is still an issue as more and more children suffer from trauma, poverty, and other social ailments that prevent them from focusing in school and teachers are getting no support in their work with children and families. Meanwhile, businesses, corporate interests, and governments continue to devise reforms that take more and more control away from teachers to determine how best to run their classrooms while they institute more confining accountability systems.

Investigating the impact of these increasingly restrictive accountability systems on teachers, schools, and the students they serve must be a priority if we ever hope to achieve meaningful change.

NOTES

1. The following quotes are from conversations I have had with aspiring and new teachers over the years.
2. Dana Goldstein, *The Teacher Wars: A History of America's Most Embattled Profession* (New York: Penguin Random House, 2014), 33.
3. Goldstein, *The Teacher Wars*, 34.
4. Goldstein, *The Teacher Wars*, 30.
5. Goldstein, *The Teacher Wars*, 32.
6. Goldstein, *The Teacher Wars*, 45–46.
7. Goldstein, *The Teacher Wars*, 49–50.
8. Founder and CEO of the non-profit organizations StudentsFirst and the New Teacher Project.

Chapter 2

The Impact of Accountability Systems on Teachers and School Culture

The most important things that need to be managed can't be measured.

—Ed Deming

In the introduction of this book, you met Quay—a new teacher who, in his first year of teaching, was left longing for the school year to end and hoping that he would survive that long. As he said, "It was so hard to get to that point—where I was satisfying the kids and satisfying the system at the same time."

To satisfy the kids, most of whom were poor and disengaged from school, Quay used culturally responsive teaching methods. He created lessons that mirrored their experiences, such as the time he taught his third graders how to annotate text by using newspaper articles about Michael Brown's shooting. Finally, with these texts, the kids were engaged and excited to learn. However, to satisfy the system, Quay had to teach reading at grade level even though the majority of his students were not there yet. This required sticking to the script, reading grade level books that didn't relate to the kids' lived experiences, and lots of mock testing.

Quay never knew if he achieved the right balance until after the annual six weeks of PARCC testing. As he describes it, during those six weeks teaching and learning "shut down, motivation becomes depleted. The culture of the school is gone," and the kids are stressed, although he blames himself for stressing out the kids. He questions whether he pushed them too hard because of the pressure on him.

Pressure to get a top score on his evaluation, which would allow him to earn that $25,000 bonus that his district gives teachers who rate high. Pressure to make sure his students' scores reach the "predetermined level" required by the federal government for "priority schools" like his. It was these things that pushed Quay to long for a new experience, one where he wouldn't be part of a failing school, and wouldn't have to focus so intently on preparing kids to pass a test.

Quay is not the only teacher struggling with the accountability systems required by federal law through the No Child Left Behind Act in 2002, and Every Child Succeeds Act in 2015. Even though the 2015 law relaxed the requirement for standardized testing, today every state requires that some type of standardized test be given in grades three through eight and once in high school.

Many teachers feel that this overreliance on testing has taken the independence, creativity, and professionalism out of teaching. Ann, a first-year teacher, describes what testing has done to teaching in her school:

> We spend time every day doing rote exercises. Forget ever doing hands-on activities, science or math games, or creative writing experiences. We do one hour of sit and drill in each of the subjects of math, reading, and writing. We use a basal reader, math workbook pages, and rote writing prompts. It is all step by step; the same thing every week. Every day for one hour the whole school does the exact same direct instruction lesson. The children sit and get drilled over and over in a scripted lesson that my principal makes me use. You can't improvise, add, or take away. You do exactly what it says. This is how testing has impacted my school and my teaching. I don't have a choice to deviate from this awful test preparation.[1]

Another teacher echoes these sentiments, elaborating in frustration:

> All of the most powerful teaching tools I used to use every day are no good to me now because they don't help the children get ready for the test, and it makes me like a robot instead of a teacher.[2]

Here is a teacher from Florida describing her experiences with the Florida Comprehensive Assessment Test (FCAT).

> These tests, and all of this pressure to make kids do well on the tests. . . . It's an insult. It's saying that we aren't a profession. That we can't be trusted to do our jobs, so high-pressure tactics are necessary to make us behave. They're treating us like children; they're turning us into bad teachers, taking away every bit of pride.[3]

The same is happening in Colorado:

> I felt demoralized and unappreciated by all of the negative press in the newspapers. . . . I feel pulled from many directions—to make education more personal, but then for CSAP—to standardized student learning—forcing them into a box

The Impact of Accountability Systems on Teachers and School Culture

whether they are ready developmentally or not. I find that it is a demoralizing, stressful situation.[4]

This teacher from North Carolina describes the context within which teachers must prepare children:

> Teachers do not flee the classroom because they lack expertise but because they feel unbearable frustration and stress. Under great pressure to raise test scores, teachers are held accountable for student progress [but they get less and less support for classroom management]. Teachers must deal daily with increasing numbers of troubled, disruptive students who suffer the same ills that torment current society: poverty, abuse, violence, drug and alcohol use, etc. These young people need help, but no teacher, however well-trained, can provide that help while simultaneously instructing twenty-five to thirty other children.[5]

From California, one teacher describes behaving in ways that go against her values and the reasons she became a teacher in the first place. The teacher stressed over the need to have her students score better on that year's tests, was teaching math concepts, but one student was having trouble understanding. She explains, "I said, somewhat sharply, 'don't you get it?' He just looked at me with his big brown eyes. I felt terrible."[6]

Finally, in New York City, a literacy coach tells the story of working with an "energetic, smart, organized, and eager" teacher in a school on the Lower East Side that serves mostly students who speak English as a second language:

> This year the principal and I both noticed that the teacher seemed less smiley, less energetic, and less enthusiastic. I met with the teacher to discuss this with her. She told me that she had so many assessments to do for the children in her class that she has practically no instructional time, no time to implement the wonderful inquiry projects that they had been doing the past few years, and, truthfully, no time to enjoy her teaching. As soon as she is finished with one assessment, it's time to do running records.
>
> These assessments give her much less information than she was getting when she had time to spend with the children and understand their interests, learning styles, and learning frustrations. When she had these observations, she was able to plan appropriate activities and interventions. We've spent time learning how to collect work for portfolios, but, she told me, there's not much time for the children to actually do the work that would go into these portfolios.[7]

These stories from across the country highlight the various impact high-stakes testing has had on teachers and their profession. The myriad testing requirements have led to a loss of professionalism for teachers, along with the independence, creativity, and use of the expertise teachers draw upon to diagnose children's learning problems and develop solutions to remedy them. This experience erodes teachers' confidence in their abilities and leads them to question their professional choices.

Being held accountable for children's educational outcomes, when everyone knows that those outcomes are impacted more by what happens outside of the classroom than by what happens inside the classroom, leads teachers to experience unbearable stress. This stress, which results from being held accountable for things that are out of one's control, leads to negative emotions such as sadness, anxiety, anger, and even guilt.

Feelings of guilt result from teachers who worry that the pressures they feel around testing cause them to inadvertently do things that end up hurting their students as the examples from Quay and the teacher from California illustrate. Finally, prolonged negative experiences like these erode trust between teachers and administrators, leading to degraded school culture. Working in a school culture marred by distrust, feeling stressed, and being criticized for prolonged periods impacts teachers' health and well-being.

These negative and hurtful experiences have an outsized impact on teachers because of what they bring to the profession. Many teachers see themselves as following a calling to serve and support children. Research shows that teachers tend to have a "deep personal commitment to [teaching] and to students."[8] For many, the choice of a teaching career grows out of a dual passion for their subject matter and for helping young people discover the joys of learning.

Teachers tend to be highly motivated to contribute to society, and they seek to achieve this noble goal through a desire to shape the up-and-coming generations.[9]

This sense of purpose is one of the things that keeps new teachers on the job despite the outsized demands and the high level of energy and effort required of teachers every single day. Public Agenda, a research organization whose goal is to help political leaders better understand public opinion on a wide variety of social issues, interviewed young people who chose a career in teaching and compared their responses to those who chose other careers. The teachers who were interviewed had up to five years of teaching experience and the non-teachers were all under thirty years old.

When talking about how long new teachers expected to stay in the classroom, 75 percent said that they saw teaching as a "life-long" choice, as compared with 50 percent of their peers who chose another profession. Only 19 percent of teachers imagined that they might change careers at some point. Many of the teachers described their desire to teach from a young age, saying things like "I wanted to be a teacher for as long as I can remember," or "There was never anything else I wanted to do."

Given this, it is no surprise that only 12 percent of the teachers said that they fell into teaching by chance as compared with 40 percent of the non-teachers. This strong desire to teach helps keep teachers in the classroom. The non-teachers, on the other hand, changed jobs a lot, with 61 percent having held two or three jobs since graduating from college. One of the only things that the teachers and non-teachers agreed upon about teaching was that "teaching is a profession people should pursue only if they have a true sense of calling."[10]

Clearly, teachers stay in the classroom because they love what they do, as 96 percent of the teachers in this survey indicated, whereas only 28 percent of the non-teachers said that they loved their current job. The data also uncovered the reasons why teachers love their jobs, it helps them "contribute to society and help others," they get a lot of personal "satisfaction out of teaching" and they work with colleagues who are "highly motivated and energetic."[11] Notice that making a lot of money does not top the list of what teachers love about teaching. Only 30 percent of teachers said it was important to them that the job pays well.

Even though 75 percent of teachers feel they are "seriously underpaid" for the work that they do, when asked to choose between working at a school where they made a "significantly higher salary" or working at a school that had "better student behavior and parental support," supportive administrators, "highly motivated and effective" colleagues or that had a "mission and philosophy" about teaching that matched their own, overwhelming majorities choose these options over making more money.[12]

When asked what they believe is the best way to improve teacher effectiveness, paying teachers more did not top the list, but came in sixth out of twelve options, after offering more professional development around inclusive teacher practices, smaller class sizes, improving consequences for student behavior, having more up-to-date technology in the classroom, and increasing professional development for teachers.[13] These data, as well as several other popular and academic studies, consistently find that "all other factors being equal, teachers of all generations tend to see teaching conditions as more important than salary.[14]

The differences between the groups say a lot about the level of commitment new teachers bring to the job. The current stressors and strains of teaching hurt teachers more than other newly employed young people because of who they are and why they have decided to teach. This all indicates strongly that when a teacher decides to leave teaching, it is not a decision they make lightly. In most cases, they leave because they are driven away from teaching.

Unfortunately, as of this moment in history when schools are suffering from the twin pandemics of racism and COVID-19, there are several things driving teachers away. If only our society could be more appreciative of the fact that the people who are choosing to teach are there because they have a calling to support children. Rather than use this well-known fact as an excuse not to pay teachers more, we should instead use our country's vast resources to provide teachers with the support they need so that they can truly fulfill their calling. As we will see, an unfulfilled calling only leads to despair.

In terms of holding teachers and schools accountable through standardized testing, teachers are not the only stakeholders who believe that the focus on testing is too narrow. Parents also share this view. First, when asked about accountability in public schools, parents do not want to talk about accountability, they want to talk about responsibility.[15] Parents, and members of the public in general, think of responsibility as a "shared duty" between institutions and the community.

When it comes to schools, parents place the responsibility for student success on four pillars: principals, teachers, parents, and students. Most parents, 76 percent,[16] believe that teachers cannot be held solely responsible for student success. In focus groups with parents, Public Agenda found that "for the parents, improving what schools and educators do is only one piece of the accountability puzzle."[17] Parents felt that it was unreasonable to expect school success without their support.

This is not to say that parents do not support standardized testing; they do. Many parents are knowledgeable about testing, and they support the administration of "mandatory testing of students in public schools each year."[18] But parents also believe that standardized tests should not be the only measure of school quality and that "testing should be put in context with other important elements of teaching and learning."[19] For parents, there are more important indicators of school quality.

For example, in a recent survey, the public rated "teaching interpersonal skills as the most important factor of school quality," whereas a school's performance on standardized tests as an indicator of quality came in last at 6 percent.[20] When it comes to preparing children for the workforce, 60 percent believe that schools have "a lot" of responsibility in ensuring that they have the right skills to be successful employees; for example, 82 percent believe that career skills classes should be offered to all high school students. In terms of academic preparation, the public wants the focus to be broader with 82 percent believing that critical thinking should be taught across subject areas.

The sad thing is that one of the reasons our political leaders instituted accountability systems based on testing was to ensure transparency for the public. They realized that the parents and the public were starting to lose faith in our nation's schools and felt accountability measures were one way to rebuild that trust. It is clear from these data that the politicians have gone too far. They are still not listening to the public. Accountability systems based on standardized testing are not what the public wants.

Educational historians have pointed to the 1983 report, *A Nation at Risk*, as ushering in the standards and accountability movement and the focus on using data to push educational reform efforts. Goldstein called the report "one of the most influential federal documents ever published," and described it as "securing a Washington toehold for the national standards and accountability education movement."[21]

She credits the report with providing the blueprint for the major reform bills that followed:

> The rhetoric and policy prescriptions of *A Nation at Risk* have proven so enduring [that] the very same assumptions and ideals underlie No Child Left Behind, Race to the Top, the Common Core, and almost every other contemporary reform effort to improve teaching.

What we tend to forget is that *A Nation at Risk* called for several categories of reform, not just the focus on teachers, which has come to dominate today's reform agenda. The first category focused on content, specifically on improving the rigor in English Language Arts (ELA) and Science, Technology, Engineering, and Math (STEM) and called on subject area associations to create updated and innovative curriculum.

The second focused on standards and called for the creation of tests of achievement to make sure they were being met. This recommendation specifically called for "other diagnostic procedures that assist teachers"[22] in evaluating student progress, which is a far cry from what we have today—a system that punishes, rather than assists teachers. Most interestingly, five of the eight recommendations in this category focused on textbooks and called states and school districts to "require publishers to . . . furnish evidence of the quality and appropriateness of textbooks based on results from field trials and credible evaluation."[23]

We all know what happened instead. A few major publishing companies, mostly from one state, Texas, have come to dominate the textbook publishing field. This has resulted in textbooks that are homogenous and an industry devoid of competition.[24]

The third category of recommendations focused on time, specifically more time to teach content and, most telling, more time for teachers. The report specifically recommended that "the burden on teachers for maintaining discipline," and "administrative burdens on the teacher . . . should be reduced."[25] Clearly, the writers of *A Nation at Risk* were aware of the simple equation that in order to spend more time teaching content in engaging and innovative ways, teachers would have to spend less time on administrative duties and managing student behavior.

What happened instead? Teachers must still contend with busy work and disciplinary duties, while dealing with the new burden of extensive testing, which takes even more time away from teaching content.

Teachers were the focus of the fourth category of recommendations. As the report stated, the seven teaching reforms were "intended to improve the preparation of teachers" and "to make teaching a more rewarding and respected profession." The report noted that "the professional working life of teachers is on the whole unacceptable" and characterized by low pay and "little influence in critical professional decisions."[26]

To remedy these deplorable conditions for teachers, the report recommended that districts build in more time for teachers to engage in curricular and professional development and that

> Salaries for the teaching profession should be increased and should be professionally competitive, market-sensitive, and performance-based. Salary, promotion, tenure, and retention decisions should be tied to an effective evaluation system that includes peer review so that superior teachers can be rewarded, average ones encouraged, and poor ones either improved or terminated.[27]

Finally, the report ended with a recommendation for more funding from both the state and federal governments; not more funding for testing, but more funding to implement *all* the report's recommendations!

A Nation at Risk was a groundbreaking and popular report because of the problems it uncovered about the state of education and the way it articulated those problems. The public felt that the report was right, and its claims were true. Not surprisingly, teachers felt mixed about the report. They welcomed the calls for increased salaries, improved working conditions, and even some forms of teacher evaluation. Even one of the largest teacher's unions at the time, the AFT was open to some of the report's recommendations such as peer review.[28]

The recommendations that grew out of *A Nation at Risk* called on all sectors of the educational spectrum to contribute to the reform efforts, from local and state officials to the federal government, from teachers and administrators to curriculum and content experts, and from parents to the community at large. Their efforts were focused on the entire educational pipeline from elementary school to college. The report began as "An open letter to the American People" and ended with a call to all of society to play a role in education reform.

Unfortunately, implementing the report's recommendations hit the same roadblock that stymied other national education reform efforts up to this point: a lack of will to invest in public education. Because federal and state legislatures resisted providing the needed funds for the public schools, the business community, and other policymakers, such as governors, were able to hijack the implementation of the report's recommendations.

Without adequate funding to implement the report's innovative and wide-ranging recommendations, Goldstein points out that "policymakers focused on teachers alone, their training, their evaluation, and their pay." Thus, the current version of the standards and accountability moment was born, and we are still dealing with the fallout of those decisions today.

It is cold comfort to know that *A Nation at Risk* actually recommended the types of evaluation methods that teachers have always supported. Contrary to popular opinion, teachers are not against being held accountable, nor are they against testing in general. According to recent polling,[29] teachers believe that testing is a valuable component of any educational endeavor. For example, 80 percent of teachers support high school exit exams.

What bothers teachers the most is both the intensity and the extent of the required testing in today's schools. Teachers are equally dismayed that results from a single test have become the main indicator by which schools, and teachers, are judged. The majority of teachers, parents, and the public believe that school quality is better assessed by student achievement over time.

Teachers understand that accountability and testing are not the same. Teachers want to be held accountable, but in ways that respect their professional autonomy and expertise. Teachers know that there are other forms of accountability that school systems can and should implement. In fact, the 2015 Every Student Succeeds Act (ESSA), which replaced No Child Left Behind (NCLB), allows states to replace the "outcome-based" accountability model of NCLB and to implement more "innovative" assessments. It also requires that states assess higher-order thinking skills. The ESSA Summary of Final Regulations states:

> Our final regulations strike a balance by offering states flexibility to eliminate redundant testing and promote innovative assessments, while ensuring assessments continue to contribute to a well-rounded picture of how students and schools are doing. Tests must measure *higher-order thinking skills*, such as reasoning, analysis, complex problem solving, critical thinking, effective communication, and understanding of challenging content. States have *flexibility to develop new assessment designs*, which may include a series of multiple statewide interim assessments during the academic year that result in a single summative assessment score.[30]

Unfortunately, the majority of states have not yet adopted alternative approaches to accountability even though there are models available. Up to this point, most educational accountability systems are based upon one model—outcome-based accountability. Lerner and Tetlock review four methods that can be used to hold someone accountable. These methods, discussed below, can help us understand how the various models of accountability work to facilitate change in individuals.

- *The presence of another*—the expectation that one's work performance will be observed
- *Identifiability*—a worker's expectation that their work outcomes will be known to others and attributable to themselves
- *Reason giving*—a worker's expectation that they will have to explain their work outcomes
- *Evaluation*—a worker's expectation that their performance will be assessed by another according to a certain standard and that consequences (either good or bad) will result from that assessment[31]

These methods, when applied to the various models of accountability, help us understand which accountability models are a better fit for teachers, given who they are and what motivates them. Outcome-based models of accountability, where the teacher is held accountable for the outcome of student test scores on a one-time assessment, rely upon the methods of identifiability, where teachers are identified by their student's test scores; and evaluation, where they either receive bonuses and merit pay, or negative evaluations and ultimately the loss of employment.

The charter-school movement has attempted to hold schools accountable using a market-based model of accountability where the school strives to attract parents as "clients" based on how well they explain their programs and how easily parents can identify desirable outcomes associated with the school. Those schools that offer the best reasons a parent should choose their school often win out. Unlike the way that public schools use outcome-based accountability, where the teacher is held solely responsible, market-based models of accountability rely on the whole community—teachers, students, parents, and administrators—to explain and identify what works about their school.

Another vehicle for ensuring accountability is through the profession itself. Professional accountability systems draw on all four methods listed above. By promoting reason giving and the presence of another, professional accountability systems build on peer review activities that encourage teachers to learn from each other. Professionals are also often identified through their membership in professional organizations and enter the field through some sort of certification or exam.

Doctors and lawyers, with their medical rounds and teamwork on complicated legal cases, come to mind when thinking about professional accountability systems. In fact, professional accountability models come closest to what *A Nation at Risk* had in mind through its mandate that teacher accountability "be tied to an effective evaluation system that includes peer review." This is supported by data that shows that over 70 percent of teachers would "prefer to work in a school where there is a lot of collaboration and guidance from other instructional experts."[32]

When teachers are held accountable in ways that respect their professional knowledge and expertise, they actually support differential payment methods, especially when performance-based pay is awarded school-wide, rather than given to individual teachers.[33] Teachers also support the idea of paying teachers who work in challenging schools, or with high-need students, higher salaries.

Finally, nearly 70 percent of teachers believe that talented teachers, those who consistently improve student academic performance, should receive merit pay or bonuses. They believe the same for teachers who are certified by the National Board for Professional Standards.[34] These data show that teachers support their colleagues who excel. Their main concern is that the methods by which differential payments are determined are fair, clearly delineated, and determined by a process that is controlled by both teachers and administrators.

What teachers are strongly opposed to is being held accountable for things that are out of their control. Teachers, like the parents quoted above, know that they alone cannot be held solely responsible for student performance. Many teachers, especially those in high-needs schools, state that a significant proportion of their students are dealing with deeply entrenched social and economic issues that severely impact their ability to learn. In many cases, teachers get very little or no support in their work with children who are suffering from poverty, trauma, and other societal ailments.

Ninety percent of teachers feel that there are "too many kids with social and emotional needs"[35] in their classrooms to teach effectively. This is especially true for our nation's most troubled and difficult-to-reform schools. This is such a large issue for teachers that we devote the next two chapters to exploring the impact of social and emotional trauma on student engagement and behavior in today's classrooms.

NOTES

1. Sharon L. Nichols and David. C Berliner, *Collateral Damage: How High-Stakes Testing Corrupts America's Schools* (Cambridge, MA: Harvard University Press, 2007), 37.

2. Sharon L. Nichols and David. C Berliner, *Collateral Damage* 41.

3. Mary Alice Barksdale-Ladd and Karen Thomas, "What's at Stake in High Stakes Testing: Teachers and Parents Speak out," *Journal of Teacher Education*, 51, no. 5 (2000), doi: 10.1177/0022487100051005006

4. Nichols and Berliner, *Collateral Damage*, 101.
5. Nichols and Berliner, *Collateral Damage*, 167.
6. Nichols and Berliner, *Collateral Damage*, 154.
7. Nichols and Berliner, *Collateral Damage*, 105.
8. Jennifer L. Cohen, "Teachers in the News: A Critical Analysis of One US Newspaper's Discourse on Education," 2006–2007, *Discourse: Studies in the Cultural Politics of Education,* 31, no. 1 (February 2010), 114.
9. Loene M. Howes and Jane Goodman-Delahunty, "Teacher's Career Decisions: Perspectives on Choosing Teaching Careers, and on Staying or Leaving," *Issues in Educational Research*, 25, no. 1 (2015), 23.
10. Steve Farkas, Jean Johnson, and Tony Foleno, *A Sense of Calling: Who Teaches and Why: A Report from Public Agenda,* Public Agenda (2000), 40.
11. Farkas et al. *Sense of Calling*, 10–12.
12. Farkas et al. *Sense of Calling*, 34.
13. Jane Coggshall et al., "Retaining Teacher Talent: The View from Generation Y," *Learning Point Associates & Public Agenda*, (2010), 7–16.
14. Jane Coggshall et al., "Retaining Teacher Talent"; Farkas et al. *Sense of Calling*; E. Hirsch, and S. Emerick, "Teacher Working Conditions Are Student Learning Conditions," *A Report on the 2006 North Carolina Teacher Working Conditions Survey* (2007); J. Rochkind et al., "Lessons Learned: New Teachers Talk about Their Jobs, Challenges and Long-Range Plans," *Issue No. 3, Teaching in Changing Times* (2010).
15. Jean Johnson, Jonathan Rochkind, and Samantha Dupont, "Don't Count Us Out: How an Overreliance on Accountability Could Undermine the Public's Confidence in Schools, Business, Government and More," *The Public Agenda & The Kettering Foundation* (2011).
16. William J. Bushaw and Shane J. Lopez, "A Time for Change," *Phi Delta Kappa* (2010) 19.
17. Jean Johnson, "Will It Be on the Test? A Closer Look at How Leaders and Parents Think about Accountability in the Public Schools," *The Public Agenda & The Kettering Foundation* (2013), 11.
18. Jean Johnson, "Will It Be on the Test?" 13.
19. Jean Johnson, "Will It Be on the Test?" 14.
20. Rebecca Silliman and David Schleifer, "Our Next Assignment: Where Americans Stand on Public K–12 Education," *Public Agenda* (2018), 11.
21. Dana Goldstein, *The Teacher Wars: A History of America's Most Embattled Profession* (New York, NY: Penguin Random House, 2014), 208.
22. The National Commission on Excellence in Education, *A Nation at Risk: The Imperative for Educational Reform* (Washington, DC: US Government Printing Office, 1983).
23. The National Commission on Excellence in Education, *A Nation at Risk,* 25.
24. Bernie Froese-Germain, "Educational Accountability with a Human Face," *Canadian Teachers' Federation* (Ottawa, 2004), 7.
25. The National Commission on Excellence in Education, *A Nation at Risk,* 25.
26. The National Commission on Excellence in Education, *A Nation at Risk,* 20.

27. The National Commission on Excellence in Education, *A Nation at Risk*, 26.
28. Dana Goldstein, *The Teacher Wars*, 183.
29. Jean Johnson, Ana Maria Arumi, and Amber Ott, "Reality Check 2006: Issue No. 3: Is Support for Standards and Testing Fading?" *Education Insights at Public Agenda* (2006), 5.
30. U.S. Department of Education, "Every Student Succeeds Act: Summary of Final Regulations," https://www2.ed.gov/policy/elsec/leg/essa/essaassessmentfactsheet1207.pdf, 1.
31. Jennifer S. Learner and Philip E. Tetlock, "Accounting for the Effects of Accountability," *Psychological Bulletin* (1999), 255.
32. Jane Coggshall, Amber Ott, and Molly Lasagna, "Retaining Teacher Talent: Convergence and Contradictions in Teacher Perceptions of Policy Reform Ideas," *Learning Point Associates and Public Agenda* (2010), 7.
33. Jane Coggshall et al., "Retaining Teacher Talent: The View from Generation Y," *Learning Point Associates & Public Agenda* (2010), 2.
34. Jane Coggshall et al., "Retaining Teacher Talent," 7.
35. Jane Coggshall et al., "Retaining Teacher Talent," 8.

Chapter 3

Students

The Impact of Social-Emotional Struggles, Trauma, and Learning Difficulties on Classroom Behavior

This book opened with the story of Liquarry,[1] a third grader who was shot and killed by his seven-year-old cousin. Because he lived in a neighborhood that was systematically deprived of resources, Liquarry attended school with many children suffering from similar social problems. When children who experience trauma are all together in one classroom, the impact of the trauma becomes amplified.

This results in behaviors that make it almost impossible for teachers to teach and for the other children in the classroom to learn. One student suffering from trauma is enough to disrupt an entire classroom. Sadly, many classrooms in our nation's most troubled schools have four, five, or more such students, creating an environment of chaos that many teachers are not equipped or trained to manage.

Classroom teacher, instructional coach, and blogger, Angela Watson knows this firsthand. Ms. Watson described, in an early 2012 blog post, one of the worse days in her teaching career and the realizations that grew out of that experience.

Ms. Watson was teaching second graders, many of whom were reading at a kindergarten level. Inexplicably, the school had a no-recess policy—for seven-year-olds! Compounding this was the fact that she was teaching in a classroom without windows. She described the school environment as chaotic and unsafe due to fighting in the hallways and the cafeteria. Even though things were better in her own classroom, she still struggled to get and keep the children on task most days.

On that fateful day in 2012, Ms. Watson was attempting to teach a social studies lesson. When she asked the class to get out their social studies books, the following chaos ensued:

One child "burst into tears . . . crawled under the desk" and proceeded to "bang his head against the floor."

Another boy called the teacher "the B-word" under his breath causing the students sitting near him to call out.

One child accidentally dropped his book on the floor, causing the students near him to laugh, which prompted him to swear and punch one of them, who punched him right back. This led to chants of "fight, fight!"[2]

Across the room, another boy was ripping the pages out of the social studies book.

Everywhere there was noise, finger-pointing, and kids running around the room. The teacher couldn't even begin to focus on the kids who were actually raising their hands for attention. As she tried to figure out "which fire to put out first, . . . a voice came over the intercom. Lockdown, Code Three. Lockdown, Code Three," which meant that police were swarming the neighborhood, and she had to move all children away from the door.

At this moment, Ms. Watson realized that although she was managing the class, she wasn't teaching, and she would not be able to teach. She was already seven weeks into the year and this behavior was still happening "all day, every day." She received no assistance from the school in supporting traumatized students or those who were falling below grade level.

The worst part for her was that all new teachers "in the district were required to stay in the same school for the first three years." This meant that she would not be able to escape the stress and anxiety she faced every day for two and a half more years. She ultimately decided to leave the school in the middle of the year. Yet, leaving the kids made her feel guilty and selfish, as though she had failed as a teacher.

What is most interesting about Ms. Watson's story is the reaction it generated from teachers all over the country. The post received over 264 comments and reads like a record of teacher despair. Her story resonated with so many teachers because it revealed the major struggles teachers face when their classrooms are filled with children who have social, emotional, and learning needs.

In far too many cases, teachers are expected to manage the behaviors that grow from their students' unmet needs on their own, with no support from the administration or other school personnel. The teacher's stories reveal the cumulative impact of the realities that plague this nation's most troubled schools. But these realities were not shaped by the usual suspects: underfunded schools, poor neighborhoods, and "bad" or unprepared teachers. Rather, they were shaped by the convergence of growing poverty, national and state policies, and corporate greed.

Let me explain. Two unrelated developments began in the 1990s that set the stage for the worsening conditions in schools that started to emerge between 2006 and 2017, the repercussions of which are still being felt today. The first development was the shift in our understanding of how to treat general or "non-cancer" pain.[3] Throughout the 1990s, two organizations, the American Pain Society and the Veterans Health Administration, began and promoted a campaign called "pain as the fifth vital sign."

This was designed to improve the treatment of chronic noncancer pain. Based on this campaign, an organization called The Joint Commission, whose mission is to "continuously improve health care for the public" created standards for the treatment of pain along with assessments that would allow healthcare providers to better manage pain control. These standards mandated that doctors provide "humane treatment" for pain, which led to more reliance on opioid medications. Finally, the Drug Enforcement Agency relaxed its oversight of opioid prescriptions in the hopes that doctors would be less reluctant to prescribe them.

These important developments for improved treatment of chronic pain led the pharmaceutical companies to deem opioids as a "humane treatment" for pain. We all know what happened next.

Between 2000 and 2006, opioid use grew in every state, and the opioid death rate grew between 1 and 7 percent in every state that tracked such growth. By 2006, doctors were dispensing between 50 and 129 opioid prescriptions per 100 people in every state except New York, Hawaii, and the District of Columbia. These trends worsened between 2006 and 2017, when opioid deaths grew between 10 percent and 33 percent in twenty-three states, between 2 percent and 9 percent in fifteen states, remained flat in thirteen states, and dropped in only one state, Oregon.[4] Finally, in 2017, the US Department of Health and Human Services declared a public health emergency to deal with the opioid crisis.

The second development grew out of the publication of the landmark education report, *A Nation at Risk* in 1983. This report introduced the idea of testing the academic achievement of all students (not just disadvantaged and poor students) based on a set of educational standards that would be shared nationwide. A Nation at Risk led to shifts in how both the states, and those who publish standardized tests, operated in regard to student academic performance.

Throughout the 1990s, the states began designing and implementing performance and content standards; they began collecting data on student performance, and they began testing students every year. In order for this to be successful, the states needed publishers, such as Pearson,[5] to design better high-stakes assessments that could be scored and interpreted quickly in "increasingly complex combinations of norm-referenced and criterion-referenced data."[6]

By 2000, the Federal Department of Education had approved the standards development process of forty-eight states and the District of Columbia. These developments culminated in the passage of No Child Left Behind (NCLB) in 2001. Among other things, under NCLB funding was now directly tied to a school's testing outcomes. The standards movement, now codified by NCLB, also called for more challenging curricula focused on reasoning, critical thinking, content knowledge, and real-world applications.

In order for students to successfully demonstrate their knowledge and skills in relation to these new assessments, teaching and learning had to shift from a focus on instrumental processes such as memorization to more active processes that required the learner to make sense of new learning independently. "Students were expected to reason aloud, to explain their thinking, and to monitor and reflect on their own learning. These substantially more challenging curricular goals placed heavy demands on both the content knowledge and pedagogical skills of teachers."[7]

Finally, while both opioid use and standardized testing were growing exponentially across the country between 2000 and 2012, poverty was also growing. There are two key measures of poverty in this country. The Department of Health and Human Services (HHS) sets the poverty guidelines each year based on the Federal Poverty Level (FPL), which is determined by the Census Bureau. In 2019, a family of four was considered poor if they made less than $25,750 a year.

There is also a measure of what is called extreme or deep poverty, which is defined as having an income that is below 50 percent of the FPL. A family of four living in extreme poverty would make less than $12,875 a year. Between 2000 and 2011, the rates of both poverty and extreme poverty grew between 2 and 8 percent in forty-three states.

Thirty of these states had an overall poverty rate of between 20 and 30 percent, and an extreme poverty rate of between 10 and 17 percent. Finally, there is something called concentrated poverty, which is defined as a census tract that has an overall poverty rate of 30 percent or more. Between 2008 and 2012, deep into the opioid crisis and the standardized testing movement, 18.7 million children lived in concentrated poverty.[8]

Since 2006, opioid deaths have consistently been highest among people aged 25 to 44, the major child-rearing years. Between 2009 and 2014, more than eight million children aged one to seventeen lived with at least one parent who had a substance use disorder. Throughout this time, poverty, extreme poverty, and concentrated poverty were also growing. Research has shown that these conditions undermine a child's well-being. Being poor and living in high-poverty neighborhoods hinders a family's access to healthy food, quality schools, and good medical care.

There are more environmental hazards such as lead paint in poorer homes and neighborhoods. These conditions can be more stressful and too much stress can lead to poor physical, mental, and emotional health for both children and families. Also, growing up with parental substance abuse impacts a child's emotional, behavioral, and social development because it disrupts the parent's ability to provide a stable environment for their children. Parents who suffer from substance use disorders (SUDs) are unable to fully engage with and care for their children.

This, in turn, impacts the child's ability to attach to the parental figure, which can be especially damaging to children. Unfortunately, it appears that while conditions were getting more stressful and difficult for a sizable portion of children, many of whom lived in urban and rural areas, those same children were also being tested in unprecedented ways and their teachers were tasked with transforming their practice to meet the demands of the new accountability systems being implemented across the country.

These events have contributed to the generational poverty and emotional and psychological trauma for students like Liquarry, and every day teachers like Ms. Watson deal with the impacts of this trauma.

The stories that follow are from teachers who responded to Ms. Watson's blog, and from observations and interviews with teachers in high-needs elementary, middle, and high schools. The general descriptions of chaotic classrooms are the same, no matter the source. Most of the difficulty stems from behaviors that result when a classroom has a cohort of students who are struggling with social or emotional issues.

When there are more than three or four such students in one classroom, it is very difficult for teachers to manage on their own while also continuing to teach the other children in rigorous ways. Students are still children, and in many of these instances, teachers describe how a certain percentage of the other students in the classroom get caught up in the disruptions or disengage from the lesson and socialize among themselves. As one teacher described,

> In a class of twenty-five kids you maybe have six that just aren't ready to be there and are disruptive. You have another six who are mostly on point, but are easily distracted, who could go either way, and then you have ten kids who really want to be students, so you got the six misbehaving, that overwhelms the other six, now you got twelve disruptive kids and you can't teach.[9]

Each instance of these behaviors disrupts the classroom, interrupts learning, and makes sustained teaching impossible. The stories that follow demonstrate the heavy emotional toll this has on teachers.

One second-grade teacher describes how the boundaries of her school recently changed, and with that so has the population.

Our school is now in an urban neighborhood and the number of struggling students in my classroom has tripled. I have a particularly difficult second grade class. I have three students with ADD and anxiety disorders, three who must be tested for learning disabilities, two students receiving counseling, and three more who require constant non-crisis intervention. Finally, I have another three students on behavior plans. The stress of dealing with students that never stop talking and getting out of their seats; the incessant fighting and bullying; almost daily, something happens at lunch, recess, or in the hallways. Despite these challenges, I have gotten very little help from the administration in dealing with the student's needs. The administration is new; both the principal and the assistant principal are in their first year. They started the year strong but seem to have turned around in regard to student behavior and are taking an attitude of "deal with it in your classroom." As I struggle, endure, and reflect, I wonder, how much should I be expected to have to deal with myself? When should I expect administration support? I believe what we tolerate becomes our standard; with this in mind, it seems we are setting a low bar when violence and other dangerous behaviors are not addressed.[10]

A fourth-grade teacher describes how classroom behaviors prevent her from fulfilling her teaching plans and responsibilities:

I love teaching, but I am not able to "teach" anything because of all the issues. I wrote a grant for a free field trip—all expenses paid—for my second through fifth graders and only five of my students were able to go because of discipline issues or in-school suspensions. We also run out of food at times on late lunch (fourth grade) so I have to then hang out until they send more food so my students can eat. This happens at least once a week, and it is truly hard for the kids to focus on learning when they are hungry, so in that class, we only cover about 60% of the lessons I planned for the week. I get supplies but they get depleted quickly because the classroom has no storage. One day, one student chased another while I was breaking up a fight and knocked over my laptop and destroyed it. Out of seventeen fourth graders, I have three who are at grade level, and the other fourteen range from first grade to the beginning of third. Common core says we should be doing two and 3-digit multiplication, but I only have one student in my class who can do one digit above 75% at least one time. We have specials, such as art or cooking, but the kids get sent back to me if they act up, which happens every day, so I never get a break to plan during the day.

This elementary school teacher is thwarted in her efforts to teach by a lack of resources and a constantly changing administration.

I have been teaching elementary school for seven years. I have thirty-eight kindergartners in a room that does not have enough tables and chairs. Our school just hired yet another new administration. Discipline in our school is out of control and getting progressively worse year after year, and the kids can't have recess when it rains outside. They are only six years old, and they need to release their energy—but not on rainy days! I don't know how I can handle another year of this chaos and stress, with no support from the administration.[11]

This next elementary teacher, because she is skilled at managing disruptive student behaviors, describes how the administration assigns many of the most difficult students to her classroom and the effect this has on her and the other students.

I am currently in my eighth year of teaching in the same district. I have gotten excellent reviews every year. I love teaching! I always give 110% every day. I wake up each day ready to work and extremely excited and happy to go. Perhaps this is why students with behavior issues have always been assigned to my classroom (right from my first year of teaching!).

I've always dealt well with the students and have turned around quite a few. I've been told by the administrators that they know I can handle the behavior. What this actually means is that they know I won't send the children to the office; that I'll handle it myself in my classroom. However, at the end of the last school year, I specifically asked to be given a break from the students who have behavior issues—after eight years!

Again, they told me that I can handle the issues. I thanked my principal for the compliment but told him I am burning out and needed a break from it for just one year. Well, I didn't get a break. The next year, I had five students who had documented behavior issues assigned to my classroom. Five students are a lot. Five students who can't stay in their seats, who constantly walk around the room engaging others while I am trying to teach, who bully other children and start fights, and who throw things. Five students throw off the whole balance of the classroom.

When at least three of them are absent, we have a great day. I can teach and the other students can learn. When they are all present, I feel like a babysitter instead of a teacher. I spend more time trying to keep students out of trouble than I do teaching. I feel awful for the students that do the right thing each and every day. The massive amount of stress I feel dealing with these five children all on my own has caused my migraines to flare out of control. I wake up in the middle of the night with dread in the pit of my stomach.[12]

The teachers above are *not* certified to teach students with moderate disabilities, they are general education teachers who end up with students who have social or emotional issues. Teachers who are certified to teach students with moderate disabilities struggle even more because rather than having four to six struggling students, they often end up with a class full of students who need extra support. The examples below demonstrate the unique struggles they have in the classroom.

Example #1

I'm a third-year, special education teacher who works with children who have moderate learning disabilities. Basically, I can't teach. My kids will not sit down for longer than two minutes at a time. I get hit, kicked, bitten, and scratched on a daily basis. The administration put a violent second grader in my classroom, which is full of mostly kindergarteners, and I spend all day stopping him from hitting and knocking them down. I don't get a real lunch break and never have time to plan.

The administration acts like I should be able to handle all of the behaviors while still meeting all of their individual learning goals and the common core assessments. I literally cry on my forty-minute commute to work every day. I can barely spend time with my own toddler when I get home because I'm frantically trying to figure out how to restructure my classroom. And nobody will help me. I feel like I'm drowning every single day.[13]

Example #2

In my school, I teach all the second graders with Individualized Education Plans[14] (IEPs), and so the administration also assigned the lowest achieving second-graders, without IEPs, to my classroom as well. I have major behavior problems which constantly result in suspension. (I still could not fathom suspending second-graders).

My days consist of me reteaching the same procedures, filling out incredible amounts of data on behavior contracts I have created and chosen to implement, and just trying to keep my students safe from one another both physically and emotionally. It's a year-round school so it doesn't end until the end of July. I am so overwhelmed, completely exhausted, and so unhappy every day, all day at work. The administration is completely unorganized and provides me with no support at all.[15]

Example #3

I am a first-year teacher of students with multiple disabilities in elementary school. For weeks I was understaffed; and then I was given my most difficult student from a more experienced teacher's classroom without any extra aid support. Administration turned me down when I said I needed another instructional assistant. I work twelve hours a day and have IEP meetings with students who have thirty goals to master.

I am physically exhausted every day by my students; some of whom have aggressive behaviors. I have no planning time during the day and for most of the year, I have not gotten a lunch break. During the first few weeks of school, when I was understaffed, I couldn't even use the bathroom all day. On top of that, I am on a provisional license, and am taking graduate courses at night so I can earn my full teaching license.

If all of this wasn't enough, I have become extremely depressed. I no longer have the energy or time to do anything I like. I work all day and all weekend. I became really sick in November and all the following months. Every time I was almost better, I would get sick again. I was told I was the hardest-working first-year teacher that my coach has ever seen in special education. I care a lot about my students, my paraprofessionals, and my coworkers. But I think I care too much, and I can't turn it off. The effect of this job is taking so much out of me that it is negative.

I have many suicidal thoughts and constantly fantasize about getting in some kind of an accident. I was never like this before I took this job; I was bright and happy. Now I feel SO responsible for my students, and the weight is impossible and unbearable. I feel like no one knows how hard this job is, and I feel like I have no-to-little respect. What I want more than anything now is to be myself and truly smile again.[16]

As is clear from these stories, behavior and learning issues start in the lower grades—kindergarten through second—and although not confined to those classrooms, many of the most severe learning and behavioral challenges take place in classrooms that serve kids who have moderate disabilities. When reading these examples, one is left with the feeling that a crime is taking place.

The children in these classrooms are being neglected and abandoned by the school system, often leaving one teacher as the sole adult responsible for providing the support they need. In many cases, the children who exhibit the most challenging behaviors have *already been diagnosed* with a host of social, emotional, and academic issues, but rather than get the supports they need, it appears that the school's administration expects the teacher to manage and contain them until they can be moved onto the next grade or out the door. This is a crime! But it is not the only one.

In these dysfunctional classrooms (and sometimes the whole school is dysfunctional), the teacher is often dealing with three different groups of children: those who are suffering from a diagnosed medical/learning issue or an experience-based trauma that impacts their ability to learn and pay attention; those who *may not* have a diagnosed medical or trauma based issue, but who may come from a home where their parents are struggling in some way, either with poverty, language barriers, overwork, or mental health or addiction issues and thus are not able to focus as much on their child's schooling or pay attention to other issues involving their child.

These children are the ones who often get distracted and may join in when those who are diagnosed act out in class. Finally, you have the children whose parents are focused on school and who can prioritize the kinds of behaviors that lead to success in school. These children know how to be students; they know how to learn, and they want to learn, but they can't because of the chaos happening all around them.

The next crime committed is that the struggling children in the school are kept together without any extra support! Children who are suffering from real, diagnosed disorders, health issues, or trauma are left to navigate the classroom without the vital support they need. The other children, who are not suffering from a diagnosed disorder (but may have undiagnosed trauma) may not have as much self-control or may be easily frustrated when they don't understand the content.

In many cases, these innocent children stay with each other all through elementary school, and what is the biggest thing they learn? They learn that they can join in class disruptions and perhaps mask their own insecurities and deficiencies. They learn that they do not have to pay attention in school. They learn this because their teachers are legitimately struggling with the kids who have traumatic, medical, social, emotional, or learning diagnoses. They learn this as early as elementary school because they are kept together in the same classrooms.

By the time they get to middle and high school—even though they are capable of doing the required schoolwork—they no longer know what good work looks like. They have not been challenged; they do not know how to be students by this point. So, although they are older and more capable, the behaviors they have always known continue in the upper grades. The following examples demonstrate how this truly vicious cycle continues.

Example #1

> The high school I work for is chaotic. There are limited consequences for students' actions. I went into education with such a passion and desire to help students learn but find myself burdened by the behaviors I can no longer control, the continuous testing, the data that must drive our instruction 24-7, the lack of classroom support, and administrators that are so focused on compliance that they ignore the challenges we face in our classrooms.
>
> Some students throw stuff at teachers and curse them out and will be back the same day, with no consequences. The administration does nothing! I have been a teacher for 9 years, and the stress is unstoppable. Most days I put in between 12–15 hours and don't feel I even make a dent in my workload. The teachers get blamed for low test scores, but half the kids do not complete the tests, mostly because of the school's low attendance rate, and there is no administrative plan for how to improve attendance. I have missed over a week of work due to stress and illness and have lost a significant amount of weight.[17]

Example #2

I taught middle school at the same school for eight years, and I loved that school. They hired me straight out of college. I feel like my co-workers watched me grow up. But last year was my breaking point. I broke. I was teaching an elective that the kids did not get to pick, Creative Writing.

My classes were huge (thirty-five and up), and I was stuck in a windowless room, in the back of the school. For some reason, I'd gotten a really challenging crop of kids. There was very little disciplinary support from the front office, and very few rules I was allowed to actually enforce with any authority. I was charged with making my own curriculum, but not given any direction, then I got slammed by administration for not being on pace with a non-existing learning schedule. I had one functioning computer for the students to use while the other elective in my grade level had a full production graphics design studio.

Every one of my classes had at least thirty-five thirteen-year-olds in the room. I love children. I love learning, and I am constantly searching for new ways to reach my students. I don't think it was unreasonable that when I asked for help, I expected to get it. But all I was hearing was "No." During this time, I was serving as the yearbook advisor. My yearbook kids were hard-working, sweet, and dependable.

Additionally, I was working a part-time job because my salary was slashed 10% in the last three years of my employment with the county. When you're not making much to start, 10% hurts. It really hurts. As teachers, we are here to serve the needs of others. You can't possibly do that if you're unhappy. You can probably skate by for a while, but if you can't give 100%, then there's no way you'll get 100% back.[18]

Finally, a male high school teacher describes his teaching situation.

Example #3

I got my first job teaching science in an urban high school. I was assigned an extra subject to teach a few days before school started so I was not able to plan for that subject over the summer. I also had no access to the online attendance system for the first two months of school which means I did not have a list of who my students were. I learned the hard way that discipline is next to impossible if you don't have a list of students, especially if they're being switched from class to class for the first month.

The behavior in my class was very challenging. One-third of my students were diagnosed with severe social/emotional issues. I have very little support from the administration; there is NO policy for discipline or behavior at the school in general. At this point I'm working over 100 hours a week, staying at the school until 11 pm on Fridays to plan. I was also making an hour of parent phone calls every day, and three to four hours on weekends.

I felt full of empathy, compassion, and drive as I made my way through ed. school. Yet, once in the classroom, the enormity of the job cast a shadow over what until then was unabashed idealism. In the end, I decided that teaching was not for me. When I was in college, I taught and tutored for years, and I thought I'd do this for my entire life. I never thought I'd leave.[19]

As these examples show, the pressures of teaching students who are dealing with learning or other social/emotional issues while also having to prepare those same students to succeed in this rigorous testing environment while getting no support from administration or classroom aids are taking a great toll on teachers' mental and physical health. Schools need to take children who are struggling with social/emotional issues seriously in the early grades and get them the services they need. Period!

At the most basic level, struggling children cannot be bunched into classrooms with only one teacher and then kept together for their entire elementary career. Even a very well-prepared teacher will stumble in these situations. Teachers need more support to be able to teach when their classrooms are occupied by students who are suffering from a wide range of social and emotional difficulties.

It is vital that we, as a society, understand the types of experiences that lead to learning, behavioral, and social/emotional disorders in children. The truth is we know very well what those experiences are; we know how they impact children's health and their mental, physical, and emotional well-being.

Many people blame the parents when children misbehave, but we know that these behaviors are caused by the ways in which poverty, stress, and trauma impact the brain. Even in the pandemic, when children's mental health issues were exacerbated, this remains true: a student cannot learn when trauma is front and center. The next chapter describes how these processes hurt children, and the impact they have on student learning in detail.

NOTES

1. Scott Allen and Maria Cramer, "Crime Consumed a Family, and an 8-Year-Old Is Lost," *The Boston Globe* (August 2007): A.1.

2. Angela Watson, "Why I Quit My Teaching Job Mid-Year (No, It Wasn't the Testing)," *Truth for Teachers* (November 22, 2012), https://truthforteachers.com/why-i-quit-my-teaching-job-mid-year/.

3. Mark Jones et al., "A Brief History of the Opioid Epidemic and Strategies for Pain Medicine," *Pain and Therapy* (April 24, 2018) 15.

4. Kaiser Family Foundation, "Opioid Overdose Death Rates," *KFF.org* (2006–2017), https://www.kff.org/other/state-indicator/opioid-overdose-death-rates/?currentTimeframe=0&sortModel=%7B%22colId%22:%22 Location%22,%22sort%22:%22asc%22%7D; Centers for Disease Control and Prevention, *CDC.gov* (2006–2017), https://www.cdc.gov/drugoverdose/deaths/index.html.

5. Pearson is a British-owned education publishing and assessment company that produces material for schools and corporations throughout the world.

6. Margaret A. Jorgensen, and Jenny Hoffman, "History of No Child Left Behind Act of 2001 (NCLB)," Pearson (August 2003), 5.

7. Lorrie A. Shepard, "A Brief History of Accountability Testing," 1965–2007, in *The Future of Test-Based Educational Accountability*, ed. Katherine E Ryan and Lorrie A. Shepard (New York, NY: Routledge, 2008), 36.

8. Annie E. Casey Foundation, "Children Living in High-Poverty, Low-Opportunity Neighborhoods," *The Anne E. Casey Foundation www.aecf.org* (2017).

9. Quote from a teacher who teaches in an urban high school in a mid-sized city.

10. Angela Watson, "Why I Quit Teaching."

11. Angela Watson, "Why I Quit Teaching."

12. Angela Watson, "Why I Quit Teaching."

13. Angela Watson, "Why I Quit Teaching."

14. An IEP is a plan for children with an identified disability that ensures that they get the specialized instruction and other services that they need in order to learn.

15. Angela Watson, "Why I Quit Teaching."

16. Angela Watson, "Why I Quit Teaching."

17. Angela Watson, "Why I Quit Teaching."

18. Angela Watson, "Why I Quit Teaching."

19. Angela Watson, "Why I Quit Teaching."

Chapter 4

What Ails the Children?

The types of student behaviors we saw in the previous chapter thrive in certain social conditions. These conditions lead to 90 percent of the out-of-control student behaviors we see in the classroom. They are poverty, family structure, and community. Poverty, family structure, and community are bound together in ways that are not easily disentangled. The experiences of the child raised in poverty are shaped by the family structure s/he is born into and the community in which s/he is raised.

It is one thing to be raised poor in a safe community with two supportive parents or by an educated single mother, and quite another to be raised by a single mother who dropped out of high school in a poor and unsafe community. Depending upon the context, the most damaging effects of poverty—stress and trauma—can have devastating effects on children's health. Outside of the family, teachers and nurses are the public servants most impacted by these health effects. In the classroom, children suffering from stress and trauma can make it very challenging for teachers to do their jobs, even when supports are in place.

Without support, teaching, as we normally define it, is simply not possible. The rest of this chapter presents the numbers, and details the impact, that poverty, stress, and trauma have on child well-being.

This chapter explores the reasons why we are seeing the kinds of behaviors described above, but before we dive into those reasons, we need to set the record straight about parents.

Chapter 4

IS IT THE PARENTS? NO!

When we ask the question of why children misbehave, for many, the answer is the parents. Sadly, one of the most common refrains is that the "parents just don't care." Society, from policymakers to teachers, to other parents, tend to blame the parents when a child's behavior is out of control or too difficult to manage. They say things like the "parents are the first teachers," and today's parents don't discipline children like they did in the old days. These comments about how parents were more responsible in the old days, really irk me.

What we need to realize as a society is that the image we tend to have about the "old days" never existed. In the "old days," policymakers and politicians did what they do today when confronted with parental behavior that they do not like. They enact laws that allow society to do what the parents cannot or will not do. According to policymakers, parents, especially poor and immigrant parents, have never done what they were "supposed" to be doing in terms of their children's education.

Let's take a close look at that history for a moment. Education in this country began as a parental responsibility with each early colony establishing its own small schools. These schools were created by religious leaders and controlled by parents, many of whom had left Europe because of religious persecution. The curriculum in these schools focused on religion, reading, and writing.[1]

In 1642, Massachusetts passed the first law requiring all parents to educate their children in reading, religion, and a trade. What the state found, however, was that these parent educators tended to focus more on religion and work skills in their lessons and less on reading. The ultimate conclusion was that not all parents could teach their children how to read. At this point, Massachusetts passed another law that mandated towns of fifty or more to hire a teacher, to be supported with public funds, to teach reading.

This realization, that parents may not have the skills to teach their own children, became more apparent in the 1890s, when European immigrants began flooding the country in droves. These parents did not have the skills to teach their children how to read or write. This prompted leaders in other states, such as Thomas Jefferson in Virginia, to call for public funds to support the education of every child in the state.

By 1852, Massachusetts passed the first compulsory education law in the country. Supporters of these laws argued that all children needed to have basic reading, writing, and communication skills in order to be able to participate as capable citizens in a democracy. For example, Jefferson feared that "un-informed citizens could easily become the pawns of political activists."[2] Other states passed similar laws, but they only mandated education through the elementary years and enforcement was weak.

This all changed with the growth of the industrial revolution. Poor and immigrant families, who needed money to survive, put their children to work in the factories, in the mines, and on the farms to supplement the family income or to work the land for food. In these cases, poor and immigrant families literally could not afford to send their children to school. To make things worse, immigrant children were seen as "cheap" labor by factory owners. It wasn't until labor unions pressured politicians to enact child labor laws that things began to change.

But it wasn't enough to pass laws against child labor because children who were now not working, especially teenagers, who were also not required to attend school, began hanging out in the streets, especially in urban areas. Because of the prevailing negative attitudes about immigrants and young people of color, especially males, these large groups of boys started to make people in the cities feel unsafe. Politicians dealt with this by passing compulsory attendance and truancy laws.

Every state had these laws on the books by 1918 allowing immigration officials to team up with schools to share the status of new immigrants across agencies to ensure compliance with the laws. Finally, many states extended the school day, keeping older children in school for more hours.

The steps described above were taken because policy makers felt that parents were either (1) not capable of properly educating their children, (2) not motivated to focus on what the state felt was an important educational aim, (i.e., the teaching of religion or job skills versus the teaching of reading), or (3) could not be trusted to send their children to school because they needed the children to work to support the family.

These laws were enacted to keep mostly poor and immigrant parents from having a full say over their children. This demonstrates that there was never a time when the authorities and poor or working parents worked together in harmony over the educational fate of their children. Back then, they passed laws that allowed schools and teachers to do what the parents could not (teach academic skills), or would not (choose school over employment). I argue that we could do the same thing today.

There has been other legislation designed to do what parents could not. The Elementary and Secondary Education Act (ESEA) of 1965 was such a law. ESEA was designed to mitigate the impact of poverty on Black, Latinx, and other disadvantaged children, who in the law were defined as "low-income, migratory, foster and neglected or delinquent" children. Thankfully, our country had evolved some by 1965 and realized that parents were hampered by poverty.

The Federal government realized that poverty prevented parents from providing what their children needed to succeed in school, so they stepped in to force, but also to *compensate*, schools and communities that agreed to assist with the "war on poverty" by providing what the parents could not, since they were poor and possibly uneducated themselves. As Johnson said when he signed the law, "by passing this bill, we bridge the gap between helplessness and hope for more than five million educationally deprived children."[3]

Like the earlier education reform laws, including more recent ones like NCLB, ESEA focused on academics. It provided funding for more books, libraries, tutoring, and extra academic support for low-income children. The new laws have gone even further, by mandating academic testing and even parent involvement. Unfortunately, these laws are becoming less and less effective in terms of improving America's educational outcomes because they continue to ignore the non-academic aspects of children's lives and how these aspects impact children's ability to learn.

Unfortunately, circumstances have changed little in the twenty-first century in terms of the stressors on poor and immigrant parents. Even though we have a larger social safety net many are still overwhelmed and stressed because of their circumstances. This makes it very difficult for them to also provide the types of structures and supports their children need in order to thrive in school. We also know so much more today about the impact that stress has on children and families.

In the historical example above, families were stressed by poverty so dire that even very young children had to work to help support the family, whereas today the toxic stress that many families experience results from other social ills that grow out of poverty, such as drug abuse, violence, and trauma. Families mired in these stressful circumstances are not able to provide the kind of environment that is best for children, regardless of whether their inability results from a lack of skill or a more overwhelming need.

Given this, it is irresponsible for us to continue to blame parents. Rather, we need to do what we have always done. We need to pass laws that mandate school and community support for what parents are not able to provide for their children, regardless of the reasons for their inability.

We can all understand that a certain percentage of poor and immigrant parents might not have the academic skills needed to prepare their children for school. However, given all of the parent blaming out there, it appears that it is much harder for people to understand how other needs might usurp a parent's ability to provide support for their child's schooling. In the case of what was happening during the industrial revolution, it was not simply that parents did not want to send their kids to school.

It was that there existed a more immediate need to feed the family. Likewise, for many families today, what might look like an ill-informed choice, or worse, a lack of care for their own children, is really an act of desperation caused by either economic or social conditions. These conditions have a direct link to student behavior in the classroom.

THE PATH OF CHILDHOOD MISFORTUNE: POVERTY BY THE NUMBERS

Poverty is an economic condition that, when combined with certain family structures and community contexts, leads to many unhealthy outcomes for children. These outcomes have a tremendous impact on a child's behavior in school. In 2018, there were eighteen million poor children in this country (26%). Just under 70 percent of poor families subsist at the federal poverty level, which for a family of four is $26,200. This goes up by about $4,000 for each additional family member.[4] (This is in contrast to those families considered low income, which is $52,400 for a family of four.)

The really sad news is that 30 percent of these eighteen million children live in extreme poverty, surviving on an income that is half the amount for a family of four or $13,100. When one looks at children of color, nearly 60 percent of poor children are Black (32%) or Latinx (26%). This is compared to 11 percent for both White and Asian children.[5] When we look at immigrant children, who make up 25 percent of children in the US, 20 percent live in poverty.[6]

Poverty is intertwined with family structure in that poor children are more likely to be raised by single parents, mostly mothers (50%).[7] These parents also tend to be younger on average, to have lower educational attainment, and to work in minimum wage jobs or to be unemployed. In 2018, 30 percent of single African American mothers were poor, as were (14%)[8] of Latinx single mothers. Poor children who are raised in these conditions are more likely to suffer from a host of unhealthy ailments.

They are more likely to have chronic health conditions. They are more likely to suffer from lead poisoning. They are more likely to have emotional and behavioral difficulties in school, and they have higher rates of learning disabilities and ADHD.[9] These outcomes can be mediated by the parent's level of education or support. Those with only a high school degree or less are more prone to react in ways that diminish the family's relational health. Likewise, single mothers who have the support of family or state services are more likely to be relationally healthy.

Without these mediating factors, the pressures on poor families can spiral out of control. For example, research has shown that financial struggles can lead to depression, family conflict, and stress.[10] This stress can become toxic, impacting the children's development, physical health, cognitive abilities, emotional and behavioral outcomes, and school achievement.[11]

One of the unfortunate truths about poverty in this country is that it tends to be concentrated in certain geographic areas. Forty percent of all poor children live in areas where the poverty rates are 30 percent or more. Children of color are more likely to live in neighborhoods of concentrated poverty.[12]

In 2018, 35 percent of Black children and 17 percent of Latinx children lived in these neighborhoods, as compared to 4 percent of White children.[13] This is why poverty is a community issue. Communities shape the overall impact of poverty.

These neighborhoods are often referred to as "distressed" communities. Fifty million, or one in six Americans, live in a distressed community, with another fifty-six million living in communities labeled "at risk."[14] Distressed and at-risk communities are distinguished by high percentages of adults who did not graduate from high school (22% and 16%), of unemployed working-age adults (42% and 33%), and by their high rates of poverty (26% and 18%).[15] The vast majority of distressed communities are located in the South, followed by urban areas in the Northeast, Midwest, and West. Distressed communities have the highest percentages of Black (56%), Latinx (46%), and Native American (58%) populations.

Sadly, poor children, including high numbers of poor children of color, tend to cluster in these same areas, with states in the South and West having the highest rates of children who live in concentrated poverty.[16] For example, twelve out of the fourteen states that have the highest poverty rates for children of color have rates of 40 percent or more. Even though the percentages of childhood poverty are highest in rural states, urban areas have the largest number of children living in concentrated poverty.[17]

Communities that have high rates of poverty also tend to be unsafe, with high rates of violence and crime. They tend to be unhealthy, with high rates of both physical and mental illness. They tend to foster despair, with high rates of drug abuse and unemployment.[18] They tend to have under-resourced schools which leads to diminishing educational outcomes.

Growing up in these conditions sets children up for two of the most pernicious outcomes of poverty. First, these children are more likely to experience trauma, and second, they are more likely to react to their experience of trauma in ways that amplify their misfortune. This happens because of the ways the body reacts to stress. We can think of this as a path of misfortune that begins in the wider society and travels through poor communities, infecting first the mother and then her children.

What starts as a community, or social, phenomenon ends up as a biological condition. This condition influences, but does not determine, a child's behavior and coping methods. Mediating factors can have a tremendous influence on childhood outcomes in these circumstances, but unfortunately, society has not yet figured out how to harness the power of those mediating factors, creating misery for millions of children and their teachers. Several researchers have documented this path of misfortune.

STRESS AND ITS IMPACT ON THE BRAIN

The brain grows tremendously in the first two years of life, more than doubling in size. Much of this growth involves the overproduction of "synaptic connections" between neurons in different parts of the brain. These neurons form pathways between brain structures. As the brain grows, some of these pathways, or neural networks, become stronger from continual use, while others grow weaker and die away from lack of use.

These pathways are like a cellular telephone network in that they set up a communications system that links different brain structures to each other. These pathways relay sensory information (anything we can hear, see, smell, touch, or taste) to the various brain structures. The sensory information moves along these pathways, or systems, in one of two forms, either through electrical impulses or through chemical neurotransmitters.

One system, called the limbic system, plays a key role in regulating our emotional responses. The limbic system consists of three major brain structures that regulate the body's "stress response"; these are the amygdala, the hippocampus, and the prefrontal cortex. These three brain structures make up what is called the HPA axis, which is the body's stress response system. This physiological system controls the body's "fight or flight" response and plays a key role in how children respond to stress, which in turn influences their behavior.[19]

The amygdala is the part of our brain that responds to threatening or fearful environmental events. One can think of the amygdala as an alarm system that gets activated by stressful stimuli. When the amygdala detects fearful or stressful sensory input, it activates the stress response system, which sets in motion the release of a cascade of chemicals and hormones that travels from the brain, down through the body.

These chemicals include adrenaline, dopamine, and cortisol. These chemicals and hormones play key roles in regulating various aspects of human behavior. Cortisol is the most significant one for this discussion given how it interacts with various brain structures, especially the hippocampus.

The hippocampus plays a critical role in the formation, organization, and storage of new memories, and thus new learning. It also plays a role in connecting certain sensations and emotions to these memories. The hippocampus helps us determine the importance of an experience by comparing new experiences to memories. An example of this is when a certain smell triggers a specific memory. The connection between the smell (sensory input) and the memory is formed in the hippocampus.

However, once the amygdala sets off the alarm by releasing cortisol, the cortisol interacts with the hippocampus in a way that facilitates fear-based memories. In response to stressful stimuli, the hippocampus is triggered to remember the emotional and fearful aspects of the situation so that we can better avoid similar situations in the future.[20]

Finally, the prefrontal cortex is part of the limbic system because it can help the body mediate the impact of stressful stimuli and fearful memories through rational thought. The prefrontal cortex helps us control our behavior by contributing to our ability to reason. This is the part of the brain that helps us inhibit inappropriate actions and regulate our behavior so that we can respond to our environment in appropriate ways.

Using its access to both working memory and long-term memory, through its connections with the hippocampus, the prefrontal cortex can draw on events that have just occurred and are stored in working memory, or draw on information held in long-term memory and use this information to help us regulate our behavior, our thoughts, and our emotions. This behavioral regulation helps us carry out the following mental actions:

- Coordinate and adjust our behaviors
- Plan next steps
- Focus our attention
- Predict the consequences of our actions
- Anticipate the outcomes of environmental events
- Control our impulses
- Manage our emotional reactions
- Suppress urges
- Set goals and work to achieve them

Under normal conditions, these three brain structures—the amygdala, the hippocampus, and the prefrontal cortex—help us recognize, evaluate, and properly deal with stressful situations by preparing the body for a "fight or flight" response in reaction to the environmental event. Two key things happen in the body to facilitate this reaction. First, the body is prepared by the chemicals and hormones released by the amygdala and the HPA axis to physically deal with the stressful situation through a faster heart rate, a rise in blood pressure, and an increase in glucose which increases energy and inhibits pain.

Second, the hippocampus is triggered by the cortisol to remember emotional and fearful aspects of the stressful situation and compare those to past experiences, so that it can better understand the situation, know how to react in the situation, and avoid similar situations in the future. Finally, the prefrontal cortex evaluates the alarming messages coming from the amygdala and the hippocampus to determine if flight or fight is necessary, and if not, allows the organism to come up with a rational explanation and/or healthier behavioral response to deal with the stressful situation.[21]

As is clear from this description, the amygdala and the release of cortisol activate the stress response system, but the hippocampus and the prefrontal cortex can deactivate the system by evaluating sensory input and returning the release of cortisol to normal, healthy levels. Things can go terribly wrong, however, when an individual experiences too much stress, like the second grader who had a temper tantrum in Ms. Watson's classroom. As we learned above, the stress response can be mediated by our memories, through the hippocampus, and by our rational thoughts, through the prefrontal cortex.

There is also a third mediating factor for stress, and that is the presence of a caring and supportive adult who can help the young child process the stressful situation. At this point, it is important to focus this conversation on the stress response in infants and very young children. When young children experience toxic stress, which is defined as "strong, frequent or prolonged activation of the body's stress response system,"[22] it shifts the way that cortisol works in the body.

Specifically, it makes the HPA axis more sensitive, causing it to release more cortisol with each stressful episode, causing the cortisol to stay in the body for longer periods of time and making it harder for "stress-induced" cortisol to return to normal levels after the stressful situation ends,[23] resulting in a body and brain that is basically swimming in a toxic pool of cortisol.

The hippocampus is especially impacted by cortisol because it has a large number of what are called "corticosteroid receptors." Because it has so many receptors, too much cortisol can destroy neurons in the hippocampus, causing it to have less volume and damaging its ability to form new memories, which is central to learning. This is especially significant for cognitive learning and memory which has been shown through neural imaging to reside in the hippocampus.

Too much cortisol can make it harder to retrieve memories, particularly impacting the retrieval of neutral memories over emotional ones. Finally, cortisol and stress enhance the consolidation of emotionally charged memories which also enhances the memory of whatever successful behavior ended the stressful situation and "coding" this behavior as a habit. This pattern can make children vulnerable to maladaptive behaviors[24] that work during stressful situations but are inappropriate in everyday life.

Cortisol also weakens the prefrontal cortex because it damages the pathways between it and the hippocampus. This hurts memory consolidation and the ability of the prefrontal cortex to accurately represent information in working memory,[25] which further damages the ability to learn. Too much cortisol also decreases the volume in a part of the prefrontal cortex[26] that is central to emotion and social regulation. While cortisol causes both the prefrontal cortex and hippocampus to lose functioning through weakened pathways, it actually strengthens the pathways and increases the volume of the amygdala.[27]

This results in a strengthening of the brain structure that promotes the stress response and a weakening of the structures that inhibit that response. This gives the amygdala more power in determining behavior because it changes how the brain mediates our behavior. The amygdala consolidates emotionally relevant information and regulates the fear response whereas the prefrontal cortex consolidates thoughtful and reflective information and regulates the rational response.

In other words, when the brain gets overloaded with cortisol-induced toxic stress, it switches from a top-down to a bottom-up regulatory system. Behavior is now driven by the rapid, emotionally driven reflexes of the amygdala rather than being driven by the more thoughtful and deliberate reflections of the prefrontal cortex.

Finally, there are two other ways that too much stress-induced cortisol impacts the developing brain. Although not part of the limbic system, they also have a tremendous impact on learning and behavior. The first is that cortisol disrupts sleep patterns in young children. One function cortisol plays in the body—when it is not directing the fight or flight response—is to regulate the body's sleep-wake cycle. In normal conditions, cortisol is released in the body on a daily, 24-hour cycle.

Cortisol levels are at their highest in the morning and gradually decline throughout the day, reaching their lowest levels around midnight. This helps the body feel awake in the morning, stay alert throughout the day, and sleep better at night. Toxic stress can cause the amygdala to be continually activated, signaling the HPA axis to continually release cortisol and disrupt the sleep-wake cycle. When this happens, young children don't sleep at night, can't wake up in the morning, and can't pay attention in school.

Second, children who suffer from too much stress have both a smaller and underdeveloped prefrontal cortex and a smaller hippocampus. The corpus callosum, a bungle of fibers that allows the left side of the brain to communicate with the right side is also smaller when children experience overwhelming stress.

> The result of a smaller corpus callosum is that children can "reside" in only one hemisphere of the brain, rather than shifting seamlessly between the two . . . A lot of individuals who have survived childhood trauma reside in their left hemisphere when they function well. But when traumatic thoughts arise, they retreat into their right. . . . They can get very emotional, without any of the logic of the left side there to guide them.[28]

Children who experience an overload of toxic stress on a regular basis end up with neuronal connections, or brain pathways, that prime them to respond emotionally to fear-based situations. Whereas the brain pathways that might help them respond to these situations more rationally are much weaker from lack of use during their early years. The growth in neuronal connections is a genetic process, but the strength of those connections in the growing brain is impacted by the environment, that is, by what comes in by way of sensory input.

An out-of-control stress response system has the biggest and most negative impact on children who experience stress at very young ages, including in utero. Maternal stress exposes the fetus to cortisol which can impact the early development of both the amygdala and the hippocampus, sensitizing the child's stress response system to react fearfully and emotionally to stressful stimuli and damaging the brain structures that enhance memory and learning. Poverty, single motherhood, and domestic violence are all conditions that raise maternal stress. This is an example of how the brain develops in response to its environment.[29]

High levels of maternal stress hurt the developing infant on two fronts. First, it shapes the infant brain in ways that make it more vulnerable to stressful situations. Second, it prevents the mother from helping the baby regulate its own emotional and stress-based responses. Babies are born with a biological instinct to seek out the mother or primary caregiver when the baby experiences discomfort or stress of any kind.

How the mother responds to the baby during these periods helps the baby to develop an internal working model of how he or she will be treated by others, especially when they are in need. The mother's response also teaches the baby how to regulate its own emotions when confronted with distressing situations. Babies are not born knowing how to regulate their emotions; rather, the baby uses the emotional signals it learns from caregivers to guide their behavior.

When a child is experiencing environmental stress, the presence of a caring and supportive adult can help the young child process the stressful situation and help them cope with their emotional responses. Over time this teaches the infant how to regulate their emotions. Parents who are experiencing toxic stress themselves are often not able to effectively model appropriate emotional regulation. This deprives their children of the necessary emotional scaffolding to eventually be able to process their own emotions in a healthy way.

Chapter 4

POVERTY, STRESS, AND TRAUMA

Living in poverty makes life more stressful for both parents and children under normal circumstances. When neglect and abuse enter the picture, children not only lack the modeling and support they need to learn how to regulate their own emotions, but they may also experience harsh, inconsistent, and insensitive parenting. Neglectful caregivers can lack empathy or be unresponsive to the child's needs. Abusive caregivers can be both emotionally and physically threatening and completely unpredictable.

These types of responses and behaviors are traumatic for children. They generate harmful emotions, such as fear, despair, guilt, and frustration, that quickly trigger, and then overload, the body's stress response system. Experiencing early trauma leads to toxic stress, resulting in the continual release of cortisol and the related damage to the limbic system as described above. The damage does not stop there. Toxic stress also damages the child's development, physical health, cognitive abilities, emotional and behavioral outcomes, and school achievement.[30]

One of the most significant studies to look at the long-term effects of child abuse and neglect was published in 1998 and called "The Adverse Childhood Experiences Study (ACEs)." This study was conducted by the CDC and the Kaiser Foundation,[31] but unfortunately it did not get much attention from national health organizations until 2011, and even now, the federal response to its own study is sorely lacking.[32] Those who are paying attention to the study's findings are mostly healthcare workers and community advocates.

Except for in a few states and isolated districts, schools have also only recently been introduced to the power and promise of the ACEs study. The ACEs study identified ten types of adverse childhood experiences. They include three types of abuse (sexual, verbal, and physical), five types of family dysfunction (having an alcoholic or drug-addicted parent, having a mentally ill parent, having a mother who is a victim of domestic abuse, having a family member who has been in jail and losing a parent through divorce or abandonment) and two types of neglect (emotional and physical).

These forms of child maltreatment are the same types of experiences that cause the amygdala to overproduce cortisol. The experience of ACEs is traumatic and leads to unhealthy outcomes for all children regardless of income, race, or ethnicity. However, children who are poor, and who live in single-parent homes and distressed neighborhoods, are more likely to have adverse childhood experiences than children who are not poor. So, do we know how many children suffer adverse childhood experiences?

The numbers indicate that in 2018, just under 20 percent of children in this country, ages 0 to 17, had experienced two or more ACEs. This represents a total of thirteen million children. In addition, caregivers for just over 10 percent of children, or 7.5 million, were reported for child maltreatment. These numbers come from numerous national and state reports that have been compiled by the Anne E. Casey Foundation and the Department of Health and Human Services.

We also know that statistically, reported instances almost never represent the true prevalence of any crime. Child abuse and neglect are no different, with many children suffering in silence. Because child maltreatment damages the brain, we also have to look at the prevalence of brain-based emotional, behavioral, or developmental conditions, such as depression, anxiety, ADD/ADHD, aggression, and other conduct problems. When we do, we see that the numbers are even higher, with 20–30 percent of children in forty-seven of our United States suffering from these conditions.[33]

BEHAVIORAL OUTCOMES INDUCED BY STRESS AND TRAUMA

Countless research articles have documented the impact that trauma and stress have on young children's behavior and schooling. We have to remember that children who experience abuse, family dysfunction, or neglect have spent the first five to six years of their lives learning how to cope with, and stay safe in, their dysfunctional environments, which can include both their homes and their neighborhoods. For these children, this is a lifetime of learning about how relationships work, how to interact with others, and how to be in the world. For many maltreated children, the learning starts before their first birthday.

Fifteen percent of all maltreated children are under one year of age when the neglect or abuse begins. Twenty percent are aged one to three at the onset of abuse, and 12 percent are aged four to five. These ages correspond with a period of tremendous brain growth, structuring the brain in ways that enable the children to survive, and even thrive, in their worlds. Survival in these cases often means learning how to adapt in an atmosphere of persistent fear and chaos. The children bring this learning to school with them. Unfortunately, behaviors that have worked for them for their entire lives often do not work in school.

Children who have these experiences can appear to be inattentive in class; teachers and peers can experience them as overly aggressive; they often struggle with self-regulation; they can have trouble forming relationships with peers and adults, and they can be anxious and have difficulties with memory and other cognitive processes needed for learning. What we have to remember is that these children's brains have been shaped by their early experiences. As demonstrated above, children who are used to living in a state of persistent fear process information differently.

For example, when in the classroom, rather than focusing on the words spoken by the teacher or by their peers, these children are primed to focus on non-verbal information. They pay attention to facial expressions, emotions, and hand gestures.[34] They do this because they have learned that in their world, non-verbal information is more important to one's survival and safety, than verbal information; it is adaptive for them to direct their attention in these ways. In the classroom though, it results in behaviors like this:

Scenario #1: A 5-year-old boy sees a peer coming toward him with an angry look on his face. He immediately focuses in on the peer. The peer is angry because he just lost his favorite pencil. The 5-year-old assumes that this boy is coming toward him to fight with him, so he strikes out first by hitting or tripping the child.

In *Scenario #2*, our 5-year-old is sitting in class trying to listen to what the teacher is teaching, but the teacher is stressed because of an incident that happened earlier in the day. The child, because he is primed to focus on emotions, can only attend to her depressed facial expression and her strained responses.

Because of this, he is unable to take in anything that she is saying. He becomes consumed with worry and fear about what he did to make the teacher upset, raising his anxiety levels. Yet when the teacher notices that something is amiss and tries to comfort him, he will not let himself be comforted. He lashes out at the teacher, refusing, or unable, to engage in any reciprocal relational interaction.

The extreme, but all too common incidents of classroom disruption in the previous chapter can be explained by the impact of trauma and stress on the developing brain. Did you notice that most of the stories involved children in early elementary school? They involved second graders who fight at the slightest provocation, children who had trouble forming relationships with the teacher or their peers; children who break down and cry or injure themselves for seemingly unknown reasons.

Unfortunately, given the focus on testing and accountability, these highest-risk children are not safe anywhere. As Perry points out, their home life is chaotic, neglectful, and sometimes abusive, their community is fragmented and plagued by gang violence[35] and their schools are not able to keep them safe, choosing to put all resources into the academic aspects of schooling while neglecting the social and emotional supports these children need. Students who can read, write, and compute well are better able to think themselves out of difficult situations and to use their cognitive abilities to solve problems and make better and more informed choices about life.

Students who can regulate their emotions are better able to navigate daily frustrations without resorting to aggressive behavior. Students who develop a strong and healthy relationship with just one teacher do better in school. Schooling is the last resort for children who need these vitally important mental, emotional, and relationship resources. Unfortunately, the social and emotional needs of children have been lost in the forest of accountability.

The good news is that teachers know this. Something interesting started happening with teachers in 2018; they began striking, not for more pay, but for more support for themselves and their students. In 2018 there were eleven major teacher strikes involving 485,000 teachers. By 2020, this number ballooned to forty teacher strikes, most of them happening in the West, Midwest, and South.

The teachers who choose to strike are from states whose students have experienced the most maltreatment, have more emotional and behavioral conditions, and are poorer on average, than the children in states that did not have any teacher strikes during this period. These states also have more students who scored below basic in literacy on high-stakes tests. Perhaps it was these conditions that lead the striking teachers to fight equally as hard, and sometimes harder, for support for the students in their care.

A majority of the schools demanded that their districts hire more nurses, social workers, school psychologists, and counselors for the students, as well as pay raises for these support staff. They demanded smaller caseloads for special education teachers and counselors. They also fought for more "mental health" services and improvements in the stress levels and health and safety conditions in their schools. Given the behaviors described in the previous chapter, we must assume that the teachers asked for these services for both themselves and their students.

Clearly, the teachers were concerned with student support, but they were also concerned about creating safe, healthy, and stimulating environments for their students such as more green space for schools and more extracurricular activities for students such as music, art, and sports. Finally, some of the strike demands focused on social and racial justice issues with teachers demanding wraparound services and sanctuary protections for their immigrant and refugee students. One set of striking teachers also demanded legal services for immigrant students and their families.

Many of the striking teachers partnered with parent and community groups to demand more community schools, fewer charters, and more money for educational services, not just teacher pay raises. Wonderfully, teachers won most of their demands during these actions, giving them more power and hopefully more confidence to fight the continued attacks and defunding of public education.[36]

CONCLUSION

We now understand the processes by which trauma and stress impact young children. Trauma causes the brain to release cortisol; trauma unchecked leads to the continuous release of cortisol and cortisol damages brain functions that enable self-control and thoughtful, reasoned, responses. This information presents a picture that is crystal clear. The seemingly out-of-control children in our nation's classrooms are suffering from trauma and toxic stress. These children have been traumatized from experiences at home, and surely from neglect at school.

They cannot learn because their brains are physically overloaded with cortisol. Teachers know this, or they at least know that something is wrong; something that is beyond their control to "fix" through high-quality teaching alone. But the powers that be—school administrators, local and state boards, and federal policymakers—keep pretending that accountability and testing will solve the problem. They keep punishing teachers, especially the ones who are truly committed to serving our most needy students.

How ironic and sad that the teachers who have committed to teaching those most in need are being driven from the classroom, or at least out of urban and rural schools. Unfortunately, these conditions are very stressful for teachers and leave them vulnerable to the effects of toxic stress. We discuss how stress impacts teacher health and well-being in section two.

Previous chapters have explored how forces outside of the school building, and outside of the teacher's control, impact what teachers do in the classroom. The next chapter looks closely at the act of teaching and explores how the cognitive complexity of teaching can hurt a teacher's sense of competence *if* the school does not provide sufficient classroom support for teachers. This is especially true for new teachers, who need to develop a sense of teaching competence in order to believe that they can teach all students effectively.

NOTES

1. Diana Hiatt, "Parent Involvement in American Public Schools: A Historical Perspective," *School Community Journal*, 4, no. 2 (Fall/Winter, 2000), 1642–2000.

2. Diana Hiatt, "Parent Involvement in American Public Schools," 3.

3. Dana Goldstein, *The Teacher Wars: A History of America's Most Embattled Profession* (New York, NY: Penguin Random House, 2014), 136.

4. US Dept. of Health and Human Services, "Poverty Guidelines 2020," *ASPE Office of the Assistant Secretary for Planning and Evaluation (*2020), https://aspe.hhs.gov/poverty-guidelines.

5. Anne E. Casey Foundation, "Children in Poverty by Race and Ethnicity in the US," *Kids Count Data Center*, https://datacenter.kidscount.org/data/tables/44-children-in-poverty-by-race-and-ethnicity#detailed/1/any/false/37,871,870,573,869,36,868,867,133,38/10,11,9,12,1,185,13/324,323.

6. Anne E. Casey Foundation, "Children in Poverty."

7. D. Blackwell, "Family Structure and Children's Health in the US: Findings from the National Health Interview Survey, 2001–2007," *National Center for Health Statistics* (2010), 9–17, Figures 5 and 6. (Single parent homes include homes where the mother lives with a parent or sibling—called extended families.)

8. Statista, "Poverty Rate in the United States from 1990–2021," *Statista*, https://www.statista.com/statistics/200463/us-poverty-rate-since-1990/.

9. Blackwell, "Family Structure and Children's Health," 17–25.

10. John Pascoe et al., "Mediators and Adverse Effects of Child Poverty in the US," *American Academy of Pediatrics Technical Report* (2016), 9–10.

11. Jeanne Brooks-Gunn and Greg J. Duncan, "The Effects of Poverty on Children," *The Future of Children*, 7, no. 2 (Summer/Autumn, 1997).

12. John Pascoe et al., "Mediators and Adverse Effects," e6.

13. Anne E. Casey Foundation, "Children in Poverty." The 35 percent figure combines black and multiracial children.

14. Kenan Fikri and John Lettieri, "From Great Recession to Great Reshuffling: Charting a Decade of Change across American Communities," *Economic Innovation Group* (2018).

15. Distressed Community Index, *Charting a Decade of Change across American Communities* (2018).

16. Annie E. Casey Foundation, "Children Living in High-Poverty, Low-Opportunity Neighborhoods," *The Anne E. Casey Foundation* (2017), www.aecf.org.

17. Annie E. Casey Foundation, "Children Living in High-Poverty."

18. John Pascoe et al., "Mediators and Adverse Effects."

19. Mary Ann Stephens and Gary Wand, "Stress and the HPA Axis: Role of Glucocorticoids in Alcohol Dependence," *Alcohol Research: Current Reviews*, 34, no. 4 (2012), doi: 2013-28231-001.

20. Kara E. Hannibal and Mark D. Bishop, "Chronic Stress, Cortisol Dysfunction, and Pain: A Psychooneuroendocrine Rationale for Stress Management in Pain Rehalibiltation," *Physical Therapy*, 94, no. 12 (2014), doi:10.2522/ptj.20130597.

21. Amy Arnsten, "Stress Signaling Pathways That Impair Prefrontal Cortex Structure and Function," *Natural Review Neuroscience*, 10, no. 6 (2009), doi: 10.1038/nrn2648.

22. Jack P. Shonkoff and Andrew S. Garner, "The Lifelong Effects of Early Childhood Adversity and Toxic Stress," *American Academy of Pediatrics*, 129, no. 1 (2012), 236, doi: 10.1542/peds.2011-2663.

23. Mary Ann Stephens and Gary Wand, "Stress and the HPA Axis," 472.

24. Mary Ann Stephens and Gary Wand, "Stress and the HPA Axis," 471.

25. Amy Arnsten, "Stress Signaling Pathways," 28.

26. Danya Glaser, "The Effects of Maltreatment on the Developing Brain," *Medico-Legal Journal*, 82, no. 3 (2014), 6, doi: 10.1177/0025817214540395.

27. Amy Arnsten, "Stress Signaling Pathways."

28. Raja Mishra, "Gauging Toll of Abuse on a Child's Brain," *The Boston Globe*, December 15, 2000, A8.

29. Danya Glaser, "The Effects"; Anne Peterson, Joshua Joseph, and Monica Feit, "New Directions in Child Abuse and Neglect," *The National Academies Press* (2013), http://www.nap.edu/catalog.php?record_id=18331.

30. Jeanne Brooks-Gunn and Greg J. Duncan, "The Effects of Poverty."

31. V. Felitti et al., "Relationship of Childhood Abuse and the Household Dysfunction to Many of the Leading Cause of Death in Adults, The Adverse Childhood Experiences (ACE) Study," *Journal of Preventive Medicine*, 14, no. 4 (1998), doi: 10.1016/s0749-3797(98)00017-8.

32. Jane Ellen Stevens, "The Adverse Childhood Experiences Study: The Largest, Most Important Public Health Study You Never Heard of—Began in an Obesity Clinic," *ACES Too High Blog* (October 2012).

33. Annie E. Casey Foundation, "Children Living in High-Poverty."

34. Bruce Perry, "The Neurodevelopmental Impact of Violence in Childhood," in *The Textbook of Child and Adolescent Forensic Psychiatry*, ed. D. Schetky and E. Benedek (Washington, DC: American Psychiatric Press, 2001), 230.

35. Bruce Perry, "The Neurodevelopmental Impact," 230.

36. Madeline Will, "How Teacher Strikes are Changing," *Education Week* (March, 6, 2019), https://www.edweek.org/steaching-learning/how-teacher-strikes-are-changing/2019/03.

Chapter 5

Cognitive Complexity and the Need for Competence

The previous chapters have demonstrated how important it is that teachers have a sense of autonomy in the classroom. A teacher's sense of autonomy enhances her sense of competence about her ability to teach children well. But teacher competence is not only tied to the degree of autonomy they have in the classroom. Autonomy does not guarantee that a teacher will feel competent to teach. For teachers, competency grows out of three key components of teaching, successful teaching, sufficient support, and collegial collaboration around the content and student needs.

Let's go even further; successful teaching *depends* upon support and collaboration. One reason this is true is that teaching is incredibly cognitively complex. Without support, and caring and collaborative colleagues, the cognitive complexity of teaching can destroy a teacher's sense of competence.

Those of us who are familiar with the day-to-day work of teaching know that teaching is extremely cognitively complex. But what exactly makes the process of teaching so cognitively complex? Is it the content that teachers teach, or the knowledge they need to master? Is it the pedagogy or the skill of teaching? Is it the student interactions that the teacher must manage; or keeping track of how each student learns? Where does that complexity lie, in the knowledge, the teaching skill, or the learner? It turns out that the complexity of teaching does not reside in the main tasks of teaching.

Rather, it resides in the spaces between those tasks and the interactions among them. It resides in the shifts from one task to the other, in the stops and starts, the pauses and interruptions, and in the decisions teachers have to make while teaching. It is these moves that make teaching cognitively complex because they interrupt, and in worse cases, disrupt, the teachers' thought processes and mechanisms.

Ideally, a teacher approaches the day's lesson with a plan for what she will teach. This plan contains the content knowledge the teacher will draw upon as well as strategies for how the teacher will teach the material. Maybe she will start with an individual activity, then provide a bit of direct instruction, then a whole class discussion, then small group work on a similar activity, with a share out at the end. The plan might also include various scenarios that might arise while teaching.

These scenarios might be focused on student learning, such as gaps in student knowledge, student confusion about the content, or wrong answers that might confuse and derail the understanding of some classmates. They might focus on the contextual elements of the classroom such as behavioral challenges or student dynamics. Finally, the plan might end with some notes on how the teacher will assess student understanding throughout the lesson.

To carry out a lesson well, that is, to ensure that the lesson results in student learning, the teacher will have to engage the following cognitive skills: She will have to have a strong *understanding* of the content's conceptual map. This means knowing how the content's concepts relate to each other, knowing what concepts will be difficult for the students to grasp, and knowing what students will misunderstand based on their prior knowledge, of which she also has to be aware.

She will have to pay very close *attention* to her students' facial expressions and *listen* intently to their responses and questions, and then place what she hears in the context of the content's conceptual map. The information the teacher gains from paying attention and listening closely to anywhere from twenty to thirty-five or more students, will allow her to *reason*, that is, *think* about, make *judgments* and *inferences* about, student understanding based upon what she sees and hears.

As she learns more about how students are receiving and reacting to the lesson, the teacher will have to *problem solve* on the spot; asking herself questions such as, does she adjust her lesson? Does she introduce a new instructional strategy? Does she introduce new content or review previous content? The solutions she chooses will be designed to advance student learning in the context of their own levels of understanding and despite their confusion and misunderstandings.

These cognitive skills, *understanding, attention, listening, reasoning, thinking, making judgments and inferences, and problem-solving* are enabled by specific mental processes. The processes that are key to teaching and learning are working memory, processing capacity, and executive function or control. Let's start with working memory and processing capacity. Working memory has been described as a short-term cognitive system for processing and storing information.

Working memory acts as both a parking lot and a workspace for information that an individual is using to make sense of their environment. For example, when trying to understand, learn something, or solve a problem, working memory consciously holds the relevant information in mind so that the brain can focus on it, which allows the brain to process that information, such as by connecting it with other experiences we have had or with information that is stored in long-term memory.

Teachers rely on working memory in several ways. For example, working memory allows us to make sense of what takes place over time. To do this, the teacher's working memory must "hold in mind" what happened earlier in the year, the month, the week, or the day, and use that information to understand what is happening in the present and what might happen in the future. For a teacher, this involves remembering the previous learning trajectory and behavior of each student so that she can better understand that student's current learning and behavior.

Whenever teachers incorporate new information about a student or a class, into their current thinking, and then use this information to come up with an alternative approach to teaching that student or class, they are relying on working memory. Finally, working memory is necessary for teachers to assess the level of student understanding by making connections between what the students say during class discussions about the content, the student's actual work, and what the teacher is trying to teach.

The second mental process that also impacts working memory is processing capacity. Working memory has a limited amount of processing capacity. Most people can only consciously process four to seven items in working memory for about twenty minutes at a time. Teachers and other experts who have an increased knowledge base in a certain area can process information in working memory for much longer.

Once the processing capacity of working memory reaches its limit, it becomes harder for a person to process, or think about, the information with which they had been working. One thing that limits processing capacity is when we have to attend to more than one aspect of our environment at a time. For teachers, the capacity to process the information in working memory is increased by the deep level of content knowledge they possess. However, the more a teacher has to split her attention between following her teaching plan, monitoring student learning, and managing classroom interruptions and disruptions, the less capacity she will have in working memory.

The last mental process we will discuss here is executive function or control. Executive function is a set of mental processes that allow us to plan, focus our attention, and multitask. Executive function can be thought of as a set of brain-based skills that are involved in helping us to maintain mental control and self-regulation.

In order to maintain mental control, we must be able to ignore distractions, manage our impulses, and prioritize the tasks we have to complete by setting goals and monitoring our ability to achieve those goals. Executive function is dependent on working memory. The more we are able to use working memory to process incoming information, the more we can stay on track, achieve our goals, and manage our day-to-day tasks.

Teaching is a profession that requires strong skills in executive function. All day, teachers must *monitor* their teaching performance and measure that performance against both their teaching plan and their observations of student learning. Based on what they observe, they must decide whether to *shift* their plans so they can move seamlessly from one teaching approach to another. This requires them to instantly *generate* new responses or problem-solving strategies to implement on the spot.

For teachers, executive function kicks in whenever they have to make a decision or troubleshoot while teaching, which happens every day, all day. New teachers, who do not have a lot of teaching experience or practice, must rely even *more* on their executive functions to carry out their teaching plan. If there are too many attentional demands on a new teacher, she will struggle more with executive control.

As with processing capacity, the more working memory gets tied up by attentional demands, the less working memory will be able to process any new information that impacts executive control. Teaching becomes increasingly cognitively complex when it is interrupted by the shifts, stops, starts, and pauses, as well as the decision-making that is required when trying to teach twenty-five or more individual learners at the same time. When there are too many interruptions, teacher well-being is negatively impacted, with severe consequences for both student learning and teacher persistence.

The following examples of teaching mathematical concepts to fifth graders, one from a veteran teacher and one from a novice teacher, demonstrate what the cognitive complexity of teaching looks like during the act of teaching.

A VETERAN TEACHER TEACHES RATE TO FIFTH GRADERS

We must start with the context because environmental demands can either constrain or facilitate teacher thinking. Our veteran teacher,[1] Magdalene Lampert, who has been teaching for ten years, teaches in a small, neighborhood school, having only two classes per grade. The school is located in a small city. The twenty-six students in her class are racially, ethnically, linguistically, and economically diverse, with about eight White, eight Black, and eight immigrants in attendance.

The desks in her class are arranged in small clusters of five to six students where they can face each other when working on problems but can also easily see the board at the front of the room for demonstrations. Her class meets after recess with students moving directly from the playground to the classroom, entering math class with all the frenetic energy that students expend after running around for thirty minutes outside with their friends.

When they enter the room, the students are expected to go to their desks and copy the problem of the day from the board into their notebooks. Once copied, they are to immediately begin working on the problem for the first half of the class. They can either work alone or with peers who share a desk cluster.

While they are working, Dr. Lampert walks around the room listening in on the discussions and observing how the students are approaching the problem. She will use the information she gathers to aid the discussion during the second half of the class. Dr. Lampert teaches through discussion, meaning that students are expected to share and talk about their work on the problem, while Dr. Lampert asks questions and teaches in response to what the students say and do.

She knows that *routines* help both herself and the students. They help the students focus and cut down on behavioral issues, and so far, her students have followed the routines she has established, causing very few disruptions as they start work on the problem. The routines make space in working memory, allowing Dr. Lampert to focus on the multiple ways that her students are solving the problem as she walks around the classroom *listening and observing* each cluster of desks.

This is the point when Dr. Lampert focuses her *attention* and *mentally reviews* her teaching plan. Dr. Lampert knows that in the discussion to follow, she wants to focus on the "halving process" specifically, the strategies that students use to divide both common fractions and decimals to solve the problem. This primes her to be on the lookout for any new insights or misconceptions about multiplying and dividing fractions, or about working with denominators or remainders when doing long division.

As she leans in to focus on the discussion from one group of peers, she notices that Steve is trying to explain how he got the remainder from the long division problem on which his group is working. Steve seems to misunderstand which number to divide by, a fourth or a half. She sees that his mistake has led him to the wrong answer, but she also notices that only one person in Steven's group seems to be questioning his thinking, which leads her to remember that Susie and Tyrone exhibited the same confusion two days prior, telling her that misinterpreting the remainder might be a common misunderstanding among other students in the class.

This, in turn, leads her to conclude that she now must modify her teaching plan so she can ask questions about this confusion in the discussion part of the class. She asks the students some questions to try to push their thinking but decides not to fully correct the misunderstanding at this time. Instead, she will have them introduce their thinking during the discussion so she can use their example to teach the whole class.

Dr. Lampert moves on, listening in and interacting with the other groups and continuing to attend to, think about, and problem-solve on the spot about how she will adjust her discussion during the second half of class. She must hold everything she is learning in mind so she can use the information while teaching the students. Dr. Lampert's ability to plan, focus her attention, and multitask while teaching depends upon the effective use of her *executive function*.

As explained above, executive function is a set of mental processes that helps us regulate our behavior, which involves maintaining mental control. This is what allows us to ignore distractions, manage our impulses, and prioritize tasks. Executive function also allows us to monitor how well we are doing these things. Our ability to exercise mental control is dependent on working memory. In fact, it is Dr. Lampert's *working memory* and *processing capacity* that makes her mental actions while teaching possible.

As explained above, working memory both processes and stores information that the teacher needs to keep in mind so that her brain can deliberately think about the information she is gathering by connecting it with other instances of each student's learning that are stored in her long-term memory. It is her working memory that allows her to make meaning out of her students' responses over time. Dr. Lampert can hold all this information in her working memory because her processing capacity has not yet been used up.

You may remember that once processing capacity reaches its limit, it will be much harder for her to retain, much less deliberately think about, the information she has been collecting about her students' understanding and how all of it relates to her teaching plan for the day. Not having to deal with disruptions such as student behavior also eases the strain on her executive function and allows her to continue thinking about what she has been learning through her observations, and using that information to make decisions about her teaching.

After thirty minutes have passed, Dr. Lampert goes to the front of the room and rings a small bell to let the students know that it is time to transition to the second half of class where they will analyze the problem together, sharing the strategies they used to solve it with each other.

The bell is another routine, used throughout the school, that helps to keep the students on track. Dr. Lampert leads and participates in the discussion, asking questions, affirming student thinking, and teaching. To do this, she draws not only on everything she learned from the day's observations but also on everything she has learned over the course of the school year about each one of her student's mathematical understandings.

Her students remain focused on, and engaged in, the discussion. They follow the thread of thought, listening quietly and raising their hands when they want to participate. They ask questions of her and each other. They volunteer to go to the board to share their illustrations. Because there are so few distractions, Dr. Lampert can continue monitoring student comments and actions and use that information to aid her instruction.

This is very important because it allows Dr. Lampert the mental space to consider another very important aspect of teaching, who her students are and what each one of them needs from her to develop fully as students *and* as human beings. For example, there is Richard, an African American boy, who raises his hand in response to Dr. Lampert's request that someone add to the diagram they are discussing on the board. As she is deciding on whom to choose from the various raised hands, she recalls that

> Richard does not often volunteer to say something in whole-class discussions. He is friendly and cooperative in his small group, but he does not contribute much in the way of mathematical assertions to his classmates' conversations, and he does not write much in his notebook. He is new to the school this year, and I am still trying to figure out what he can do.
>
> I can never look at him without remembering that on the first day of school, when he introduced himself to the class, he said math was his "worse subject." I cannot predict precisely what he will do with this problem or know exactly what it will mean to him socially to come up to the board. But because it is my aim that all students understand mathematics, I call on him to show us on the diagram how far the car will go in fifteen minutes.

Here, Dr. Lampert considers Richards's social needs, not just his need to learn math. She remembers his past behavior. He is a student who does not participate much, plus he has defined himself as someone who is not good at math. Even though she is unsure how he will contribute to the discussion—he might say something that causes more confusion—she takes a chance by calling on him, putting his social needs above her teaching needs.

When Richard makes an error while adding his answer to the diagram, this creates another dilemma for Dr. Lampert. Now she must not only consider his social needs but also how her next actions might contribute to how the rest of the class sees Richard. Rather than correcting his error, she asks the class if anyone can explain what Richard was thinking. She explains that she often asks this type of question in her discussions as a way for her students to "practice how to talk about mathematics."

Of the several hands that are raised, Dr. Lampert notices that Catherine wants to say something. She does a quick mental review of what she knows about Catherine. "My experience with her contributions to class discussions lead me to expect that she will be polite and articulate, whatever she says, possibly helping me out of the impasse with Richard."

However, rather than explain Richard's thinking, Catherine says, "I disagree with that" and makes it clear that she wants to tell the class why. But then Catherine pauses and looks at the teacher. Dr. Lampert hesitates. She knows enough about Catherine as a student to know that "if I did tell her to continue, she would provide not only the correct solution but also a clear and correct explanation of why her solution made sense." But Dr. Lampert wonders,

> What effect would that have on Richard? How would it affect Catherine if I did not let her continue? What effect would either course of action have on what the rest of the class could learn about math, as well as what they could learn about Richard and Catherine or about the racial and gender groups to which these students—an African American boy and a Caucasian girl—belonged?

This self-questioning indicates that Dr. Lampert does not want to damage either Richard's or Catherine's mathematical self-efficacy, and by extension the mathematical self-efficacy of the other girls and students of color in the classroom. These are critical questions that every teacher should consider, especially in today's high-needs classrooms. Dr. Lampert has the mental room to consider these questions because she has few interruptions or attentional demands that divert her thinking from teaching math, with all its implications.

Throughout this lesson, Dr. Lampert is holding many things in mind. She remains focused on what she wants to teach and how she wants to teach it. She thinks deliberately about the content in terms of each student's understanding and misconceptions, and how to teach the content based on this information. She also thinks deliberately about individual student feelings and how students might perceive each other and their peers' racial and gender identities in relation to math.

Specifically, she thinks about how her actions as a teacher might contribute to students' perceptions of each other. Finally, she problem-solves the best ways to approach her lesson based on her thinking. During this teaching episode, Dr. Lampert can rely on her executive function skills to maintain her mental control while her working memory and processing capacity help to manage her cognitive load. It also helps tremendously that her students are engaged in the lesson and following the class plan, which prevents her mental system from being overtaxed by multiple disruptions that increase her attentional demands.

A NOVICE TEACHER TEACHES FIFTH GRADERS HOW TO MULTIPLE FRACTIONS

Robin, our novice teacher, is in her first year of teaching. She had been teaching for six months when these observations took place.[2] However, in many ways, we can think of Robin as a second-year teacher because she earned her teaching credential through a graduate teaching residency program in an urban school district. As part of this program, she taught for the entire school year, under the guidance of a more experienced mentor teacher, while simultaneously taking graduate courses focused on the practice of teaching.

Her mentor teacher practiced the most up-to-date, researched-based teaching methods, such as the workshop model. Robin learned and taught using these same methods during her resident teaching year. When she was hired, she asked about the teaching methods used in her new school and was told by fellow teachers on the hiring committee that "she could use whatever methods she thought would be successful with the children."

Robin teaches fifth graders in a large urban elementary school, with six classes per grade. Her students are racially, ethnically, and linguistically diverse, but not economically diverse. Her classroom had thirty-four students, the majority of whom were African American and Latinx, with a handful of White and Asian students. Many of her students speak English as a second language and about one-fourth are on IEPs.

The desks in her class are arranged similarly to Dr. Lampert's, in small clusters of four to five students where they can work together on problems but can also see the board. Like Dr. Lampert's class, her class also meets after recess. Robin picks her students up on the playground and leads them in a long line through the school to her classroom, this march gives them some time to transition after running around for thirty minutes outside with their friends.

When hired, Robin decided that she wanted to use the math workshop model, just like her mentor did. She liked the model because she liked the idea of facilitating learning rather than direct teaching. It was also important to her that her students had choices and the chance to be creative in their thinking as they developed their knowledge of math. Finally, Robin believed that students did better when they learned with and from their peers. With this model, students start the class by focusing on a particular math problem that connects to the teacher's lesson.

This is followed by whole-group instruction through a mini-lesson. Next, students work independently or collaboratively to solve problems at various learning stations placed around the room. The station activities are based on the teacher's lesson. While students are completing the station activities, the teacher is supposed to be working with small groups of students at her desk to address specific learning needs. Robin included this step at the beginning of the year but then realized that her students worked better at the stations when she was present and walking about the room, so she does that instead. The lesson ends with a wrap-up and review of the day's activities.

The lesson described here focused on multiplying fractions. When her students enter the room, they are expected to go to their desks and complete the problem of the day for about ten minutes. They can work alone or with their peers. Robin has worked hard to build *routine* into her math lessons by making sure that students have an opening activity every day. Like Dr. Lampert, Robin listens in on the discussions and observes student approaches so that she can incorporate their understandings, or misunderstandings, into her mini-lesson.

Because her children can be boisterous, Robin looks around to make sure everyone is on-task before focusing on individual groups. She notices some trouble brewing among a few groups and makes one more announcement about staying on task.

From the beginning of the lesson, Robin must split her attention three ways: between *listening* to what the students are saying and doing as they solve the problem of the day, while also *mentally reviewing* her teaching plan in case revisions are necessary based on what she is hearing, and finally, by *attending* to outbursts of student disruptions from around the room. The problem of the day contains two examples, one that serves as a review of previous work, and one focused on the new task they will be covering that day.

The review problem asks students to change mixed numbers into improper fractions. At one cluster of desks, where the students are working independently, Robin notices that some of the students are multiplying the whole number by the numerator, instead of the denominator, leading them to the wrong answer. She decides to check in on another cluster to see how widespread the misunderstanding is.

She looks around to find a group who is working together on the problem, hoping to hear what students are thinking by listening in on their discussion. As she heads over to the new group, she hears Noah and Ariana arguing over a pencil. "Shut up!" Noah yells and throws the pencil across the room. Robin immediately heads over to quell the disturbance, but before she gets there, Ariana gets up to run after the pencil and trips.

A group of boys who had just settled down starts laughing loudly, causing the whole class to laugh, at which point Ariana rolls over on her back and starts to do some kind of dance on the floor, which sets the whole class off. Robin raises her hand to get everyone's attention, but the students don't seem to notice, forcing her to raise her voice so she can be heard above the din.

Robin does not like to "yell" at the kids, causing her to get frazzled every time she has to raise her voice. By the time she restores order, six minutes

Cognitive Complexity and the Need for Competence

have passed. This forces her into *decision* mode. Does she give them more time to finish the problem of the day or does she start the mini-lesson? She decides to start the mini-lesson, determining that since at least half of the students in the group observed made the same error, enough of the other students might have also. She mentally modifies her mini-lesson to review multiplying mixed numbers.

Robin's mini-lesson was about twenty minutes long. She used an overhead projector and taught through a combination of direct instruction, question-asking, and demonstration by having the students go to the board to work out the problem. Halfway through the lesson, Robin asks Darius, an African American male and one of the first students she observed making the original error, to work out the problem on the board. She intends to use his attempt to talk the students through the correct way to do the problem and to get a sense of where the whole class is when it comes to this particular misunderstanding.

Just as Robin starts to talk through Darius's work, Hakeem announces that he doesn't feel well and tells the teacher that he threw up at recess. At this news some of the students exclaim "Yew," and one of the boys, who witnessed the event, starts telling the whole class about it, resulting in more "Yews." Robin quickly quells the outburst and sends Hakeem to the nurse. It takes her about a minute to restore order.

When she turns back to the problem on the board, she has forgotten how she was going to relate this misunderstanding to her overall lesson and must pause to collect herself. Robin hates when this happens and gets frustrated with herself. She feels that her lessons must be fast-paced to keep the kids' attention, and if they are not, the kids get distracted again which leads to more problems. This worry interferes with her ability to think clearly about where she was in both her thinking and her lesson, causing her to take more time to get herself back on track.

After what feels to Robin like an hour but was just a few seconds, she is able to collect herself and proceed with the lesson, but she switches to direct instruction. She also stops directing her questions to the whole class, directing them instead to students who she knows will provide the answers she wants. This decision leads her to ask Eva, an Asian female who Robin can always count on to provide the right answer, and Mark, a white male who usually does a pretty good job of explaining how to do the math problems the class is working on.

Robin feels bad about this decision. She had wanted to ask Darius, an African American male, to explain his thinking about the problem first because she saw during the stations that he was almost there in understanding the math, and she believed that having him explain the problem would boost his confidence in his math abilities, which she felt he really needed.

She was hoping to follow up with Jaynce, an African American female who does not speak much, but who Robin noticed was doing the problem correctly. Jaynce and Darius were friends and Robin felt that calling on them together would give them both more confidence to talk about the math. However, because of the earlier disruptions, Robin chose to call on students who could quickly provide answers because she wanted her lesson to move along at a faster pace in the hope of avoiding additional distractions.

When the mini-lesson ended, the students began working in the math stations that Robin has set up around the room. One of the stations asked students to multiply and divide fractions with mixed numbers. Robin remained focused on helping students understand how to translate mixed numbers and improper fractions because she knew understanding this is crucial for working with fractions overall. Robin plants herself at that station to see if her mini-lesson improved student understanding.

The first group to arrive took a few minutes to get settled but then got right to work. Robin was thrilled to see that one of the students remembered the discussion about the diagram on the board. She was listening intently to their discussion when an argument broke out across the room. Isaac, Lucia, and Tony were arguing about how to do the activity at their station. Each of the boys had a different understanding of the directions, but they would not listen to Lucia, who was the station captain.

Station captains are responsible for making sure everyone understands the task and reaching out to the teacher if there is confusion. Before Robin could get to their station, Tony had pushed Isaac, and Isaac was just about to push him back when Robin caught him mid push. Someone yelled "fight," which caused the students from all the other groups to gather around.

While holding Isaac, Robin calmly told them all to go back to their stations; most of them did, but some wandered off across the classroom and Robin did not have the energy or time to call after them; she still had to deal with Tony and Isaac. She took them to her desk for a talk. Robin discovered that they had also been arguing at recess and had continued the argument when they got to the station. She settles them down, asks Tony to go to a different station, and sends Isaac back to his previous station.

The whole ordeal takes ten minutes to resolve. As Robin makes her way back to the mixed numbers station, she sees three boys sitting at a table playing some game on their phones, and notices that a few other students are sitting quietly at their desks rather than joining the stations with their peers. She focuses on the boys playing the game because they are getting louder and louder and ushers them back to their stations, letting the other students stay at their desks.

She tells herself that because they are being quiet, they will benefit from working alone. Finally, back at the mixed numbers station, Robin has trouble paying full attention to the conversation, because she keeps scanning the room in an attempt to stem any behavioral issues before they start. Finally, she decides that rather than trying to listen to her students thinking, she will just review the station worksheets when they come in and spends the rest of the station time walking about the room making sure that students are staying on task.

When the students are done with the stations, they return to their desks and complete an assessment focused on the problems they tackled at the stations. The assessment has three questions on it. Robin stops the students halfway through and asks them to substitute one of the questions for a new question that she has written on the board. This causes a round of chatter and confusion, but eventually, everyone gets back on track. Robin wraps up the class by asking the students to do a turn and talk about what they learned at the stations.

She knows that most of the students will not talk about the math, but she has to get them, and herself, ready to teach social studies, and she wants the students to get some of their energy out so they will be able to focus on the next lesson.

Like Dr. Lampert, Robin is holding many things in mind as she teaches this lesson. She tries to remain focused on what she wants to teach and how she wants to teach it by thinking deliberately about the content and how students are approaching the problem. She also mentally relates this to her upcoming lesson, thinking about how she will modify it based on the information she is gathering from the students. While thinking in these ways, Robin must also deal with several behavioral disturbances that interrupt her thinking.

These interruptions put more pressure on her *working memory* and on her *capacity to process* both how she will teach the content based on student understanding *and* how she will manage the classroom behavior in a way that allows all students to learn. This extra pressure also compromises her *executive function* which hurts her ability to manage her impulses and monitor whether she is accomplishing her goals for the lesson.

There are so many stops and starts and shifts and pauses because of the attentional demands on Robin's thinking that her working memory reaches its capacity. When this happens, Robin's well-thought-out teaching plan gets compromised in the following ways:

First, Robin concludes early on that she just cannot sit at a desk teaching a smaller group of students, while the rest of the class works at the stations, so she abandons that step of the math workshop model opting instead to monitor the groups while they are working. Robin explains that she felt good about this decision because it allowed her to listen in on how students were thinking about the math as they worked with each other in each station.

It also gave her the opportunity to talk with individual students about math. In this instance, Robin was able to justify her decision based on her knowledge of how best to teach math content to children, allowing herself to feel good about the decision that she had made.

Second, after the first disturbance with Noah and Ariana, Robin has to make a decision about what to do next; does she let the students finish the problem of the day and lose time for the rest of the lesson or does she move on to the mini-lesson? This requires a shift in Robin's thinking about how the lesson will proceed. Shifts like this, coupled with added decision-making, use up one's working memory which increases the cognitive demands of teaching. When the working memory gets tied up, the executive function gets weakened.

Remember that executive function kicks in whenever a teacher has to make a decision or troubleshoot something while teaching. New teachers, who do not have a lot of teaching experience or practice, must rely even *more* on their executive functions to carry out their teaching plan. If there are too many attentional demands on a new teacher, she will struggle more with executive control. This is what happened to Robin in this lesson. It would have required too much cognitive energy to get the students back into their groups to finish the problem of the day, plus she would also have had to figure out how to adjust the lesson with less time. It was easier, cognitively, to just start the lesson.

Third, after she sends Hakeem to the nurse Robin forgot where she was going with the lesson and has to take a few seconds to regroup. This happened because her working memory is now full, she has no more processing capacity, and therefore is unable to use her executive function to remember, and then pick up, where she left off. This gets compounded by her frustration. She is concerned now that her pace will not be fast enough and there will be another outbreak. This worry further diminishes her processing capacity, making it almost impossible for her to focus on the lesson she is trying to teach.

This leads to her fourth compromise; instead of continuing to ask questions, Robin switches to direct instruction for the remainder of the lesson. With limited processing capacity for working memory, and unable to effectively draw on her executive function, Robin can no longer cognitively handle uncertainty. This is why she stops asking questions to the whole class and instead directs her questions to the students who she knows will answer in a way that allows her to continue her lesson as planned.

Given how the brain works, this was not a planned decision on Robin's part. It was a decision made of underlying panic and fear about having to deal with another behavioral incident and not being able to carry out her teaching plan. Because Robin can no longer rely on her working memory to help her process the lesson, she switches to doing what is safe, because the brain always brings us back to safety.

Fifth, having decided to call upon students whose answers she could predict, prevents Robin from focusing on Darius and Jaynce, two students whose learning she was hoping to advance through the discussion. Robin's working memory is so full, that, unlike Dr. Lampert, she is unable to think about the racial and gendered implications of her decision. That thought, literally, does not even enter her mind until after the class is over and she has time, with help, to process what happened.

The sixth compromise happens after the disturbance at the stations, when Robin lets the students who are sitting at their desks and not working at a station as they should be, stay at their desks. She does make the group of boys who were playing the game return to the stations, most likely because they were making noise which could lead to another disruption. At this point, behavioral disruptions, in Robin's mind, have become the thing to avoid at all costs.

The other students, because they are sitting alone at their own desks, are unlikely to cause a disruption, whereas trying to get them to rejoin the stations might. Because Robin's rational brain is now on overload, preventing her from thinking rationally about her lesson, her instinctual brain takes over with its focus on safety. In Robin's case, safety means getting through the lesson without any more disruptions.

The seventh compromise happens when Robin abandons her plan to listen in on students thinking about the math at the stations. She decides instead to use the worksheets to figure out the students' thoughts. She makes this decision so that she can spend more time moving around the room, keeping her students on task and monitoring for behavior. On the one hand, this decision does ensure that the students will be more engaged in doing the math, but on the other hand, it prevents Robin from gaining insight into student thinking while they are doing the math, which could prove valuable in her attempts to teach them.

The final compromise happens when Robin decides to end the lesson with an ineffective exercise that does not really have the students reflecting on the math. She acknowledges this, but because of the state of her brain, she is unable, at the moment, to think about a more effective wrap-up. After the class, when she has more brain capacity, she is able to list two or three effective review wrap-ups that would have accomplished her goal of allowing the students to release some energy while also giving her a few minutes to regroup for the next lesson.

THE FIVE ACTS OF TEACHING

These descriptions of Dr. Lampert's and Robin's lessons demonstrate how the act of teaching is incredibly cognitively complex and the different ways that teachers navigate that complexity. There are five aspects of teaching that enhance the cognitive complexity of teaching. One of these aspects is the context within which the teaching takes place. The other four aspects can be thought of as cognitive and emotional tasks. These tasks can be organized into the following categories:

- Interactive Decision Making (IDM)
- Student Focused Thoughts (SFT)
- Mental Activities that Require Effort (MARE)
- Exerting Self-Control (ESC)

These categories help us understand the flow of Dr. Lampert and Robin's mental processing while teaching. They also show us how that flow can get redirected from focusing on the content to focusing on student behavior. This is how it works: The process starts with Interactive Decision Making (IDM), which is another way to describe teaching itself. It represents the decisions a teacher makes while teaching. The examples above illustrate the differences in the decisions that Dr. Lampert and Robin made while teaching.

Interactive Decision Making

During her lesson, Dr. Lampert's *interactive decisions* revolve around student understanding of the content. While listening in on the group discussions she is thinking about what she is hearing and observing about the student's math abilities. For example, she can mentally unpack how student thinking led them to a wrong answer, or she can anticipate where students are going when they appear to have detoured during their discussion and decide whether to let them continue or stop them. All these decisions require mental processing.

While teaching, Dr. Lampert makes decisions about how best to word a question she wants to ask, how to explain a concept, or which math problem to use as an illustration for maximum learning. She can think about what the students draw on the board and decide how to incorporate that information into her teaching plan. When she asks questions, she has the mental space to think about each student's history in the class, the extent of their mathematical knowledge, how they might answer her questions, and if their answers will aid her in teaching the lesson.

Based on all of this, she can decide whether or not to call upon them in the discussion. Finally, she is also able to think about the personal and social backgrounds and experiences of each student and how their mathematical self-efficacy as children of color or female students in a math class might be impacted by the way she teaches and whom she calls upon. Again, she uses this information to decide which students to call upon and which examples to use.

Finally, she makes decisions about her own actions, such as if she should wait until the next day to introduce a new concept, or if her explanations are taking too much time. All of Dr. Lampert's decisions focused on student content understanding and personal growth rather than student behavior. This is of course because Dr. Lampert's students were not engaging in the types of behaviors that had to be managed.

Most of Robin's *interactive decisions* during her lesson revolve around student behavior and engagement. From the very beginning of the lesson, Robin must split her attention between three mental activities. Like Dr. Lampert, she listens to the group discussion and mentally reviews her teaching plan for possible revisions, but unlike Dr. Lampert, she must also attend to student behaviors. At the beginning of the lesson, Robin is better able to focus her decisions on content understanding, as is illustrated when she looks for a group that is working together rather than individually so that she can hear what they are thinking about the problem.

From there, the behavioral incidents become more frequent. In addition to having to split her attention between teaching and managing student behavior, Robin also has to contend with her frustrations. She gets upset with herself at three points in the lesson, first when she "yells" at the students, second, when she forgets where she was going in the lesson, and third, when she does not call on Darius and Jaynce.

Frustration actually shuts down working memory, crippling both processing capacity and executive function, because it causes our protective brain to take over. When this happens, our brain goes into survival mode, preventing us from thinking about anything else. Now of course Robin is not in danger, but her brain does not know that and fights to keep her focused on those aspects of her day that are troubling to her—which is student behavior. This is what leads to the seven compromises she ends up making for the remainder of her lesson.

Each of those compromises—from deciding not to work with a smaller group of students while others completed the stations, to deciding not to have students finish the problem of the day, to deciding to switch to direct instruction, and so forth—involved a decision that privileged managing student behavior over *determining* student content understanding. Of course, Robin had to attend to and manage her students' behavior because learning was not, and could not, happen without that management. But attending to behavior, while also trying to teach, overloaded her cognitive processing systems, preventing her from focusing on, and privileging, student understanding of the content in her thinking about the lesson.

Student Focused Thought

As we can see from these examples, to make the best decisions possible, the teacher has to ask herself questions about the students, about the knowledge and temperamental differences between them, about how they think or how they will behave in certain circumstances. Those questions tend to be focused on either student content understanding or student behavior. In this way, Interactive Decision Making (IDM) requires Student Focused Thought (SFT). We know that a teacher cannot teach well without thinking about who her students are as learners in the context of her classroom.

To make the best decisions possible, the teacher has to remember each student's learning history, quirks, and level of content understanding. We also know that a teacher cannot teach well if student behavior becomes unmanageable. To make the best decisions in terms of having the least disruptions possible, the teacher has to remember each student's past behaviors, along with their temperament and levels of tolerance. Student-focused thoughts are a constant for teachers. The focus of those thoughts determines the quality and effectiveness of a teacher's lesson.

Mental Activities That Require Effort and Exerting Self-Control

Another requirement for effective interactive decision-making (IDT) is the teachers' engagement in Mental Activities that Require Effort (MAREs). MAREs take up space in working memory and require executive function. The following mental activities require great effort from teachers:

- When they have to resolve a conflict
- When they have to switch from one task to another
- When they have to control their attention
- When they experience time pressure
- When they have to keep several ideas in mind at once
- When they are interrupted and then have to get back on track
- Finally, when they have to use their working memory

Both Dr. Lampert and Robin engaged in many MAREs during their lessons, but Dr. Lampert's were focused on student content understanding whereas Robin's were focused mostly on student behavior and engagement, with some focus on student content understanding. If too many mental activities are required, it impacts the teacher's ability to Exert Self-Control (ESC) while teaching.

Being able to exert self-control while teaching allows the teacher to think deliberately about her next move, plan the next steps while teaching, make sure routines are followed, and even pay attention to the words and actions of specific students. This is exactly what happened to Robin as she attempted to teach her lesson. She had to engage in so many MAREs that she was not able to exert self-control when it was most needed.

For Dr. Lampert, because there were few, if any, unmanageable behavioral disruptions during her lesson, her mind was able to process and make sense of the information without the shifts, starts and stops, pauses, worries, and decision-making that overloaded Robin's working memory and processing capacity preventing her from following her teaching plan *and* managing the class's behavior. This inability also led to Robin's frustrations and disappointments with her own behaviors while teaching her lesson.

For example, she was unable to control her thinking in a way that would have allowed her to mentally search for other alternatives to raising her voice in her attempts to get the students' attention. This also happened when she let her worries about the pace of her lesson determine how she taught that lesson. Because her working memory was at capacity, she was not able to exert self-control in these instances.

In conclusion, when the teacher's student-focused thoughts shift from *thoughts about the students' content knowledge to thoughts about the students' behavior or engagement with the class*, this overwhelms the teacher's working memory, processing capacity, and her ability to rely on her executive function. This shifts the teacher's ability to think about, and make decisions about, student behavior and student content understanding. In these situations, because of how the human brain works, the teacher will get stuck in thoughts about student behavior.

This in turn impacts her interactive decision-making process leading to an unhelpful feedback loop. Figure 5.1 illustrates how this works.

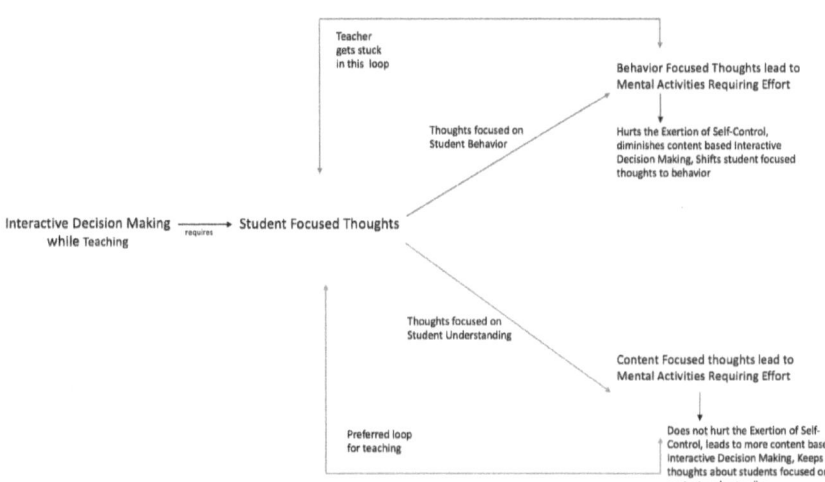

Figure 5.1. The Two Pathways of Student-Focused Thought while Teaching

As Robin's example shows, when the day-to-day cognitive complexity of teaching becomes unmanageable, overloading the teacher's working memory and shutting down her ability to process information, this leads to feelings of incompetence, which sets off an emotional process that can severely impact teacher well-being *if* the teacher gets no support in dealing with the emotions that result from this process. These impacts are seen in multiple ways and on many levels.

The next section explains how this experience, along with the other experiences described in this section, thwarts teachers' psychological needs, triggering an emotional process that damages teacher well-being and ultimately hurts students and schools.

NOTES

1. This example is adapted from Magdalene Lampert's book *Teaching Problems and the Problems of Teaching* (2003). Dr. Lampert is a veteran elementary math teacher turned professor who describes in detail a lesson on teaching the mathematical concept of rate to fifth graders.

2. Robin's classroom was observed on a regular basis for three months.

Part II

Teacher Health and Well-Being

The stress that sickens students in our nation's most under-resourced classrooms also infects teachers. A teacher's brain is impacted similarly by overwhelming stress through the release of cortisol that damages brain and bodily functions. The stress that teachers face has multiple causes and manifests in all aspects of a teacher's life.

It starts on a relational level with the realization that one's family, friends, and society, in general, are critical of the teacher's career choice. Loved ones' judgments about a chosen career can lead to feelings of isolation, defensiveness, and anger.

Next, when they get their first job, many teachers must deal with the sleep deprivation and exhaustion that comes from the overwhelming workload and lack of time to plan and prepare during the workday. Although these emotions are counteracted by the excitement of starting a new profession, early career teachers, like Quay, who work in our most troubled schools, have to learn how to manage the stress that comes from working in what can be chaotic environments with very little support.

Finally, once they gain enough experience to be considered a professional, teachers still have to deal with the frustration, despair, loss of pride, and guilt that comes from knowing that there is a better way to teach, assess and support children, but not being allowed to follow best practices because they have to follow scripted curriculums and prepare students for predetermined assessments that give them very little autonomy to make the professional choices they were trained to make.

When teachers realize that their professional knowledge is not respected, and they are not afforded the autonomy nor allowed the creativity to practice their life's work, this hurts them on a personal level. These experiences of rejection are stressful. They cause teachers to question their calling, and they lead to negative emotions such as sadness and frustration.

Finally, teaching children whose backgrounds and life experiences are different from their own causes teachers to face deeply personal issues around race, class, and social justice. When teachers are left to grapple with these issues on their own, it causes damage on many fronts. It hurts student learning and leads to lost opportunity and potential for many young people. It hurts teachers' psychological health and well-being and leads to a lack of retention and economic loss.

It hurts society by devaluing public education while perpetuating racist stereotypes that lead to structural barriers and systemic oppression of poor and racialized children. Over time, those who choose to teach in high-needs schools experience a slow build-up of personal, relational, and professional stressors that end up impacting their physical and psychological health.

Complicating these experiences for teachers is the fact that many of them chose this profession because they were called to teaching.[1] People are "called" to certain professions because the work "contributes to a personal sense of meaning or purpose and can be used to serve others." A calling has also been defined as growing out of a sense of personal "destiny (teaching is what one was meant to do) or perfect fit (teaching is an ideal match for one's values, skills, and interests)."[2]

People whose life's work also fulfills a calling have been shown to have greater job satisfaction, to see their work as more meaningful, and to be more committed to their profession. In addition, people who can fulfill a calling through their work are more satisfied and happier with their lives in general.

One cannot talk about teachers without talking about the notion of a "calling." As shown in chapter 2, a majority of teachers see themselves as following a calling to serve and support children. Teachers tend to have a deep personal commitment to teaching and students. Teachers also tend to be highly motivated to contribute to society, a goal that they seek to accomplish by working with young people.

This sense of being on a mission is one of the things that keeps teachers on the job, especially teachers who choose to work in urban, rural, and other high-needs schools, despite the outsized demands and the high level of energy and effort required of them every single day. When a calling goes unrealized, because it is thwarted by multiple aspects of the job, this takes both a psychological and a physical toll on teachers.

Why are these experiences so damaging? There are several reasons. First, they thwart the basic psychological needs that all humans require in order to maintain a positive self-image. Second, they force teachers to engage in practices that contradict their personal values and professional training, causing them to experience toxic stress, unhealthy emotions, and harmful levels of cognitive dissonance on a daily basis.

Finally, the stress and negative emotions generated by these experiences not only damage an individual teacher's physical health, they also infect and further degrade relations between school staff, teachers, and administrators, eroding school culture in the process.

Clearly, teachers are getting more and more frustrated by policymakers' refusal to see the connection between a healthy workplace for teachers and teacher well-being, and to put reforms that ensure teacher well-being front and center. This is evidenced by the growth in teacher strikes. As explained in the previous chapter, recent teacher strikes are different. Rather than striking for more pay, teachers are striking for better policies that can transform the school environment in ways that better support students, school staff, and themselves.

This is also evidenced by the fact that in 2017 Congress introduced the Teacher Health and Wellness Act which was sponsored by both Democrats and Republicans. This Act directed the National Institutes of Health to conduct a study on reducing teacher stress and increasing teacher retention and well-being. Congress implemented this Act based on the following findings:

> High levels of stress are adversely affecting teachers' health. Teachers with high levels of stress are less effective in raising student achievement than their healthier peers. Elementary school teachers who have greater stress and show more symptoms of depression create classroom environments that are less conducive to learning. Stress is contributing to the high turnover rate among teachers, which causes instability for students and communities.
>
> This leads to higher costs for school districts to train new teachers and hinders students' academic success. School organization, low job *autonomy*, and a lack of ability to access teacher leadership opportunities are main sources of teacher stress. If teachers are unable to manage their stress levels, this leads to lower-level teacher instruction, which then impacts student well-being. High teacher turnover brings down students' math and language arts scores.

Congress also cited a 2014 Gallup survey that found that "46 percent of teachers experience high daily stress during the school year. This percentage is *tied for the highest rate of daily stress among occupations* and is a significant increase from teacher stress levels in 1985."[3] Certainly, Congress is aware of the tremendous stress teachers experience, yet there is very little will to do much about it. For example, this legislation, although enacted, was not funded, and there is no information on the bill's outcome.

This section explores the ways in which the experiences described in Section One hurt teachers psychologically. It examines the specific ways that teachers' needs are thwarted, as well as the psychological processes that damage teacher well-being.

NOTES

1. Steve Farkas et al., *A Sense of Calling: Who Teaches and Why: A Report from Public Agenda,* Public Agenda (2000).
2. Ryan Duffy et al., "Calling and Life Satisfaction: It's Not about Having It, It's about Living It," *Journal of Counseling Psychology,* 60, no. 1 (2013), doi: 10.1037/a0030635.
3. Gallup, *State of America's Schools the Path to Winning Again in Education* (Gallup, Inc., 2014), 24.

Chapter 6

How Under-Resourced Schools Thwart Teachers' Basic Human Needs

This is Stephanie's story.[1] She taught for fourteen years as a White teacher in a high-needs, high-poverty school. The school had strong leadership, collaborative colleagues, and respectful relationships with parents. It was "the most ethnically, racially and linguistically diverse" school in the state. Stephanie's classes were part of a language immersion magnet program that integrated Spanish-speaking and native English speakers who attended the mostly immigrant and African American neighborhood school.

Stephanie and her colleagues also created an after-school program that provided language instruction in Spanish to support the English instruction for Spanish-speaking students school-wide. She worked with a team of ten diverse teachers who wrote their own curriculum units that included original, rubric-based assignments that were culturally relevant and aligned with state standards. Stephanie "relished the challenge of teaching math and science in a Spanish-language immersion classroom."

> [She found it professionally fulfilling to] help her students access the specialized vocabulary and concepts of science and math in a foreign language through manipulatives, [such as building blocks], or dramatization, and real objects of nature. She and her colleagues worked closely with families to ensure that meaningful, authentic learning opportunities were abundant.[2]

Stephanie felt invigorated by her teaching. She felt that her work allowed her to use her content knowledge to help students become absorbed by their learning and able to make real world connections between that learning and their lives outside of school. She loved collaborating with her colleagues on a shared goal.

She also valued the relationships she developed with her students and their families and felt that her ability to teach her students well depended upon those relationships. She described how her knowledge of her students informed her teaching:

> When I was at my best, it was my understanding in the back of my head of where I needed to get my students. My ultimate goal was . . . my interaction with the kids so that I was responding to where they were and what they needed individually and as a group to get to that place. It sounds kind of messy . . . it wasn't just teacher directed. I wasn't standing up giving information, but designing the environment and the activities and the experiences so that the kids would acquire the skills they needed and the kind of stances in their thinking about things that I felt would serve them.[3]

Stephanie started teaching in the mid-1990s, a time when teachers had the autonomy to use their expertise to determine best teaching practices. Things changed for Stephanie and her school when No Child Left Behind was implemented in 2001. She describes the shift as gradual. For example, when Virginia implemented state-based standards, Stephanie worked with a team of teachers to align the district's review packets with the Science Standards for Learning. However, over time, to Stephanie's "dismay, those packets, originally intended for review purposes" not only became central to, but ultimately dictated, the third-grade curriculum. Stephanie explains,

> The supplemental test preparation materials that she had a hand in creating became the curriculum itself. Discovery and inquiry-based science approaches that relied on experiments were phased out to make room for ensuring students learned the "facts." A teacher-directed model of instruction in which textbooks dictated the content and pace of learning subsumed the collaborative approaches that had been the norm for Stephanie's team.[4]

Despite these changes, Stephanie and her colleagues tried to close their doors and continue teaching using student-engaged practices, but the pressure to have kids pass the state tests became too great, and there was not enough time in the day to focus on both facts and teach the students "how to think about math." Stephanie hung on for two more years but just couldn't do it anymore. She explained,

> Education is about people and it's kind of messy and not quite as standardized as someone might think. I am fundamentally not interested in enacting other people's plans. There is no creativity in that; there is no opportunity to use what I know in that situation, and also, it is a slap in the face to me as a professional.[5]

Stephanie finally left teaching three years later.

What happened to Stephanie, has happened to good teachers throughout this country. What they love about the challenge of teaching—getting to know students well enough so that they can help them make connections between the content and their experiences and focusing on the intricacies of student thinking, so that they teach them how to think in ways that allow for higher-order analysis and complex problem solving—requires relationship building, creativity, and planning.

This is one reason why teachers are professionals, they understand the complexities and convolutions of student thinking, and they can figure out how to help students navigate these twists and turns as they learn how to think like engineers and lawyers, and doctors.

The teachers you have met in this book, Stephanie, Quay, and Robin, have all hit roadblocks in their attempts to teach well and to carry out their professional duties to do right by the children who are under their care. Even though each one of them faced very different challenges, in different professional contexts, the psychological outcomes have been the same—frustration, bewilderment, and self-doubt about their profession, their competence, and their commitments.

These types of feelings cause psychological pain that impacts health and well-being in very negative ways. This chapter explains the psychological processes behind the negative experiences that teachers have while teaching, and clarifies why these experiences are so psychologically and physically damaging to teacher well-being.

One of the strongest motivations we have as human beings is to see ourselves as good people, as people who are consistent, competent, and ethical and whose actions conform to the cultural and social norms of our communities.[6] The beliefs we hold about ourselves help us maintain the sense that we are a good person in the domains that matter to us, be they work, family, friends, or community. These beliefs make up our *self-concept*, which consists of our *goals and aspirations*, our accomplishments, our values, and our *personal and professional standards*.

Our self-concept represents our knowledge and perceptions of ourselves and allows us to answer the question, who am I? It not only represents who we are as people in terms of our gender, race, or occupation, but also how we feel about who we are and how we, and others, evaluate the roles we play in the valued domains of our lives. These self-evaluations are based upon our behaviors, in that our behavior within a certain domain becomes a personal measure of how well we reflect our self-concept within that domain. This impacts our *self-esteem* because how we feel about ourselves in a certain domain impacts our ability to behave effectively within that context.

This book, with its focus on teaching, is mainly concerned with the domain of work. Our work impacts our self-concept because we come to see our behaviors at work as an affirmation of our values and standards, as proof that we are a good person within that domain, that we are competent, and that our actions confirm that we are a good citizen within the cultural and social norms of our work context.

Research has shown that the ideas and beliefs we have about ourselves and our abilities are what sustain us when it comes to being able to take effective action in our lives, this includes in our working lives. This sense of *self-efficacy,* the belief that we can successfully and competently complete required tasks, is what gives us the confidence that we can do our jobs well, and that we can act effectively at work. For example, teachers who have a strong sense of teaching self-efficacy are better educators because they believe that they can teach the content, and/or the students, well.

Related to this is the fact that as human beings, we all have a set of innate, *psychological needs,* that when met, increase our overall health and well-being. These needs are the need for autonomy, the need for competence, and the need for relatedness.[7] The need for *autonomy is* the need to have a sense of ownership over the decisions we make and the actions we choose to take, rather than being or feeling pressured to act in certain ways by outside forces.

The need for *competence* is the need to have sufficient knowledge, judgment, or skills to make meaningful decisions that impact one's life and environment. Finally, the need for *relatedness is* the need to feel connected to others by seeing oneself as a member of a group, family, or another social affinity.

Just as the need for water and food is essential for our survival, these needs are essential for a healthy self-concept and high self-esteem. *These psychological needs reinforce our self-concept either positively or negatively.* For example, if work is a valued domain in a person's life, and that person can meet their need for autonomy, competence, and relatedness at work, then that person will have a healthier self-concept and higher self-esteem than someone who is not able to meet these needs in the workplace.

Humans also have a natural inclination toward psychological growth, identification with others, and well-being. Psychological growth is growth that advances an individual's ability to achieve their goals and gain a sense of internal fulfillment. Identification with others takes place when we unconsciously assimilate the values, beliefs, feelings, or attitudes of those whom we frequently associate with into the self and adopt them as our own.

Well-being is defined as living a healthy and happy life that brings one a sense of satisfaction. The extent to which people can grow in these areas is based on how well they are able to satisfy their need for *autonomy, competence, and relatedness.*

These needs are met through our environmental and relational experiences. In other words, *context* is important and can either inhibit or facilitate growth and well-being. One way that environmental influences hurt our self-concept is by thwarting or frustrating our basic psychological needs. This is crucial for well-being because the ability to meet our psychological needs is what provides us with *meaning* in our lives. Some psychologists have defined human beings as meaning makers.[8]

What they mean by this is that people long to feel part of a coherent cultural worldview. This coherence helps people to not feel alienated from the world around them and to feel like they belong to a community of others who view them as members with similar values and beliefs. The meaning that comes from affiliation gives people a *sense of certainty* in their lives. It helps people to "know" that their beliefs, attitudes, and behaviors are "correct" and that their understanding of how the world works is accurate.

Meaning, and the certainty that it provides, helps us to feel confident about our personal and professional decisions. It raises our self-esteem because it signals to us that we "fit" within our particular context. Meaning and certainty are reinforced when our needs for autonomy, competence, and relatedness are met in key life domains, and our efforts to maintain meaning are greater when the domain is personally and/or professionally relevant to us.

Finally, meeting our needs and having a sense of meaning and certainty enhances our motivation to do our best in a particular domain. An inability to meet these needs in a highly relevant domain diminishes our self-concept, lowers our self-esteem, and reduces our motivation because it deprives us of the sense of certainty that we can predict and control our worlds.

This process of needs satisfaction leading to psychological growth and well-being is common to all humans. People can fulfill these needs for autonomy, competence, and relatedness through their personal interests, through their family and social circles, or their work. In this country, because of the outsized role that work plays in many people's lives, being able to fulfill these needs at work becomes crucial for a strong self-concept and a healthy sense of well-being.

This is especially true for those who consider themselves to be professionals, and who have undergone extensive schooling or other forms of training to prepare for the work that they do. Because teachers fall into this category, this discussion focuses on how the satisfaction of autonomy, competence, and relatedness needs at work impacts teachers and teaching. The following discussion demonstrates how needs satisfaction impacts motivation.

NEEDS SATISFACTION AND MOTIVATION AT WORK

Research has shown that people who are able to fulfill these needs at work are more motivated to do their best and to contribute in positive ways to workplace goals. On the other hand, "when people do not feel capable and effective at work, their *motivation* plummets and they suffer from psychological distress which in turn impacts their health."[9] Because motivation is a key outcome of successful needs satisfaction, those who study work and the role it plays in our lives, have focused specifically on motivation and its relationship to the three psychological needs.

They have focused on two types of motivation, intrinsic and extrinsic. Workers are intrinsically motivated when the tasks they do at work are inherently interesting and enjoyable in and of themselves, as opposed to extrinsically motivated workers, who perform work tasks for external reasons that are not inherently rewarding. Research has shown that having intrinsically motivated employees leads to a successful, satisfying, and productive workplace, and that intrinsic motivation is enhanced when workers can meet their needs for autonomy, competence, and relatedness on the job.[10]

This brings us to teachers. Teachers are more intrinsically motivated than most because many have been "called" to teach, making them more committed and determined in their work with young people. The fact that teachers begin their careers with such high levels of motivation is very advantageous for both student success and the overall working environment of a school. We know that workplaces with highly motivated professionals are more productive, more collaborative, and better able to meet the overall goals of the organization.

It turns out that maintaining high levels of intrinsic motivation at work requires a supportive work environment that is characterized by working conditions that foster competence, autonomy, and relatedness. For teachers, competence is cultivated through supportive feedback, clear communication, and collaboratively determined incentives. But having a sense of competence about one's teaching ability is not enough to sustain intrinsic motivation.

Teachers must also have a sense of autonomy which comes from being trusted to make independent decisions about how they teach the content, and the ability to use the knowledge and skills they have acquired in making those decisions.

Some education reformers have criticized the idea of autonomy as encouraging individualism and a go-it-alone attitude. But when we talk about teacher autonomy, we are not talking about teachers who close their classroom doors to others and do whatever they want in the classroom. This is a misunderstanding of the concept of autonomy. Autonomy, as a psychological need, does not mean that we desire to act independently, regardless of what others want. It *does* mean that, as humans, we have a need to act with "a sense of choice and volition, even if doing so means complying with the wishes or others."[11]

When we choose to act collaboratively, in conjunction with colleagues, our need for autonomy is satisfied. This is why working in the community and building relationships at work enhance a teacher's sense of autonomy. It is only when teachers are actively denied a sense of autonomy that they retreat to the confines of their classroom. Intrinsically motivated teachers delight in the knowledge that they have the competence *and* autonomy to solve the complex educational problems that trouble our nation's most challenging schools.

Having responsibility for what they teach is what enhances and maintains a teacher's sense of intrinsic motivation, not the external rewards such as merit pay that have become the norm in many school accountability systems. In fact, research has shown that receiving external rewards for work performance diminishes one's sense of autonomy, thus hindering intrinsic motivation.[12]

Finally, intrinsic motivation is enhanced for those who work in schools that foster a sense of security and relatedness among teachers.[13] This research shows how the social context of the school can support or frustrate the three psychological needs, leading to diminished intrinsic motivation in teachers.

Not all teachers are naturally intrinsically motivated to teach. However, this does not mean that they are motivated only by their paycheck or other external rewards. When teachers can personally identify with the goals of their school and feel that those goals match their values and beliefs, they unconsciously begin to internalize those values as their own, thus increasing their identification with students and colleagues. This process allows teachers who are extrinsically motivated to both identify with and integrate the school's principles and procedures, gaining a sense of autonomy in the process.

Having met the need for autonomy through identification, extrinsically motivated teachers tend to be more engaged and more competent in completing tasks. Depending on other factors present in the school environment, it then becomes easier for these teachers to satisfy their need for relatedness as well, thus increasing their overall well-being. Through the process of identification, even when teachers are extrinsically motivated, they can still deeply value and be personally committed to teaching.

Even though many teachers begin their careers with high levels of intrinsic motivation, their motivation can be compromised if they are not able to satisfy their psychological needs within the school environment. School environments that thwart the need for autonomy, competence, and relatedness breed alienation, lack of commitment, and distress in teachers. Not only is this terrible for teachers, but it also does tremendous damage to students, who lose out on the benefit of being taught by healthy and happy professionals.

Thanks to the long history of research on school reform we now have a very clear and specific picture of how organizational structures impact teachers. This research goes as far back as the 1960s with the work of Jonathan Kozol. Similar, major studies have been published each decade since, by Tyack in 1974, and Lortie in 1975, Theodore Sizer in 1980, Jean Anyon in 1997, Charles Payne's aptly titled book *So Much Reform, So Little Change* in 2010, and finally with the most recent extensive studies conducted in 2019 by Susan Moore Johnson's Project on the Next Generation of Teachers.

The findings from over sixty years of research have been consistent and backed up by those who study the psychology of work in general. Despite this overwhelming evidence of the power of the social *context* itself to effect change, there are still far too many dysfunctional schools in our nation, many of them serving our most needy children in poor urban and rural communities.[14] Charles Payne describes these schools as having "demoralized, depressed and socially chaotic environments."[15]

Ten years later, Moore-Johnson describes them as "dysfunctional and unsupportive work environments."[16] All of these researchers highlight the specific working conditions that characterize these dysfunctional schools to show why teachers leave teaching. It is also important to show that these environments are also psychologically damaging for the teachers who stay. One reason these practices hurt teachers so much is that these environments make it impossible for teachers to fulfill their need for autonomy, competence, and relatedness at work.

Let's start with autonomy. Stephanie's experiences illustrate how teacher autonomy has consistently been whittled away over the last twenty-five years due to the growth in testing and the punitive evaluation measures based on testing outcomes. Despite being highly educated professionals, too many teachers lack the autonomy to make professional decisions.

This is true even though teachers in most states are required to complete a credentialing program, along with a content degree, as well as pass state certification exams and renew their teaching license every few years. In addition, teachers participate in required professional development sessions, both throughout the year and during the summer.

Despite their level of education, too many policies and practices in use today have been imposed upon teachers, rather than collaboratively chosen with teachers. These include standardized testing, test prep, pacing guides, "teacher-proof" curricula, and merit pay. These mandated policies lead to the following types of experiences:

> Before the state testing was implemented, I could just go with the kids. If something came up that hooked them, I could follow their interests. But now, if we start in a different direction, I get worried we won't get back to the test prep, so

I have to kind of rein them in. I know they get frustrated and so do I! I think, is this what I got into teaching for?[17]

This teacher's need for autonomy has clearly been thwarted by the requirement to teach to the test. The teacher no longer feels comfortable when following student interests because of the time that takes. Even though the teacher, and all of us, know that students learn best, and retain more when the content aligns with their interests.

Another teacher explains,

I teach at a school designed for students at risk of dropping out. The kids at my school are great, but the job has become increasingly test-centered rather than student-centered. All the testing and compliance have led to a job that is 80% paperwork, and 20% teaching. Keeping track of the paperwork is incredibly difficult. I am often forced to choose between helping a student who needs my attention or completing my paperwork. I feel that too many times the students get shortchanged because teachers get audited on their paperwork once a month and are given a numerical grade based on compliance.[18]

Finally, we hear from this teacher:

We are under so much pressure to get good results there is little time for anything else. [The testing, along with the negative consequences] definitely decreases morale. I had to cease a lot of projects and other activities and programs in my room [that made learning fun for the kids] just to make time for teaching test subjects and strategies.[19]

These policies diminish teacher autonomy in ways that hurt their teaching, their personal well-being, and the overall school community.[20] In terms of their teaching, these policies lead to teachers who are nervous about "following student interests" as they teach for fear that they might shortchange teaching to the test. Think about that! Good teaching is all about knowing when to take the time to connect a student's interest to the subject matter.

This is one of the many decisions teachers make every day while teaching. "How can I connect this question or this line of thinking to the content?" "Should we stop and discuss this question so I can then use something similar on my formative assessment?" Now teachers must also consider whether following a student's line of thinking will hurt their compliance score.

A big part of teaching is designing experiences for students, the more complex, interesting, and collaborative, the better. This is what Stephanie was doing before NCLB invaded her state. Students are much more likely to remember classroom experiences that confound them or that allow them to solve problems with their peers. It takes time to both design and implement cognitively challenging and collaborative activities, yet today's teachers are forced to choose between teaching that grows out of who their students are or teaching materials that have been mandated to cover testing subjects.

In most cases, these materials do not take student backgrounds and cultures into consideration. For example, a second-year teacher was talking about the new pre-AP curriculum that schools in her district were required to adopt. This teacher was frustrated because she felt that her students did worse with the new curriculum than they had done the previous year.

She explained that in her first year of teaching, the students read full-length books in English class. Because they were reading books, the teacher and students spent more time discussing the characters, themes, conflicts, and overall message. They spent more time with the text; more time thinking about, writing about, and applying the ideas and content they were learning.

This year, with the new pre-AP curriculum, the teachers are not allowed to teach through books or novels. They must assign the short stories or short pieces of non-fiction mandated by the pre-AP curriculum. After reading and discussing these short pieces, the students must complete a writing assignment where they answer specific predetermined questions. The teacher cannot tailor the questions for her students, nor change them in any way.

As a result, this teacher is finding that her student's ability to think critically about the texts and to make critical connections in their writing has been diminished. She believes that the short stories are not enough for them to work with, partly because the majority of her urban, African American, and Latinx students cannot relate to the stories. But more crucial, she can no longer take the time to work on a deeper level with the material.

She had found that going in-depth with the books, through discussion, annotation, and writing, allowed the students to engage more with the text and thus to think more deeply about the themes found within them. Now she must follow this curriculum exactly even though she knows that her students cannot relate to it, hurting not only their engagement but also their learning. Interestingly enough, the pre-AP curriculum was originally designed for sixth graders.

It didn't work with those students, so her district started using it with eighth graders. Same problem. Now she is stuck with it as a tenth-grade teacher. Maybe the problem is not the students, but the material. Unfortunately, no one at her school can address her concerns. Most likely the state mandated this for the district, the district for the schools, and the principal for the teachers.

She is so far removed from any decision-making about this curriculum, and she is very worried that her AP students will not come close to passing the AP exam.[21] Rather than aid student learning these kinds of policies "suppress good teaching practice by prohibiting variation, discouraging innovation, barring adaptation, and penalizing independent thinking."[22]

Finally, we cannot talk about how teacher autonomy is diminished without talking about merit pay. Research has shown those merit pay policies, which have been widely implemented, deflate a teacher's sense of autonomy. When a teacher, or any self-motivated professional, is told that they are going to be given a bonus or reward pay for doing the job that they have prepared to do, it causes them to lose a sense of ownership over the decisions they make at work. As Deci and Ryan, two leading researchers on the psychology of work explain:

> Autonomy is diminished not only by tangible rewards, but also by threats, deadlines, directives, pressured evaluations, and imposed goals . . . because, like tangible rewards, [these practices reinforce the feeling that one is being motivated by external forces]. In contrast, choice, acknowledgment of feelings, and opportunities for self-direction were found to enhance intrinsic motivation because they allow people a greater feeling of autonomy.[23]

This hurts teacher well-being. The less autonomy a teacher has, the more likely they are to be anxious, worried, and frustrated. Organizationally, teachers with less autonomy respond worse to environmental stressors that cause them to feel mistreated. This makes them more likely to interpret ordinary situations as threatening and minor frustrations as hopelessly difficult.

These feelings cause teachers to experience more stress and conflict around the role they play within the school community. This can lead teachers to engage in more organizational politics[24] or behind-the-scenes strategies designed to improve their influence within the school. These tactics damage interpersonal trust and hurt relationships between teachers, leading to higher levels of burnout out and ultimately more teacher turnover.[25]

When teachers are prevented in their day-to-day work from exercising their autonomy as professionals, like both Quay and Stephanie were, their sense of competence also suffers, with similar results. For example, teachers who do not feel competent do not identify as readily with work tasks, and worse, they can come to see those tasks as less significant to the overall success of the school and student learning. Also, the less competent workers feel, the more political the work environment becomes.[26]

Once this happens, it is very hard to turn the school around, as Charles Payne, in his research on school reform in "bottom tier schools" has illustrated. Payne describes his work as an "analysis of failure" and points out that those who engage in school reform efforts lack a "systemic understanding of the causes of failure."[27] He then goes on to describe what happens in what he calls "these demoralized institutions," many of which serve poor, urban children of color.

They tend to be places governed by an overarching sense of futility and pessimism; where colleagues may distrust their supervisors and perhaps one another; where there can be a certain harshness in the way children and parents are dealt with; where many children, also many teachers seem to be disengaged much of the time; where the levels of human capital are at their lowest; where instruction is uncoordinated and uninspiring; where there are too few resources, and those few are often badly used; where *the* curriculum is narrow, boring, and frequently changing; where teachers have profound skepticism about "programs"; where there is a general feeling of instability—personnel come and go, students come and go, programs come and go—all of it is presided over by a dysfunctional bureaucracy. . . .

The problems manifest themselves in so many ways that they may obscure the fact that *many of the discrete problems are either generated by or reinforced by the sheer lack of connectedness among people.*[28]

Payne, and other education reformers, describe the problem without ever stating the obvious—reforms must start and end with the teachers. No teacher ever accepted a job with the goal of *not* practicing what they learned during their years of preparation. No teacher wants to *not* interact or collaborate with colleagues. And finally, no teacher actively tried to *not* do their best to provide what students need. Payne says that we must think of "demoralized schools as if they were clinically depressed individuals."

Teachers in troubled schools *are* depressed because they have had their professional autonomy stripped from them, along with any sense of competence and the efficacy they once felt about their ability to be a good teacher. The impact this has on teacher well-being shines through in the adjectives Payne uses to describe such schools. He describes the teachers as suffering from "collective depression" and "social demoralization" because they work in "irrational organizations" and are expected to teach young people with minimal social, cultural, and material resources in a society that is constantly judging them.

An inability to fulfill the need for autonomy and competence at work can end up corrupting the need for relatedness and belonging. This is because belongingness is such a strong need that humans will find unhealthy ways to relate when the social context impedes more healthy relations. This phenomenon is discussed in detail in the next chapter. First, let's examine what happens in schools where teachers' basic psychological human needs are fulfilled.

SCHOOLS THAT MEET TEACHERS' NEEDS

The picture is very different in schools where teachers have the autonomy to make and follow through with decisions about their teaching. These teachers identify more strongly with their role in the school and feel more supported at work. They also are better at accepting feedback because they are more confident that they will have a part in determining how the feedback is implemented. Their confidence stems from the fact that teachers who have more autonomy also feel more supported at work and have better relationships with their supervisors.

They also perceive that work procedures and interactions are fair. This gives them a stronger sense of job satisfaction, increasing their motivation and engagement at work. More important, teachers with a strong sense of autonomy are more emotionally committed to their school, making it more likely that they have a sense of shared values with their supervisors and colleagues and actually like being at work.[29]

The benefits are similar when teachers have a strong feeling of competence and relatedness at work. These teachers are more optimistic and tend to have higher self-esteem. This leads them to be more conscientious and mindful about both their own work and the overall work environment, and to feel that their work responsibilities are important to the overall goals of the school. There is also a relationship between a teacher's sense of competence and relatedness and their belief that they can teach students effectively.

These teachers have a stronger sense of teaching efficacy which has been associated with teachers' effectiveness, level of engagement, and commitment to teaching. Teachers whose needs are met in these ways feel more supported by both their colleagues and administrators and have higher levels of job satisfaction. Finally, and most importantly, these teachers have higher levels of physical, emotional, and mental well-being.

Education researchers who have studied and observed successful schools have identified the specific school characteristics that satisfy teachers' psychological needs. It turns out that schools with these characteristics are more successful in every measure than schools without them. These schools have happy teachers who work well together, successful students, and low turnover rates.

Generally, successful schools have resources that help teachers meet both the emotional and academic needs of students, have support for their development as professionals, have strong collaborative leadership, and have school-wide systems in place that encourage shared values and professional norms.

More specifically, Susan Moore-Johnson, who has been studying teachers' work environments for the last twenty years through the *Project on the Next Generation of Teachers*, has identified and defined nine school features that determine the quality of a teacher's work environment. Each of these contextual features can be measured on a spectrum from best to worst[30]: colleagues, community support, facilities, governance, leadership, professional expertise, resources, school culture, and time.

Where a school lands on these qualities often determines its success or failure. As Moore-Johnson points out "these factors can differentiate positive, sustaining work environments that serve teachers and students well from unproductive, demoralizing ones that shortchange both."[31] These qualities can also be categorized according to the psychological needs they meet, or thwart, for teachers.

For example, the need for autonomy is met by strong shared *governance* policies, where teachers have a voice in decision-making. Both autonomy and competency needs are met when teachers are viewed by their *colleagues* and the *principal* as *professionals* whose decisions about teaching and learning are respected. Teachers also feel more competent when they have *time* to meet all their professional obligations, "both instructional and non-instructional."

Finally, teachers' relatedness needs are met, first and foremost, when they work within a *school culture* that is defined by mutual trust. Mutual trust allows *colleagues* to be more collaborative, supportive, and productive in their work together to meet the schools' challenges. The level of *community support* also fulfills the relational needs of teachers by providing, among other things, validation for a teacher's commitment to contribute to society, through their efforts on behalf of children.

In other words, these schools work because they meet teachers' psychological needs. When a teacher's psychological needs are met within the school context, that teacher is more psychologically healthy. She experiences less stress at work because she is less anxious and fearful about her day-to-day interactions and less frustrated and angry with her colleagues and the school leadership.

Because she is part of a community that discusses and shares best practices and is then allowed to implement those practices in ways that work for her students, she also feels more respected at work, and like her opinions and decisions matter. All of this gives her more strength and confidence to deal with the social and emotional issues that students bring to the classroom, issues that those Robin and Quay had to deal with on their own.

Teachers in healthy schools know that they do not have to deal with the multitude of student needs on their own and that they will have the support and the resources they need. In these schools, the teacher is a healthy and happy professional who works among other healthy and happy professionals, making the overall school environment more successful for both teachers and students.

Previous research has implied that high-needs schools with high levels of minority children are, in and of themselves, failing schools, as if the students were the ones responsible for the school's failures. However, Payne and Moore-Johnson's research, let alone common sense, shows that this is not the case. High-needs schools fail because they get far fewer resources to meet the far greater needs of the students, and yes of the teachers.

Educational reform policies must put teacher well-being at the center. Happy and healthy teachers is what leads to successful schools. Rather than think of the problem as one that can be solved without teachers, policymakers must put teacher well-being at the forefront. Only then will school environments be transformed into healthy places, where teaching and learning are possible for all.

NOTES

1. In her study of teachers from high poverty schools who left teaching, Santoro (2011) interviewed 13 teachers who taught before the enactment of No Child Left Behind in 2001, and who ultimately left teaching based on their experiences with the new federal and state policies.
2. Doris Santoro, "Good Teaching in Difficult Times: Demoralization in the Pursuit of Good Work," American Journal of Education, 118, no. 1 (November 2011), 13, doi: 10.1086/662010.
3. Doris Santoro, "Good Teaching in Difficult Times," 14.
4. Doris Santoro, "Good Teaching in Difficult Times," 15.
5. Doris Santoro, "Good Teaching in Difficult Times," 16.
6. Claude M. Steele, "The Psychology of Self-Affirmation: Sustaining the Integrity of the Self," Advances in Experimental Social Psychology, 21 (1988).
7. Anja V. Broeck et al., "A Review of Self-Determination Theory's Basic Psychological Needs at Work," Journal of Management, 42, no. 5 (July 2016), doi: 10.1177/0149206316632058.
8. Steven J. Heine, Travis Proulx, and Kathleen D. Vohs, "The Meaning Maintenance Model: On the Coherence of Social Motivations," Personality and Social Psychology Review, 10, no. 2 (2006).
9. Richard M. Ryan and Edward L. Desi, "Self-Determination Theory and the Facilitation of Intrinsic Motivation, Social Development and Well-Being," American Psychologist, 55, no. 1 (2000), 6, doi: 10.1037//0003-066X55.1.68.
10. Richard M. Ryan and Edward L. Desi, "Self-Determination Theory."
11. Anja V. Broeck et. al., "A Review of Self-Determination Theory," 1198.
12. Edward Deci, L. Koestner, and Richard Ryan, "A Meta-Analytic Review of Experiments Examining the Effects of Extrinsic Rewards on Intrinsic Motivation," Psychological Bulletin, 125 (1999).
13. Richard M. Ryan and Edward L. Desi, "Self-Determination Theory."
14. Susan M. Johnson, Matthew A. Kraft, and John P. Papay, "How Context Matters in High-Needs Schools: The Effects of Teachers' Working Conditions on Their Professional Satisfaction and Their Student's Achievement," Teachers College Record, 114 (2012).
15. Charles Payne, So Much Reform, So Little Change: The Persistence of Failure in Urban Schools, Harvard Education Press (April, 2008), 23.

16. Susan M. Johnson et al., "How Context Matters," 2.
17. Sharon L. Nichols and David. C Berliner, *Collateral Damage: How High-Stakes Testing Corrupts America's Schools* (Cambridge, MA. Harvard University Press, 2007), 42.
18. Sharon L. Nichols and David. C Berliner, *Collateral Damage*, 44.
19. Sharon L. Nichols and David. C Berliner, *Collateral Damage*, 38.
20. Anja V. Broeck et al., "A Review of Self-Determination Theory."
21. Interview with a second year teacher, Olivia Difranco (March 2021).
22. Susan Moore Johnson, *Where Teachers Thrive: Organizing Schools for Success* (Cambridge, MA: Harvard Education Press, 2019), 17.
23. Richard M. Ryan and Edward L. Desi, "Self-Determination Theory," 70.
24. Anja V. Broeck et al., "A Review of Self-Determination Theory."
25. Anja V. Broeck et al., "A Review of Self-Determination Theory."
26. Anja V. Broeck et al., "A Review of Self-Determination Theory."
27. Charles Payne, *So Much Reform*, 5.
28. Charles Payne, *So Much Reform*, 23–24.
29. Anja V. Broeck et al., "A Review of Self-Determination Theory," 6.
30. Susan M. Johnson et al., "How Context Matters."
31. Susan Moore Johnson, *Where Teachers Thrive*, 11.

Chapter 7

Emotions and Cognitive Dissonance
The Psychological Pain of Teaching

One teacher spoke candidly about her psychological pain and the emotional toll teaching has taken on her, stating,

> I feel demoralized and unappreciated by all of the negative press in the newspapers and have doubted myself as an educator for the first time. . . . I feel pulled in so many directions. We have to try to make education more personal to motivate students and account for individual learning needs, but at the same time, because of all the testing, we have to standardize student learning, forcing students into a box whether they are ready developmentally or not.
>
> This leads a certain percentage of students to misbehave out of frustration and disrupt the classroom, for which we get no support. I find that it is a demoralizing, stressful situation. I know my kids are learning; they are advancing in their understanding, yet I am being judged year to year on one outcome for completely different sets of students. It is so much pressure.[1]

EMOTIONS, FEELINGS, AND NEEDS

One can hear the despair and sense of hopelessness in this teacher's voice as she describes her lived experience as a teacher. This teacher's psychological needs as a professional have been thwarted. When this happens, it sets off an emotional process that is difficult for teachers to manage without support. Even though we tend to use the terms emotions and feelings synonymously, understanding the differences between these terms is important for this discussion.[2] The process described here begins for teachers with their emotions, which are bodily sensations that we experience in response to certain stimuli.

For example, emotions can be generated when we see someone we love or when we see a spider. Emotions are physical and unconscious. They are bodily reactions that originate in the brain's amygdala and that result in biochemical reactions which alter our physical state by increasing our heart rate, causing us to feel indigestion or abdominal pain, causing us to sweat, or make certain facial expressions. For example, a teacher's heart might start racing when her students behave in certain ways or she might smile when her students successfully complete an academic challenge.

Once we experience an emotion, we interpret our bodily sensations as feelings. Feelings originate in the neocortical areas of the brain which are located in our frontal lobes. To understand an emotional reaction, our brains assign meaning to it. The meanings we assign are subjective and are influenced by our personal experiences, beliefs, thoughts, and memories. For example, volume or noise level is a stimulus that can trigger a significant response. An increase in volume can become a sign that students are getting restless and about to misbehave.

In response, the teacher's heart starts racing automatically. This might lead her to unconsciously interpret the sensation as fear because she knows she has trouble getting the kids to settle down. She might interpret it as disappointment in herself because she feels she has not engaged them enough. She might interpret it as worry because they have to take a test next and might not be able to focus as they should.

Over time, our brain begins to associate certain emotions (bodily sensations) with specific feelings (based on mental interpretations) which is why just thinking about certain experiences or events can trigger an emotional reaction which then results in a specific feeling. This process is also triggered when we anticipate certain events or experiences before they happen, resulting in the same cycle—we experience the sensation (elevated heart rate) and feel the feelings we have associated with that bodily sensation, and now with the anticipated event.

This can become a vicious cycle, especially within environmental contexts where one has the same difficult experiences over and over but has little support in processing those experiences. For example, if Robin continues to have the same teaching difficulties in her classroom day after day, she may experience anxiety every time she enters the classroom in anticipation of those difficulties. As time goes on, this will make it harder for her to teach effectively and will end up shaping how she behaves with her students.

This is a likely path for Robin because our emotions and feelings are the driving force behind many of our behaviors, both healthy and unhealthy. Our emotions and feelings influence how we act, and interact, in the major domains and contexts in which we live our lives. Needs satisfaction, or lack thereof, plays a large role in this process. As we saw in the last chapter, schools where teachers are able to fulfill their need for autonomy, competence, and relatedness work much better, with more productive and happier teachers than schools where need fulfillment is a challenge.

When we are unable to meet our psychological needs in the workplace, we experience uncomfortable emotions which we tend to explain in negative ways, leading to negative feelings. This can lead us to engage in unhealthy behaviors such as isolating ourselves from colleagues or not being open to feedback. A lack of need satisfaction also leads to lower levels of motivation and hurts one's identification with their work roles. This has vast implications for teachers because teaching is a very emotional job!

The types of school and classroom-based challenges described in this book lead to very strong emotions and feelings for teachers. These challenges compromise the teacher's ability to do the work. Teachers feel these challenges intensely because they thwart the act of teaching; they prevent the teacher from using the best methods and practices that reflect her professional training and expertise. Think about it! The teacher knows how to teach, has dedicated herself to learning the best methods for teaching the students in front of her, and has invested time and money into the extensive and ongoing training required to be licensed in most states.

Yet, when she finally gets her own classroom, she is often asked—or forced—like Stephanie was, to teach in ways that contradict her expertise and devalue her knowledge. Teachers face contradictions like this every, single day. Many are systemic, caused by educational policies, such as those around testing or behavior management. Others result from a lack of support for teachers, causing them to deal on their own with multiple classroom challenges.

Teachers' attempts to cope in these types of school cultures often lead them to act in ways that contradict their personal and professional convictions, leading some to question their commitments and abilities. We saw how these personal contradictions plagued Quay, Stephanie, and Robin.

The fact that Quay and Stephanie could not teach in ways that truly engaged the children, or that Robin reverted to behaving in ways that she did not value, such as raising her voice or calling on students whose answers she could anticipate, completely frazzled and dismayed them. In other words, these experiences set off emotional responses that result in feelings that over time damage a teacher's physical and mental health.

COGNITIVE DISSONANCE

Situations like these lead us to experience cognitive dissonance (CD). We experience cognitive dissonance when we act in ways that contradict our self-concept. This happens when our behaviors contradict our thoughts and beliefs. CD leaves one with the sensation of being off balance. It can also be experienced as a tightness in the throat, a clenching in the jaw, or a queasy feeling in the pit of the stomach. These sensations, depending upon the context in which we experience them, can lead to feelings of guilt, anxiety, doubt, uncertainty, regret, or overall psychological discomfort.

When we experience cognitive dissonance, we experience it as a threat to who we are, a threat to our values, beliefs, and standards. When we experience this self-threat in professionally relevant domains, it can cause us to question our professional choices. These *self-threats* make us feel foolish and incompetent. Worse, we lose our sense of meaning in relation to our professional identity, and our sense of certainty, not only about our work but about who we are as a person. These self-doubts diminish our sense of self-efficacy.[3]

Teachers are more likely to experience cognitive dissonance—and the feelings that accompany it—in schools that lack resources and supportive structures, and where it is difficult for teachers to meet their psychological needs. The experience of CD can take many forms. Stephanie, who had a very strong self-concept as a competent and committed teacher, and a high level of teaching self-efficacy, experienced CD when the new testing policies prevented her from taking an inquiry approach in her teaching. The first thing she lost was her sense of autonomy.

She could no longer use her professional judgment about what to teach and when to teach it; rather she was forced to follow someone else's pacing guide. As she said, "I am fundamentally not interested in enacting other people's plans. There's no creativity in that. There is no opportunity for me to use what I know in that situation." Once this happened, Stephanie started to lose her sense of competence as a teacher. She tried teaching in these foreign ways for two more years but ultimately left the profession.

Robin experienced something similar, not because of testing policies, but because of her still developing classroom management skills. Again, Robin was aware of best teaching practices but chose to follow less effective methods so that she could better manage her classroom. Robin did this in two ways, one that she was able to explain in a way that helped her avoid CD, and another that caused her to experience CD.

She was able to avoid feelings of CD when she modified the math workshop model by interacting with the students while they moved through the math stations instead of teaching a smaller group of students who needed the extra support, while the other students worked at the stations alone. This decision did not threaten Robin's self-concept as a teacher because she was able to explain her decision as a way to learn more about student thinking and to interact with her students while they are attempting to solve the math problems. This explanation was in keeping with good practice, allowing Robin to maintain her self-concept as a good math teacher.

Robin modified the workshop model again, however, when she let a group of students sit out the math stations even though she knew that working to solve problems after a lesson is one of the best ways for students to retain what they have learned. This decision did bring on cognitive dissonance because it threatened her sense of teaching competence. She knew that she was not following best practices in this case and that her actions would result in diminished student learning. This happened again for Robin when she felt guilty for not following her original plan to call on Tyrone and Jaynce while teaching.

Calling on those two students was something she had thought about and planned for, but when things got difficult, she called on the "safe" students instead. She felt so badly about this because she is aware of the achievement gap in math between African American and Latinx students and their white and Asian counterparts, and she is familiar with the research that shows how white teachers contribute to these gaps through their classroom actions.[4] She also sees herself as a non-biased and anti-racist person and teacher, and she believes that her actions in this situation did not live up to that vision of herself.

This contradiction caused her to experience more severe cognitive dissonance, leading to actual pain because of her deeply held conviction to teach in antiracist ways.

These classroom experiences threaten Robin's sense of competence as a teacher. They also threaten the meaning she has made of her decision to teach, which was so that she could play a role in mitigating the biased teaching practices that hurt poor children and children of color. This also diminishes her sense of certainty about the decisions she had made in choosing a career as a teacher.

Unfortunately, Robin had no time to process these contradictions in the moment because she had to move on with her lesson, causing her negative feelings to build up over time without resolution or reflection. She also had no support in processing her feelings around these personal disappointments. Extended experiences of cognitive dissonance are very difficult to mitigate without support, often leading to overwhelming stress that can make a teacher ill and more likely to leave the classroom.

Finally, teachers can also experience persistent cognitive dissonance when they have invested heavily in their decision to teach, but once hired, struggle to enact best teaching practices for various reasons, leading them to experience the repeated and prolonged thwarting of their psychological needs over time. Once again, this leads to a loss of meaning and certainty about the decisions they have made. For example, Robin got her teaching license through a teaching residency program where she spent one full academic year teaching a reduced load under the guidance of a mentor teacher, while simultaneously completing a master's degree in education.

This required a lot of effort, time, and expense. If Robin continues to struggle, without support, to enact what she believes to be the best teaching practices the cognitive dissonance she experiences may lead her to leave the teaching profession. As we can see from these examples, awareness of discrepancies between one's teacher beliefs and one's teaching practice threatens a teacher's sense of self, leading to feelings of incompetence which brings on the experience of cognitive dissonance. This prevents the teacher from teaching effectively.[5] The psychological discomfort felt in these situations thwarts the teacher's goals and hurts her self-esteem.

COGNITIVE DISSONANCE AS MOTIVATOR

The experience of cognitive dissonance, and the feelings it generates, motivates us to restore our sense of integrity and competence by helping us explain why we behaved the way that we did. Cognitive dissonance represents a judgment that implicates the self. These judgments arise in response to events that are important to our sense of self.[6] The first thing we do in our attempts to restore our self-concept is to attribute a cause to the feelings and psychological discomfort that result from our contradictory behaviors.

Our attributions help us explain the contradiction and why it may have happened. The explanations we produce are shaped by our prior experiences, our beliefs, our memories, and our personalities. Our dispositions, and whether we tend to lean optimistic or pessimistic, also play a role in how we attribute a cause to our contradictory behaviors.

The attributions we make about our behaviors have three defining characteristics.[7] First, we can understand our behaviors as stable, meaning that the causes of our behaviors will not change over time, or we can understand our behaviors as variable, specific to a particular time period. Second, we can attribute the cause of our behavior to factors that are either external (another person, a policy, or a context) or internal to ourselves. Last, we can explain our behaviors as being context-based or consistent across different contexts.

Depending upon our personal attributional styles, we tend to favor one set of characteristics over the other. Attributing our positive behaviors to stable, internal, and consistent factors, and our negative behaviors to variable, external, and contextual factors is psychologically healthy because this allows us to maintain our self-concept as competent and consistent people. Whereas it is psychologically damaging when we tend to attribute our negative behaviors to stable, internal, and consistent factors.

The damage this does is not only psychological; this type of attributional style also damages our health. Researchers found that people who tend to attribute their negative behaviors in this way are more prone to depression, have weakened immune systems, and have more visits to the doctor.[8]

To understand what this looks like in practice imagine two new teachers, Mark and Linda. Both worked hard on a lesson about integers for their fifth-graders that was observed by their supervisor. After the lesson, they debriefed with their supervisors. Mark's supervisor loved the class. Mark's attributional style led him to attribute his success to his own skills and abilities with both the subject matter and the students. He explains his teaching skill as internal to himself, stable over time, and consistent.

Because his attribution style is more optimistic, had Mark's supervisor been critical of his lesson, he would most likely have attributed his lack of success as external to himself—for example, the students had just returned from recess and had trouble paying attention. If the lesson had happened at another time during the day (variable) or in a different context (contextual) the lesson would have been successful. Because Mark tends to attribute his negative behaviors to variable, contextual, and external factors, he is able to maintain his self-concept as a good teacher.

Linda is the opposite. She tends to attribute her positive behaviors to variable, contextual, and external factors and her negative ones to stable, internal, and consistent factors. For example, if Linda's supervisor loved her lesson, she might be more likely to explain her success by saying that the students behaved because of the supervisor's presence. If Linda's supervisor was not pleased with the lesson, she would be likely to attribute her failure to internal factors such as it is hard for her to focus when she is being observed.

This type of attribution would tend to lead her to believe that she will also fail the next time she is observed because her failure was due to her own nervousness. Linda's more pessimistic attributional style makes it difficult for her to maintain her self-concept because she tends to attribute her failures internally and her successes externally.

Depending upon our personality and dispositions, the attributions we make can help us restore our sense of self by providing us with explanations that shield the self from criticism or threat.[9] This is not always the case, however, because sometimes the attribution itself can lead to feelings of self-threat if the cause we attribute contradicts our values or knowledge.[10] For example, if a teacher attributes student failure to a lack of studying even though she knows that many of her elementary students struggle to study at home for reasons beyond their control, her awareness of this discrepancy may cause her to experience cognitive dissonance, which can increase her experience of self-threat.

In fact, because of their calling to teach, teachers are often more aware of when their classroom behavior and their attributions contradict their teaching values. This type of "objective" self-awareness[11] is more common among teachers who feel called to teach because they tend to lead with their values, which makes them more sensitive to the relationship between how they act while teaching and their personal standards, thus forcing them to see their contradictions more clearly.

There are several ways that teachers can relieve their experience of cognitive dissonance.[12] In many cases, the teacher will change her beliefs or thoughts by seeking out and accepting alternative information that justifies her approach. Robin did this when she modified the math workshop model. Robin changed her thoughts to emphasize the importance of observing and talking with students while they attempt to solve math problems. This decision allowed her to maintain her sense of competence as a teacher, thus avoiding self-threat and the feelings that come with it.

Sometimes, teachers do not feel responsible for their contradictory teaching moves, such as when they are forced to "teach to the test" to "help" students pass standardized exams. This allows the teacher to pass responsibility for student failure onto the administration or the policy, helping them to avoid the cognitive dissonance that results from using teaching methods they don't believe in.

However, as we saw with Stephanie, this method did not work for her. She first dealt with this threat to her teaching integrity by trying to fight the system. When that did not work she tried to close her door and teach the way she felt was right. In the end, neither of these methods could relieve her feelings of psychological discomfort, causing her to quit teaching.

Teachers can also reduce their feelings of cognitive dissonance if they can trivialize the importance of their discrepant behavior. Robin may have done this when she told herself that the students who skipped working at the stations could make just as much progress working alone. Rationalizing one's behavior, however, also involves selective information processing. To make this statement, Robin must privilege the idea of independent work over peer support, which contradicts why she believes in the workshop model.

This goes hand in hand with another method for avoiding cognitive dissonance, which is simply being so distracted that the teacher forgets the discrepant event. Fortunately, or not, Robin gets more and more distracted as her class continues, allowing her to forget, at least in the moment, her contradictory teaching practices.

Finally, the healthiest way to deal with cognitive dissonance is to modify one's behavior to match one's beliefs and professional standards. This can be very difficult to do for two reasons. First, this requires mental effort, forcing the teacher to rely on information processing and working memory to resolve the feelings of cognitive dissonance. This is very difficult, if not impossible, to do while teaching. As we saw with Robin, her working memory became overloaded very quickly, leaving her unable to follow her teaching plan, leading to ineffective teaching.

Even though she was aware of her feelings, there is no way she would have been able to process them while teaching. Being unable to process, or provide explanations for self-threatening actions in the moment hurts a teacher's sense of self-efficacy and prevents effective practice over time. Given all the other pressures Robin is under as a new teacher, it is very unlikely that she will be able to properly reflect on her experience when she leaves school for the day. It is in situations like this that teachers need specific support in dealing with the factors that lead to cognitive dissonance.

The second reason why it may be difficult for teachers to modify their behavior to match their beliefs is that school policy and practice will simply not allow them to enact teaching behaviors that match their professional standards. Stephanie is an excellent example of this. The new policies prevented her from teaching in ways that conformed to her professional standards and beliefs about what her students needed. Those policies prevented Stephanie from meeting her need for autonomy *and* her need for competency.

In Stephanie's case, she couldn't get her psychological needs met under these circumstances, thus she was unable to relieve her experience of cognitive dissonance because she was consistently expected to behave in ways that contradicted her self-concept. We know the outcome for Stephanie; she left teaching. Not all teachers can leave the profession; some do not want to leave, and others cannot leave because of family and financial obligations. These teachers must find other ways to alleviate the dissonance they feel so that they can resolve the self-threat they are experiencing and restore a sense of integrity to the self.

It turns out that when human beings are not able to resolve a self-threat in one aspect of their lives, they will seek to affirm themselves in another aspect. Also, if they are not able to reinforce their sense of meaning and certainty by meeting one of their psychological needs, they will attempt to do so by meeting a different psychological need.

People can adapt to self-threat through actions that affirm the general integrity of the self, even when these adaptations do nothing to resolve the provoking (or original) threat itself. Indeed, for some threats, this may be the only adaptation possible.[13]

Researchers refer to this process as "fluid compensation." They use smokers to illustrate how it works. If a person feels foolish because they continue to smoke, even though they believe smoking to be a vile habit, they can restore their sense of competence as a person who makes good decisions by joining and fighting for a cause, thus feeling better about their abilities because of their work for that cause. Unfortunately, the process does not work in quite the same way for professionals who are strongly committed to the work they have chosen and who seek to make a difference in this world through that work.

For teachers, it is not enough to get their psychological needs met in other ways. As Steele points out, "when the very most important aspects of the self are threatened, so that there are no equally important alternative self-images,"[14] the person must find other ways to meet their psychological needs *in the same domain*.

For teachers, the most important aspects of their self-concept involve being a teacher and helping young people navigate and understand their worlds. Because many teachers are so committed, it is more difficult for them to find an equally important way to meet their need for competency and/or autonomy in a different domain or through other work.

In other words, if a teacher cannot achieve a sense of autonomy over her work and has lost her sense of competency in doing that work, it would be hard for her to enact her self-concept in other ways. In this type of situation, the teacher would have to fulfill her psychological needs in a way that not only addresses but also tries to restore the specific loss in the same or very similar domain.

There are several ways that teachers do this within the school context, some for positive effect and some, unfortunately, for ill effect, for both themselves and the school culture. One way for teachers to regain a sense of autonomy is to close their doors and do their own thing in their classroom. Stephanie and her colleagues tried this, but it is getting harder and harder to gain autonomy in this way with the focus on accountability and student achievement data. When teachers gain autonomy in this way it hurts the school culture because it discourages collaboration and alignment of curriculum.

Many teachers make up for their lack of autonomy by nurturing a sense of relatedness within the building. They do this in several ways. Some take on other roles in the building such as athletic or instructional coach, union representative, or other administrative positions. These roles fulfill the teachers' need for relatedness through close work with students and colleagues.

These roles can also fulfill the teachers' need for autonomy and competence, not through teaching students, but through coaching and working with colleagues. Other faculty, who may feel alienated from their teaching and their colleagues, may regain a sense of relatedness and autonomy by working closely with families and community organizations that partner with the school.

These roles can be positive for the overall school culture because they encourage relationships and collaboration, which ultimately supports students, and can restore a sense of competence to the teacher. Finally, teachers can meet their psychological needs by affiliating with each other for social support. Education researcher Charles Payne, calls these groups "factions" and attributes their formation to a negative school climate.

Factions usually form among groups that are already aligned in the school, such as veteran teachers or novice teachers, teachers of color or white teachers, ESL/SPED teachers or regular education teachers, and so forth. Even though negative for the school culture, factions can be a source of support for teachers, one that allows them to at least meet their need for relatedness in the context of their professional life.

COGNITIVE DISSONANCE AND TEACHER FEELINGS

CD helps us understand why teaching can be so emotionally fraught. CD can be responsible for nebulous feelings of psychological discomfort, which involve feelings that result from being bothered, disappointed, or annoyed with the self or being self-critical. CD also triggers specific feelings in teachers such as anxiety, frustration, doubt, uncertainty, regret, and remorse.

The role feelings play here has special significance for teachers because research shows that people experience a wider range of feelings in situations that are personally relevant to them, and we know that teaching has high self-relevant for teachers. The commitment and passion that teachers bring to teaching set them up to be impacted by the experience of cognitive dissonance and the strong feelings it generates in ways that are more fraught than in most professions.

Teachers need to understand and acknowledge the feelings they have while teaching because feelings impact teaching in several ways. First, emotions impact a teacher's cognitive functioning, especially in relation to what they attend to, how they problem-solve,[15] and how they use memory while teaching. Negative emotions focus a teacher's attention, diverting it from the teacher's instructional plan. They also make it difficult for a teacher to regulate her emotions in the moment. For example, we all know that new teachers, because they lack the benefit of experience, struggle with classroom management.

A new teacher in this situation may experience anxiety every time her students get off track. This will immediately flood her brain, making it difficult, if not impossible, for her to think about her lesson. Feelings like anxiety also impair a teacher's working memory, making it very difficult for her to process what is happening or to problem-solve ways to deal with challenging situations. Her focus will be solely concentrated on regaining control, causing her to unconsciously abandon her plans until that goal is achieved.

If a teacher's students act up repeatedly, like Robin's students did, this can influence and direct the teacher's memory as well. We remember emotional events better than we remember unemotional events, meaning that the memory of dealing with difficult classroom behavior can stay with the teacher from one day to the next, coloring the teacher's overall experience with her students. The impact of these effects can spiral, influencing how the teacher approaches planning and teaching, and leading her to fall back on methods that contradict her teaching values.

Finally, a teacher can end up getting trapped, quite literally, in negative emotions. This is because of a phenomenon called "mood congruent memory." If a teacher is feeling angry or frustrated, that teacher will be more likely to recall angry or frustrating memories when she thinks of her classroom. The biggest impact of all of this is on the teacher's mood over time. When teachers do not get support around their teaching challenges, the impact of negative emotions like frustration and anxiety can take over, unconsciously driving their teaching decisions.

Our emotional state influences the attributions we make. The feelings we experience impact how we explain our teaching and student outcomes. For example, if we are angry, we tend to attribute negative outcomes to others and see them as responsible for their own misfortunes. Whereas if we are sad or depressed, we tend to explain outcomes as situational, leading to feelings of hopelessness that one cannot change the situation.

This impacts how teachers react to students. If a teacher determines that a student is responsible for their own academic failure, then the consequences tend to be more harsh, and they are less likely to provide appropriate instructional or emotional support than if they believe that the student is a victim of his or her circumstances.

Finally, a teacher's level of intrinsic motivation is also impacted by her feelings. Chapter 6 discusses the benefits of intrinsically motivated teachers. Research has shown that both need satisfaction and positive emotions are necessary for intrinsic motivation. Teachers who are "constantly frustrated by ineffective administration, testing demands, etc. are less intrinsically motivated."[16] Feelings of sadness or depression about student life circumstances can also diminish intrinsic motivation.

Motivation impacts a teacher's sense of self-efficacy, and research has shown that negative feelings diminish self-efficacy beliefs. Cognitive dissonance leads to negative emotions that have wide impacts on what teachers come to believe about their own teaching efficacy and their students. In poorly resourced schools, where teachers get little support in dealing with the challenges they face, negative emotions can overwhelm a teacher, impacting not only her health but also student outcomes and overall school culture.

It is also important to look at the impact that specific negative emotions have on teachers and teaching.[17] The focus here is on negative emotions because those cause the most damage to teachers' physical and mental health.

Researchers have identified five negative feelings (frustration, anger, anxiety, guilt, and sadness), and two negative emotional states (psychological discomfort and stress) that are common for teachers to experience. It is no coincidence that five of these, frustration, anxiety, guilt, psychological discomfort, and stress, commonly result from the experience of cognitive dissonance.

Frustration is the most common feeling that teachers report experiencing. Frustration is related to goal attainment. It impacts our self-concept because it is usually experienced when we fail to meet our personal or professional goals and standards. Frustration is circumstantial; it wells up within teachers when they feel that they have no control over classroom situations that happen over and over again. Teachers also become frustrated with themselves for not being able to attain their professional goals. Finally, teachers tend to feel frustrated when they are prevented from teaching well by factors outside of the classroom over which they have no control.

Frustration can lead to anger, which is a stronger emotion and is often other-directed. Teachers are likely to feel angry when they feel someone—an administrator, a colleague, or a student—has wronged them. For example, the growth in educational reforms that privilege testing and "teacher-proof" curricula have angered many teachers like Stephanie, because they believe that the reforms are insulting, demeaning, and do not respect their professional knowledge.

The complexity and the uncertainty of teaching can lead to feelings of anxiety. There are two types of anxiety, situational and dispositional. Situational anxiety is felt in specific contexts that an individual perceives to be physically or psychologically threatening. A stressful workplace can lead to situational anxiety. Dispositional anxiety is a personal characteristic that makes one prone to anxiety in a variety of situations.

A person who has dispositional anxiety is more likely to experience situational anxiety when they feel psychological or social stress. New teachers are more likely to experience daily anxiety, especially during their first year of teaching. Uncertainty about whether or not they are doing a good job is one of the main sources of anxiety for new teachers.

New teachers also tend to be anxious about how prepared they are to teach or to deal with student engagement issues, and they tend to question their ability to meet the standards set by education reforms when their teaching and classroom management is a challenge. Feeling uncertain about outcomes, both for their students and themselves also leads to feelings of anxiety in teachers.

Finally, anticipating parent interactions can make teachers feel anxious, especially when students' racial and ethnic backgrounds differ from the teachers.[18] It is important to note that uncertainty and anxiety are related. The main reason teachers feel anxious in these types of situations is because of the level of uncertainty surrounding them. When teachers feel uncertain, it threatens the meaning that they have attached to their professional identities and prevents them from knowing if they are doing a good job.

Teachers are more susceptible to feelings of guilt than most professionals. This is because, like nurses, some teachers work from an ethic of care and a sense of responsibility toward their students. Unlike the other feelings, guilt is intimately tied to a sense of responsibility and a moral purpose. Guilt is aroused when a teacher feels that she should have control over the situation or that they have violated their values to care for and support students.

This can happen when a teacher feels responsible for student failure or feels helpless to adequately support students who are doing poorly in school because of poverty, trauma, and other systemic issues that are beyond the student's and family's control. Teachers who have large numbers of students and families in these types of situations tend to feel sad for their students. Sadness and guilt stem from concerns about one's students and families, and can ultimately lead to feelings of depression.

These four emotions, especially frustration and anxiety, are associated with an emotional state called psychological discomfort (PD) or distress. Teachers experience psychological discomfort when they are unable to cope with the demands of the classroom. It is brought on by cognitive dissonance which leads teachers to doubt their professional skills and abilities.[19]

Experiencing psychological distress is common among teachers who share three experiences: they feel that they have no control over what they do in the classroom; they get little, to no, support in dealing with the emotional burdens of teaching, and the work they do is very demanding on many levels.

In terms of overall health and well-being, psychological distress is experienced as an overall malaise that leaves teachers feeling exhausted. In fact, exhaustion is the most common physical symptom of psychological distress. When teachers feel exhausted, they feel tense, restless, and drained. They have lower levels of tolerance, leaving them easily frustrated and less empathic to the needs of their students. This hinders their ability to relax, not only while in school but also at home.

They may experience a lack of motivation, lose their interest in teaching, and have difficulty concentrating. Physically, psychological distress leads to sleeplessness, chest pain, headaches, and stomach and digestive problems. In the worst cases, PD can lead to clinical depression, somatic complaints, and other psychological conditions. All of these symptoms contribute to low self-esteem and self-doubt that can spread from impacting how one copes at work to how one copes in their personal life.

Psychological distress is exacerbated when a teacher lacks the personal and/or organizational resources to help them cope with the multiple emotions and feelings generated when teaching.[20]

Finally, we can't talk about teacher health and well-being without talking about the impact that stress has on teachers. Stress has become such an issue in teaching that Congress felt the need to introduce the *Teacher Health and Wellness Act* in 2017 to study how to reduce it. At the time, nearly 50 percent of teachers reported experiencing high levels of daily stress. This was tied with nursing, and it was the highest rate of stress reported among all occupations.[21]

Stress is the most damaging and difficult emotion with which teachers have to deal. We discussed the impact of stress on traumatized students in chapter five. Teachers who get no support in struggling schools experience similar outcomes. Stress manifests as "harmful physical and emotional responses."[22] Physically, stress leaves teachers with the feeling of tension in the body. This is because our bodies react to stressful feelings by releasing hormones such as cortisol.

These hormones make us more alert, increasing our heart rate and tensing up our muscles. Limited stress can be healthy because these bodily reactions help us manage difficult or dangerous situations. Stress becomes harmful when we can't escape the situation. Our body reacts to this chronic stress by getting stuck on high alert. The damage this does to our bodies has been well established. Chronic stress leads to heart attacks, heart disease, high blood pressure, diabetes, obesity, and depression. It can also cause exhaustion, stomach aches, joint pain, lack of energy, and headaches.

Research has shown that three aspects of the school environment are particularly stressful for teachers. Schools like the ones Payne described, with ineffective leadership, lack of resources, and little support for teachers around student engagement and effective instruction are very stressful places for teachers. The less autonomy teachers have to make decisions, coupled with a lack of true collaboration with colleagues around curricular strategies, the more stressed teachers feel.

Finally, keeping up with job demands such as high-stakes testing, dealing with penalty-based accountability systems, and supporting students who are suffering from trauma, poverty, and learning disabilities is overwhelming for many teachers, and leads to chronic stress.[23]

Stress impacts teacher performance in many ways. It hurts the teacher's ability to pay attention while teaching. It increases the teacher's cognitive load, which diminishes the capacity of her working memory, making it harder for her to think about how student responses relate to subject matter. Stress also increases anxiety and hurts the teacher's ability to properly read social cues. Finally, stress increases the tendency to react with negative emotions. Schools cannot continue to ignore the fact that teachers experience tremendous amounts of stress on the job.

NOTES

1. Sharon L. Nichols and David. C Berliner, *Collateral Damage: How High-Stakes Testing Corrupts America's Schools* (Cambridge, MA: Harvard University Press, 2007), 37.
2. Antonio Damasio, *The Feeling of What Happens: Body and Emotion in the Making of Consciousness* (New York, NY: Harcourt, Inc. 1999).
3. Claude Steele, "The Psychology of Self-Affirmation: Sustaining the Integrity of the Self," *Advances in Experimental Social Psychology*, 21 (1988).
4. Interview with Robin, a first-year teacher.
5. Karine Lavergne and Luc Pelletier, "Predicting Individual Differences in the Choice or Strategy to Compensate for Attitude-Behavior Inconsistencies in the Enviornmental Domain," *Journal of Environmental Psychology*, 44 (2015), doi: 10.1016/j.jenvp.2015.10.001.
6. Richard Elliot, "A Model of Emotion Driven Choice," *Journal of Marketing Management*, 14 (1998).
7. Sandra Graham, "An Attributional Theory of Motivation," *Contemporary Educational Psychology*, 61 (April 2020), doi: 10.1016/j.cedpsych.2020.101861.
8. Snyder and Raymond Higgins, "Excuses: Their Effective Role in the Negotiation of Reality," *Psychological Bulletin*, 104, no. 1 (1988).
9. Claude Steele, "The Psychology of Self-Affirmation."
10. G. Bradley, "Self-Serving Bias in the Attribution Process: A Reexamination of the Fact or Fiction Question," *Journal of Personality and Social Psychology*, 36, no. 1 (1978).
11. Jared, Kenworthy et al, "A Trans-paradigm Theoretical Synthesis of Cognitive Dissonance Theory: Illuminating the Nature of Discomfort," *European Review of Social Psychology*, 22, no. 1 (2011), 94, doi: 10.1080/10463283.2011.580155.
12. April McGrath, "Dealing with Dissonance: A Review of Cognitive Dissonance Reduction," *Social Personal Psychology Compass* (2017), doi: 10.1111/spc3.12362.
13. Claude Steele, "The Psychology of Self-Affirmation."
14. Claude Steele, "The Psychology of Self-Affirmation," 292.
15. Rosemary E. Sutton and Karl F. Wheatley, "Teachers' Emotions and Teaching: A Review of the Literature and Directions for Future Research," *Educational Psychology Review*, 15, no. 4 (December 2003).
16. Rosemary E. Sutton and Karl F. Wheatley, "Teachers' Emotions and Teaching," 339.
17. Mei-Lin Chang, "An Appraisal Perspective of Teacher Burnout: Examining the Emotional Work of Teachers," *Education Psychology Review*, 21 (2009), doi: 10.1007/s10648-009-9106-y.
18. C. Erb, "The Emotional Whirlpool of Beginning Teachers' Work," Paper In annual meeting of the *Canadian Society of Studies in Education*, Toronto, Canada (2002). Cited in "Teachers' Emotions and Teaching" (2002).

19. Tina Arvidsdotter, "Understanding Persons with Psychological Distress in Health Care," *Scandinavian Journal of Caring Sciences* (2015), doi: 10.1111/scs.12289.

20. Tina Arvidsdotter, "Understanding Persons with Psychological Distress" (2015).

21. Gallup, "State of America's Schools: The Path to Winning Again in Education," Gallup, Inc. (2014), http://www.gallup.com/services/178709/state-america-schools-report.aspx.

22. Steven Sauter, "Stress . . . at Work," *National Institute for Occupational Safety and Health, Publication number 99–101*, (1999), 3, https://www.cdc.gov/niosh/docs/99-101/default.html#print.

23. M. Greenberg, T. Brown, and R. Abenavoli, "Teacher Stress and Health Effects on Teachers, Students and Schools," *Edna Bennett Pierce Prevention Research Center*, Pennsylvania State University (2017).

Chapter 8

Colleagues and the Need for Relatedness in Schools

One question that kept coming up in the researching of this book was "what are colleagues for?" Are they there to help improve the work of teaching? Are they there to offer support professionally or emotionally, or both? What purpose and role do they play in each other's development and well-being?

Education researchers discovered over forty years ago that schools that had great collaborative cultures tended to have better outcomes[1] in terms of teacher satisfaction and student learning. This led to more studies showing that collaboration enhanced teachers professional development, job satisfaction, school culture, and student outcomes. Eventually, policymakers jumped on this, as they are wont to do in their desperate attempts to fix schools without consulting teachers, concluding that requiring more collaboration would lead to teacher professionalization.

These policies led to the growth of two types of collegial teacher cultures. "Collaborative cultures," where teachers work with each other in "spontaneous, voluntary, development-oriented and pervasive" ways, and "contrived collegiality," where teachers' work is "administratively regulated, compulsory, and implementation-oriented."[2] This is not surprising given what we know happens when policymakers attempt to force reforms onto struggle schools that have grown out of unhealthy school cultures without examining what made the school unhealthy in the first place.

To get a better understanding of the *role colleagues play*, we need to first distinguish the difference between collegiality and collaboration. Those who study how teachers work together describe collegiality as emotional and collaboration as professional. Collegiality involves all aspects of teacher relations, social, emotional, political, and professional. School culture and climate are established through collegial activities and reflect the character and nature of those activities.[3] Collaboration is one example of collegial activity. It is the activity of teachers working together to accomplish specific professional goals.

This is one way that colleagues support each other. Colleagues also support each other personally by providing acknowledgment, social acceptance, and appreciation. These supports validate teachers, especially those working in schools that have weak support structures and heavy work demands. In these schools, collegial support might be the only way that teachers are validated in their work. Colleagues also help teachers meet their relational needs. This fact becomes crucial in schools where teachers struggle to also meet their needs for autonomy and competency.

Key to the idea of collegiality is that colleagues are united by a common purpose and a shared identity. Of course, the ideal common purpose that unites teachers is to educate children. This is not always possible, however. As we have seen in previous chapters, teachers are not always able to unite around their goals for educating children because of certain reform policies and the difficult working conditions of some school environments.

Constraints like these complicate collegial relations because too often, the constraints and the struggles come to define how colleagues see their purpose in the school. A school's struggles can also shape its teachers' identities. All teachers enter a school with the common purpose of doing whatever they have to do to educate all students. Most teachers begin their careers with a teacher identity that is rooted in a deep care for young people and a desire to make a difference in their lives.

Unfortunately, these common elements of teacher purpose and identity can be thwarted and then warped by the school culture. The psychological factors previously discussed—the experience of cognitive dissonance, the thwarting of one's psychological needs, the attempts to fulfill those needs in other ways, the feelings aroused by negative emotions, the moral injury—play a large role in the transformation of teacher purpose and identity. When this happens, we can end up with a school whose teachers are united by the common purpose of survival or need satisfaction, rather than by the purpose of educating all children.

This changes the nature, and the function, of collegiality in that school. It also changes how the teachers in that school define their common purpose and, more seriously, their identity as teachers. Finally, this is where the psychological factors discussed in this book have a direct impact on school culture and outcomes.

The bottom line here is that if colleagues cannot support each other in ways that aid each other's development as a teacher, they *will* support each other in ways that aid the satisfaction of their psychological needs or their emotional survival. The next section explains how this process unfolds in two areas within the school. It happens in the relations between novice and veteran teachers, and it happens through the interactions that take place within teacher groups or teams.

Let's start by unpacking the experiences of novice teachers. It is important to understand how novice teachers are initiated into the profession. Many get their first jobs after completing a traditional teacher preparation program which consists of two years of coursework, either at the undergraduate or graduate level, with one semester of student teaching at the end of the two years. Today, one of the fastest-growing options for teacher preparation, especially for those who want to teach in high-needs schools, are residency programs.

Modeled after a medical residency, these programs place would-be teachers in a school for one to two years where they teach a reduced load under the guidance of a mentor teacher while taking teacher education courses in the evening. Residency programs are often cohort-based, meaning that the resident teacher is placed within the school along with a cohort of peers who are also learning to teach. The cohort provides the practicing teacher with a group of peers who share the experience of learning how to teach together, and more importantly, who support each other in what can be a stressful teaching and learning environment.

Cohorts were most likely *not* implemented for their psychological benefits, but in terms of what was discussed in chapter 6, the cohort helps the practicing teacher satisfy her need for competency, autonomy, and relatedness. This helps the practicing teacher gain more certainty about what it means for her to be a teacher, which leads to improved self-esteem and self-efficacy while she is learning how to teach. After working with teacher cohorts for over twenty years, I have found that the cohort also serves to shield the practicing teacher from many of the painful obstacles that she will most likely face when she gets her own classroom.

One thing to keep in mind is that a resident teacher is essentially a teacher. The residents do everything that a new teacher does with the main difference being that the resident has a reduced load and a full-time mentor who models how to teach, and gives them constant feedback, advice, and guidance. The cohort also provides the resident with a full-time support system of like-minded, practicing teachers who they can turn to whenever they run into trouble.

One unfortunate reality about practicing teachers is that they often enter the profession with negative attitudes about the veteran teachers who will soon be their colleagues. This is especially true with new teachers who want to teach in high-needs and poorly resourced schools. There are several reasons for this. First, even though they have chosen to be teachers themselves, many aspiring teachers have been so inundated by the public rhetoric and criticisms about teachers and high-needs schools, that they enter the field with these negative ideas in mind.

Second, many new teachers, again, especially those who have chosen to teach in high need and other Title I schools, tend to be idealists. They have chosen teaching because they feel called to give back and support young people. They also tend to be acutely aware of the struggles that Black and Brown children served by Title I schools have. This leads them to feel that they can do a better job than current teachers because they care so deeply.

Third, once they get into the building and witness for themselves some of the things veteran teachers say and do, they begin to distance themselves from the veterans without having a full understanding of why the veterans may act in certain ways. For example, those of us who prepare teachers have all heard stories about how new and practicing teachers avoid the "teacher's room" so they do not have to hear how the veteran teachers talk about students and families. Below is one example of a typical conversation among practicing teachers about eating with their veteran colleagues[4]:

Practicing Teacher 1: I eat lunch with some teachers who are so negative! And it's like God, how can you be a teacher?
Practicing Teacher 2: Yep.
Practicing Teacher 3: I know!
Practicing Teacher 1: I mean they're so down on the kids; they're so down on the schools.
Practicing Teacher 2: The whole system!
Practicing Teacher 1: Everything! They're so negative! It's like, "Why can't you be a little bit more . . . like, hopeful?"
Practicing Teacher 2: Yeah, and [my fellow cohort member] and I just sit there. And we're just sitting there looking at each going, "Oh boy."

This takes us back to our discussion about psychological needs. This is the one area where the cohort can harm novice teachers. The main need that practicing teachers struggle to meet is their need for competency. Because they are sharing their mentor's classroom and will be following their mentor's lead during their practice teaching, they do not yet struggle with their lack of autonomy. However, feeling competent can be very difficult for practicing teachers in resource-poor schools.

As demonstrated in chapter 6, our need for relatedness and belonging becomes stronger when we have difficulty fulfilling our other needs. This is where the cohort plays what seems like a positive role for the practicing teacher, but ends up being a negative role in terms of overall school relations. The cohort makes it easier psychologically for practicing teachers to distance themselves from veteran teachers during their residency year, and to feel okay, even justified, in doing so.

The practicing teachers can shun relations with veteran teachers because of the strong bond they have with each other. The cohort provides support, validation, and feedback. More importantly, the cohort serves as a community with shared values and beliefs. Their relations with the cohort lend meaning to the work of practicing teachers, helping them to achieve a sense of certainty about their professional journey and the role they are playing in the school, especially with their students.

These psychological validations can lead practicing teachers to feel that they do not need veteran teachers. This strong affiliation with the cohort is one of the things that gets the practicing teacher through their resident year. Unfortunately, the experience of having strong professional relationships and a community of support seldom follow the novice teacher into their first job, even if they get hired at the same school where they completed their resident teaching. There are several reasons for this.

First, unlike other young professionals, on day one, many novice teachers are expected to take on the full slate of tasks, teaching responsibilities, and administrative duties as veteran teachers. They often have to do this while being assigned the neediest children with the fewest resources and often in the least desirable classrooms or no classroom at all (if they are in a school where some teachers have to "roam" between classrooms) all because they are a new teacher with no seniority.

Some school districts assign a novice teacher a mentor or engage all new teachers in group induction activities that are separate from their school site. However, as Susan Moore Johnson points out, "many districts seem not to recognize how much assistance new teachers need."[5] This does not tend to be true in other professions where the newly hired are afforded a slower release into their new responsibilities. Having to jump right in often results in an overwhelming amount of uncertainty for novice teachers concerning many aspects of the school.

For example, any new employee must come to understand the "organizational culture" of their workplace. For teachers, this involves understanding formal features such as academic and role expectations as well as informal practices such as how meetings are run and the norms for social interaction. When the new teacher has to jump in feet first, they often do not have the bandwidth to pay attention to details about how the organization works. Teachers also have to deal with other levels of uncertainty.

As Lortie pointed out over forty-five years ago, "uncertainty is the lot of those who teach."[6] This could not be more true than in today's educational climate. On top of trying to understand the organizational culture, teachers also have to understand their students, who also bring a lot of uncertainty to the novice teacher's experience as they learn how to motivate them, engage them, and educate them. This is compounded many times over for those who begin their careers in low-performing, resource-poor, rural, and urban schools.

In these environments, new teachers also have to understand how racism, poverty, trauma, and systemic neglect impact their ability to teach and their students' ability to learn. Additionally, they must collect and analyze data and work within their school's accountability systems, including teaching to standards that they may not fully understand or agree with, all while the state tracks both them and their students' performance with consequences for those who do not measure up. The level of uncertainty, and dealing with the negative feelings that accompany it, are two of the most psychologically difficult aspects of the novice teacher's job.

These emotions and uncertainties have grave consequences for new teachers. We know that having a sense of certainty regarding one's professional activities brings meaning to the professional lives of novice teachers. Meaning not only enhances a teacher's motivation to do their best work but also gives them a sense of self-efficacy that they can teach the students in front of them well. Novice teachers gain meaning and certainty about their teaching practices by getting their needs for competency, autonomy, and belongingness met within the school context.

A new teacher who feels that her students are learning and that her colleagues are supportive will gain confidence, and thus certainty, over time. Without a sense of certainty and meaning, new teachers suffer from low self-esteem and low motivation. Starting as a new teacher in many high-needs schools often means, as it did for Robin, managing great anxiety and dread on a daily basis.

New teachers often experience

> overwhelming feelings of disillusionment, believing that they [are] unable to cope with the multitude of pressures encountered each day . . . and struggling to succeed within an uncertain environment of seemingly insatiable demands and scant support.[7]

And if the new teacher has graduated from a cohort-based residency program, they can also feel a sense of isolation because of their previous experiences.

> It's difficult coming out of the kind of community where you were used to being able to talk about the things you were planning, how they were going, sharing materials—to a situation where you're on your own. You don't have materials, you don't have the money to purchase everything you need, and you're not with a whole staff of people you can bounce your ideas off of.

The main way that novice teachers cope with the emotional fluctuations brought on by all of this uncertainty is by seeking support from their colleagues. However, two things get in the way when seeking support from veteran teachers. First, because most schools don't have the resources to structure this collegial support well, it is difficult for many novice teachers to get the support that they need. This is not because veteran teachers do not want to help, but rather, without an organized and structured plan for targeted mentoring and support, veteran teachers are simply too busy, or too worn out, to put in the needed time for true mentoring.

Moore Johnson recounts the experiences of two newly hired novice teachers in a large urban elementary school:

> Donnell, who taught fourth grade was able to step out and ask for help but he still found himself frustrated that he must figure out so much on his own. Referring to experienced teachers and administrators, he explained, "They assume that first-year teachers know a lot of things." When he found an inventory sheet in his mailbox and had no idea what to do with it, he was left wondering, "What am I going to do? Do I do it now? Do I do it at the end of the year? What do I do with that?"
>
> His colleague Amy recalled that she, too, was confused by all the paperwork and school procedures. But more important, she went through a good part of her first year unable to communicate with the non-English speaking parents of many of her students, because no one ever told her that she had access to a translator. She echoed a comment voiced repeatedly by new teachers: "Everyone is willing to help, but I don't even know the questions to ask. So, how can they help me if I don't know what I am supposed to be asking for help with?"[8]

Second, because of their initial alienation from veteran teachers, as well as experiences like the one described above where practicing teachers complain about being in the teacher's room, listening to the ways that veteran teachers talk about students, many novice teachers are reluctant to affiliate with the veterans in their new schools. This causes them to seek out informal collegial support from other beginners.

The support they get from like-minded beginners feeds their enthusiasm and energy, but it doesn't give them what they need in terms of developing their craft as a teacher or explicitly learning how things work in their schools. As one novice teacher who relied on informal support from other beginners described.

> It's so nice to be able to get back with people who thought like you thought, believed like you believe and just almost like touch ground with your beliefs, like Yes, what I'm doing is okay." Even though everyone else in the school might be looking at me like I'm wrong, what I'm doing is okay and it is right, and I can keep trying it.[9]

Another said,

We discuss what we are doing in [our subject area], what we are doing in other areas . . . and basically that's just a sharing time. . . . It's nice to talk with someone. It's also nice to complain about certain things to people.[10]

Her last comment is telling. She acknowledges that, among colleagues she trusts, it is helpful, or "nice to complain" sometimes. Yet she does not realize that this might be what the veteran teachers are doing over lunch when they "complain" in the teacher's room. What she cannot realize, because she has not experienced it yet herself, is that the veteran teachers in that school might be suffering from prolonged cognitive dissonance, stress, and frustration about the state of the school and their professional lives.

At this point, it is important to summarize what this novice teacher, and what most novice teachers who teach in struggling schools, are experiencing psychologically. This is important because it helps us understand how teacher teams and groups end up shaping school culture. We will start with Robin, who you met in chapter 6 as a new teacher who had the benefit of learning how to teach with a teaching residency program.

Robin also had trouble connecting with the veteran teachers in her school, causing her to feel somewhat isolated from her colleagues. This is not because her colleagues were not supportive, they were. What they did not do was validate and affirm Robin's self-concept as a teacher like the cohort did, because, as the quote above shows, they did not share the same beliefs about how best to teach the students.

Also, as Robin's math lesson showed, she started experiencing cognitive dissonance and the negative emotions that go along with it early in her first year. The struggles she had while teaching caused Robin to question her competence as a teacher. It also put her under tremendous stress, leading her to feel lots of anxiety and impacting her health.

Already Robin is beginning to experience the psychological pain of teaching. She is struggling to have experiences that affirm her teaching self-concept. She is not able to satisfy her psychological needs because she is not feeling competent in her teaching, and as a first-year teacher, she has not yet developed a sense of autonomy within the school. When the self cannot be affirmed through autonomy and competence, relatedness becomes very important because of the role our relationships play in affirming the self and helping us to deal with self-threat.

This is especially true within domains that have personal relevance. Humans are social creatures, and our actions are understood within our social contexts. We also have to remember that our reactions in these situations are unconscious. Teachers often have no awareness of why they end up behaving as they do when these things start to happen. In Robin's case, she has to be able to make sense, to make meaning, about what is happening to her as she tries to teach in a difficult environment.

People gain meaning from their relationships with others in similar domains. These facts create a need within Robin to affiliate with a group. She no longer has the cohort, but she does have her colleagues.

This creates a bind for Robin. Because she has been critical of her colleagues, to begin to affiliate with them now would lead to more cognitive dissonance, more threats to her self-concept, and more negative feelings. She could decide to leave teaching rather than deal with this dilemma, but this is Robin's first professional job, for which she spent a lot of time and money preparing.

She does not feel that she can just quit. If Robin can solve this dilemma by affiliating with her colleagues, it will provide her with many psychological benefits. For example, when we agree with professionally significant others, it helps to raise our confidence in the work we are doing thus improving our self-esteem. Groups help people maintain a positive sense of self. They help us cope with the types of self-threat that Robin faced in her classroom. Groups help us deal with self-threat because group support reduces feelings of cognitive dissonance.[11]

Most importantly, groups help us ascribe meaning to confusing and complicated social situations, reducing our sense of uncertainty about ourselves and our place within a particular social context. As demonstrated above, new teachers experience an overabundance of uncertainty during their first year on the job. Some argue that uncertainty is the main motivator for affiliating with a group[12] because group membership allows human beings to restore their sense of certainty.

One reason for this is that groups of like individuals tend to share similar opinions and beliefs, leading people to conclude that if their opinions and beliefs are shared with others, they are more likely to be correct. These psychological benefits of group affiliation are one reason why people form groups in difficult social contexts. As we all know, schools can be extremely complex social settings where teachers must educate and care for children without proper resources and amidst a tangle of externally imposed standards and mandates.

Robin's high level of uncertainty, cognitive dissonance, and psychological distress are what leads her to, unconsciously, begin to affiliate with the veteran teachers at her school. To do this in a way that prevents her from leaving the profession, she must begin to tell herself a different story about who she is as a teacher or about why she cannot implement the instructional practices she learned in her preparation program. The attributions she makes will make it easier for her to align with her colleagues and for her colleagues to affirm her self-concept.

This process will be easier for a novice teacher like Robin because as a new teacher, her teaching self-concept is not yet fully formed. Our professional identities do not develop in a vacuum. They develop in relation to our professional colleagues in a specific social context. Thus, the group helps to define, for ourselves and others, who we are. The group draws boundaries for us; it restricts who we are in a particular domain. Perhaps this is the only way for novice teachers to survive in what Payne calls "dysfunctional," resource-poor schools.

It is very important to remember a few things about this phenomenon. First, this is an unconscious process, initiated and driven by the anxiety, fear, and stress that new teachers have to contend with, often on their own. Their psychological needs go unsatisfied, they feel exhausted, emotionally drained, and ill. It is simply too much for them to be isolated and unaffirmed as well. Second, some people have a very low tolerance for uncertainty. This is especially true for those who require structure or are externally motivated.

These traits cause individuals to avoid uncertainty and motivate them to resolve it quickly when it arises. Third, what is described here is more likely to happen in the bottom 30 percent of our nation's schools. These are schools that struggle to educate children because of low resources, overzealous accountability systems, and lack of support for children's social/emotional needs.

The teachers in these schools tend to be charged with educating a majority-minority and immigrant student population without the services that would relieve the poverty and systemic discrimination from which the families and communities suffer. Finally, affiliating with other teachers in the building who may not share the novice teacher's beliefs and values about teaching does not mean that the novice teacher avoids all of the pain, emotional upheaval, and ill health associated with experiences of cognitive dissonance.

What it does mean is that, because she is now getting her relational needs met and feels a part of a team that affirms her, she can feel good about herself and maintain her sense of integrity, *not* in the teaching realm, *but in the realm of being a good colleague.* She might become the chair of her grade-level team; she might become a union officer. Becoming more deeply involved in her colleague's struggles can compensate for the needs she was unable to satisfy through the classroom alone and restore her self-concept.

She might be considered a great colleague and a good enough teacher. This is not what we want of course, but it is how teachers survive when they get no support for their psychological health in schools.

The above explains the unconscious, emotional process that novice teachers experience because of overwhelming cognitive dissonance during their first year of teaching. In struggling schools that are resource-poor, veteran teachers are not immune to the impact of cognitive dissonance and the negative emotions generated from a lack of need fulfillment. Payne describes what he calls "bottom-tier" urban schools as "irrational organizations" and the adults in them as "socially demoralized."[13]

He concludes that these schools are held back by "teacher pessimism" and a "distrust of higher administration." Payne came to these conclusions because he has spent countless hours observing and studying many "bottom-tier" schools. What he saw was real, but he *never* examined why the teachers were behaving in the ways that he noticed. Payne comes closest to the true explanation of what is going on in these schools when he says "we have to think about demoralized schools as if they were clinically depressed individuals."[14]

As demonstrated above, the psychological conditions in many of these schools actually lead to depression and other mental health issues. Payne also points out that in schools like these, "a negative climate is fertile ground for the development of factions."[15] Payne is right about this as well, but again, he mischaracterizes the cause of this behavior. It is not because the teachers are being deliberately/consciously obstinate. They have been driven together for all of the psychological reasons described above.

They are attempting to fulfill their need for belongingness as a way to affirm themselves and their self-concept. If the self cannot be affirmed through its sense of autonomy or competence, then relatedness becomes very important. Being a member of a group or "faction" improves self-esteem because agreement with others raises one's confidence. Also, collegial support reduces stress, something that is essential for teachers in the types of school environments that Payne describes.

Imagine a group of teacher colleagues who have two things in common. First, they struggle every day with the cognitive dissonance that results from not being able to do their best work on behalf of the children to which they have committed their professional lives. Second, they have been thwarted in their attempts to meet their need for autonomy and competency at work. The only psychological need they can meet now is their need for belongingness, which can give them a sense of meaning and certainty about their work.

Third, they are experiencing many of the negative feelings discussed above. Now imagine those same colleagues in meetings about aspects of their work at the school. These meetings may be spontaneous, taking place in the teacher's room or cafeteria; they may be teacher initiated, or they may be mandated by school administrators. It doesn't matter. Given the teachers' psychological state, what do you think the focus of those meetings will be? Fortunately, we don't have to guess or imagine what the focus of these interactions will be. There is research that details not only what happens in these situations, but also how it happens.

We have already learned how group affiliation reduces self-threat, affirms our self-concept, improves self-esteem, and reduces feelings of cognitive dissonance. It also provides us with a sense of certainty that because our work, opinions, and beliefs are shared with similar others, that they are correct. This boost in positive feelings about the self is enough to push people to affiliate with others. Research has shown that teachers are motivated to affiliate with colleagues when they experience a loss of autonomy and feelings of cognitive dissonance.

This is especially true when teachers are forced to contend with policies they disagree with on professional and personal terms, such as accountability and merit pay policies for example. Opposition to these policies can cause teachers to affiliate with each other as a way to both strengthen their resistance and regain autonomy. Stephanie and her colleagues attempted to do this in opposition to the standardized testing policies introduced at her school. Teachers resist these types of policies both formally, through their union membership, for example, and informally, through the conversations that take place in smaller department or grade level meetings.

However, it is very important to remember that the process through which teachers affiliate with each other is not only about policy resistance. It is also about need satisfaction and self-affirmation, especially when teachers get no support for the cognitive dissonance, stress, anxiety, and other negative emotions they experience because of a lack of resources to deal with the instructional and social/emotional struggles that their students present. These unconscious reasons for affiliation are so effective because they are often driven by something very powerful: the teachers' emotions.

Those who study organizations and work teams have identified a phenomenon called emotional contagion, which is defined as the process by which one or more people in a group can be influenced by the emotions expressed by others in that group.[16] Emotional contagion is mostly an unconscious process that takes place when individuals are exposed to the positive or negative emotions of other group members. Whether or not other group members "catch" the emotions of their colleagues is determined by several factors. First, negative emotions are more contagious than positive emotions.

This is because people respond more quickly to negative emotions and negative emotions illicit stronger behavioral and cognitive responses. People also tend to pay more attention to—and have a greater tendency to accept—negative information. Unfortunately, once negativity starts to grow between individuals, it tends to escalate, with attitudes and feelings becoming even more negative. This is why work groups often get caught up in negative aspects of their projects or jobs.

Second, individuals who express their own emotions more forcefully get more attention and therefore are more likely to spread those emotions to others. Groups that have more outspoken individuals can end up with more negative affect than other groups. Social comparison is a third phenomenon that increases the likelihood of emotional contagion in groups. This happens when individuals use the emotions expressed by others as a type of social information that helps them understand how they should be feeling about an event or situation.

New employees, such as novice teachers, are especially prone to rely on social comparisons because it helps them to understand what types of feelings are appropriate in various settings. Empathy and perspective-taking also play a role in emotional contagion. Empathetic people, who experience the emotions of others, and those who are skilled at perspective-taking, are very likely to catch a groups' emotions, especially when they work in the same contexts and are sharing the same experiences as those who are expressing the emotions. Specific personality traits can also enhance emotional contagion.

Those who are more attentive to the needs of others or who are good at reading others' emotions are more susceptible to emotional contagion, as are those who tend to be interdependent. Finally, some people are prone to unconsciously mimic the facial expressions of those around them. Individuals who do this are also more vulnerable to emotional contagion.

Negative affect hurts a group's ability to engage in mutual problem-solving and complex logical reasoning and hurts the collective sense of self-efficacy for both the group and the individuals who make up the group. Finally, negative emotional contagion also shapes how group members behave, causing members to be less cooperative and helpful, not only with non-group members but also with each other. This leaves the entire community[17] more prone to conflict overall, thus tainting the effectiveness of any group projects.

Once emotional contagion begins, it is very hard to stem, especially in work environments where employees are chronically overwhelmed and feel hopeless about the possibility of change. When people share the same negative emotions, it impacts their judgments, behaviors, attitudes, and beliefs about their work environment. These emotions play a very powerful role in work outcomes and shape how people react. Especially, in terms of how they think about their work and the types of attributions they make.

For example, emotional contagion impacts the types of social judgments group members make. Payne calls this the "principal of negative interpretation" which he describes as the practice of interpreting the actions of administration, parents, and other outgroups in negative ways. Payne says:

> Whatever other people do is interpreted in the most negative way possible. If parents don't show up at school, it means they don't care. If the principal fails to observe a class, she doesn't care. If a colleague has great relationships with

students, she is not holding them to standards. Ambiguous evidence is consistently interpreted negatively; no one gets the benefit of the doubt.[18]

Payne describes these negative interpretations as conclusions or explanations that are consciously chosen by the teachers. But this is not what is going on here. What we are seeing is what happens in an environment where teachers must continue to use what they believe to be unproductive and unhelpful teaching methods, when they are given negative evaluations when those unhelpful methods do not work, and when they get no support in dealing with the stress and negative emotions that result from having to work under these conditions.

The teachers in these schools are suffering from psychological trauma. What Payne has observed is the result of working in a psychologically unsafe environment where negative emotions such as anxiety and stress make productive professional collaboration all but impossible.

MORAL INJURY

The phenomena described above is one of the main things that leads to what has been called "teacher burnout." Burnout has been defined as a state of emotional exhaustion and a loss of motivation and commitment.[19] It is applied in situations where work that was initially experienced as "important, meaningful and challenging . . . becomes unpleasant, unfulfilling and meaningless."[20]

The term was first applied to healthcare workers, and then researchers began looking at teacher distress through the lens of burnout. Since then, burnout among teachers has been studied extensively, and today it is one of the most common reasons cited for why teachers leave the profession.

Burnout, however, is the wrong term for the exhaustion and frustration that is boiling over among today's teachers![21] Santoro describes what teachers are experiencing as "demoralization." She defines demoralization as "a process of continually being frustrated in ones' pursuit of good teaching."[22] Santoro focuses on the notion of good teaching, which she defines as the ability to reap the "moral rewards" of teaching. Teachers are able to access the moral rewards of teaching when "they feel that they are doing what is right in terms of one's students, the teaching profession, and themselves."[23]

Being able to access the moral rewards of teaching is the fundamental reason why teachers feel called to the profession. Their goal is to use their professional expertise, coupled with their knowledge about and care for their students, to teach them using methods that work for them. When teachers are asked to use mandated curriculums, like Stephanie was, they must consider whether the mandated methods are "good" for their students given what they know about them. Good in the sense that the methods resonate with the kids; that they affirm the kids. Good in a moral sense.

If the answer is no, the teacher may experience cognitive dissonance, and the negative emotions associated with it, because she has "violated her moral principles by engaging in practices that feel wrong"[24] for her students. This does not mean that the teacher is not teaching well or that her students are not succeeding on outside assessments. It often does mean that the methods are dry, irrelevant to students' lives, and not engaging. Using the concept of burnout to describe this experience is wrong!

As Santoro points out, "the insidiousness of the diagnosis of burnout is that it characterizes the problem as one of individual failure and weakness rather than a problem residing in the practice. Burnout depoliticizes a problem that is more than just personal; demoralization reflects a fundamental alteration of the practice of teaching."

Santoro's work highlights the moral dimensions of teaching. Teaching has long been understood as a moral enterprise and that is because teaching takes place within the context of human interaction and relationships. "What makes teaching a moral endeavor is that it is, quite centrally, human action, undertaken in regard to other human beings. Thus, matters of what is fair, right, just, and virtuous are always present."[25]

As shown in previous chapters, the moral nature of teaching is especially salient for those who feel called to teach, and is the main reason many teachers have chosen this profession. Philosophers have argued that "public education is a morally complex system because it is charged with transferring societies values, beliefs, and expectations to the future citizenry."[26] This could not be more true today given the weight of the economic, social, racial, and political struggles facing our nation's schools.

It is not an overstatement to say that our very democracy is at risk because of our failure to attend to the moral dimensions of educating our nation's youth.

> Widespread moral transgressions [in schools] can lead not only to moral harm for educators but also for students who must attempt to cope with and successfully navigate an immoral system. One way that both educators and students cope with an immoral educational context is by accepting and normalizing immorality. Thus moral transgressions may lead not only to distress or injury to individuals in the public education system, but to an overall moral weakening of a core democratic institution.[27]

And, to democratic society itself.

If we believe that educating young people is a moral activity, then what our nation's teachers are suffering from is a type of moral injury. Individuals experience moral injury when their actions violate their internal moral codes.

Moral injury is usually studied in the context of war but has most recently been applied to the American educational system.

Those who have studied moral injury in public schools argue that it is a phenomenon that may be increasing among US teachers given our growing racial and economic achievement gaps, education reform policies that favor high-stakes testing, and zero-tolerance discipline policies among other contentious societal issues that seem to coalesce in the school house. These policies lead teachers to engage in a "daily struggle between a desire to feel like [they] are part of a system that produces good in the world and piercing evidence to the contrary."[28] As one educational philosopher describes it:

> Teachers, because of their calling, feel obligated to take action that fulfills the demands of moral justice, but have to do so under conditions in which no just action is possible because of contextual and school-based injustices. Under such circumstances, educators suffer moral injury: the trauma of perpetrating significant moral wrongs against others despite one's wholehearted desire and responsibility to do otherwise.[29]

Schools must understand and accept the tremendous influence that emotions have on the work of teachers. They must begin to provide supports that help teachers both understand and deal with these emotions. They must do this not only to safeguard teacher health and well-being but also to build better collegial relations for all school staff.

NOTES

1. Dan Lortie, *Schoolteacher: A Sociological Study* (London: University of Chicago Press, 1975).

2. Andy Hargreaves, *Changing Teachers, Changing Times: Teachers' Work and Culture in the Postmodern Age* (New York: Continuum, January 2001), 192.

3. Lucy Jarzabkowsli, "The Social Dimensions of Teacher Collegiality," *Journal of Educational Enquiry*, 3, no. 2 (2002).

4. Deborah L. Harris and Helene M. Anthony, "Collegiality and Its Role in Teacher Development: Perspectives from Veteran and Novice Teachers," *Teacher Development*, 5, no. 3 (2001), 380–381, doi: 10.1080/13664530100200150.

5. Susan M. Kardos et al., "Counting on Colleagues: New Teachers Encounter the Professional Cultures of Their Schools," *Educational Administration Quarterly*, 37, no. 2 (April 2001), 251.

6. Dan Lortie, Schoolteacher, 133.

7. Susan M. Kardos et al., *Counting on Colleagues*, 252.

8. Susan M. Kardos et al., *Counting on Colleagues*, 265.

9. Deborah L. Harris and Helene M. Anthony, "Collegiality and Its Role in Teacher Development," 381.

10. Susan M. Kardos et al., "Counting on Colleauges," 272.

11. Steven Heine, Travis Proulx, and Kathleen Vohs, "The Meaning Maintenance Model: On Coherence of Social Motivations," *Personality and Social Psychology Review*, 10, no. 2 (2006), 98–99.

12. Michael Hogg, "Subjective Uncertainty Reduction through Self-Categorization: A Motivational Theory of Social Identity Processes," *European Review of Social Psychology*, 11, no. 1 (2000): doi: 10.1080/14792772043000040.

13. Charles Payne, *So Much Reform, So Little Change: The Persistence of Failure in Urban Schools*, Harvard Education Press (April, 2008), 31.

14. Charles Payne, *So Much Reform, So Little Change*, 61.

15. Charles Payne, *So Much Reform, So Little Change*, 27.

16. Sigal Barsade, Constantinos Coutifaris and Julianna Pellemer, "Emotional Contagion in Organizational Life," *Research in Organizational Behavior*, 38 (December, 2018), doi:10.1016/jriob.2018.11.005.

17. A. Isen and P. Lavin, "The Effect of Feeling Good on Helping: Cookies and Kindness," *Journal of Personality and Social Psychology*, 21 (1972); R. Marcus, "The Role of Affect in Children's Cooperation," *Child Study Journal*, 17 (1987).

18. Charles Payne, *So Much Reform, So Little Change*, 27.

19. Mei-Lin Chang, "An Appraisal Perspective of Teacher Burnout: Examining the Emotional Work of Teachers," *Education Psychology Review*, 21 (2009).

20. C. Maslach, W. Schaufeli and M. Leiter, "Job Burnout," *Annual Review of Psychology*, 52, no. 1 (2001), 397.

21. Doris Santoro, "Good Teaching in Difficult Times: Demoralization in the Pursuit of Good Work," *American Journal of Education*, 118, no. 1 (November 2011), doi: 10.1086/662010.

22. Doris Santoro, "Good Teaching in Difficult Times," 2.

23. Doris Santoro, "Good Teaching in Difficult Times," 2.

24. Doris Santoro, "Good Teaching in Difficult Times," 2.

25. Fenstermacher, "Some More Considerations on Teaching as a Profession" (1990), p. 133, as quoted by Erin Sugrue in "Moral Injury among Professionals in K–12 Education," *American Educational Research Journal*, 57, no. 1 (February 2022), 46.

26. Erin Sugrue, "Moral Injury among Professionals," 46.

27. Erin Sugrue, "Moral Injury among Professionals," 46.

28. Callid Keefe-Perry, "Called into the Crucible: Vocation and Moral Injury in US Public School Teachers," *Religious Education* (2018), doi: 10.1080/00344087.2017.1403789.

29. M. Levinson, "Moral Injury and the Ethics of Educational Injustice," *Harvard Educational Review*, 85 (2015).

Chapter 9

Teachers of Color and White Teachers' Experiences in Schools

Different Causes, Similar Pain

RACE AND TEACHING

Some of the most fraught instances of psychological pain, including moral injury, take place as teachers attempt to navigate race, class, and culture while working in schools. These issues will only get more complicated as the number of white students in public schools drops over the next ten years.

School districts need to do more to create structures that allow both teachers of color and white teachers to be effective in teaching students of color, and they need to recognize that those structures need to be different depending on the race and ethnicity of the teacher. Districts need to understand that teachers of color and white teachers need these structures to be in place for different reasons.

As we all know, the vast majority of public school teachers are female, mono-lingual, middle-class, and white, non-Hispanic. In 2018, 80 percent of teachers represented this demographic, with 9 percent being Latinx, 7 percent being Black, only 2 percent being Asian, and less than 1 percent of teachers being American Indian/Alaska Native or Native Hawaiian/Pacific Islander.[1] Table 9.1 shows us that teachers of color are represented in higher numbers in schools that have a majority of students from different racial backgrounds, but even in those schools, white teachers are still the majority.

All teachers need support in navigating issues of racial justice and equity in schools because all teachers are adversely impacted by the ways in which racial dynamics are enacted in school environments. These dynamics hurt both teachers of color and white teachers. Racial dynamics play out in *very* different ways and for *very* different reasons for teachers of color and white teachers, but the psychological damage is similar. This chapter examines

Table 9.1 Percentage of Teachers by Racial/Ethnic Background Compared to Percentage of Students by Racial/Ethnic Background in the Same School

Students	Percent of teachers teaching in schools that have a majority of specific student races					
Majority of the student population in a particular school	White teachers	African American/ Black teachers	Latinx teachers	Asian teachers	American Indian/ Alaska Native teachers	Hawaiian/ Pacific Islander teachers
White students	90%					
African American/ Black students	54%	36%				
Latinx students	54%		33%			
Asian students	60%			27%		
American Indian/ Alaska Native students	61%				29%	
Hawaiian/ Pacific Islander students	26%			26%		19%

Source: National Center for Education Statistics, September 2020. Race and Ethnicity of Public School Teachers and Their Students.

how teachers of color and White teachers struggle with racial dynamics in classrooms and schools.

WHITE TEACHERS TEACHING STUDENTS OF COLOR

Three things are true of White teachers when it comes to race and teaching, especially for those who teach in high-poverty, high-needs schools. First, it is clear that a majority of these teachers see themselves as unbiased, or even antiracist teachers, who are supportive of, and advocate for, their Black and Brown students. In fact, many of them have chosen to teach in high-needs schools because they have a heartfelt desire to give back in some way.

Second, a majority of White teachers are well-meaning and sincere in their desire to be an effective teacher for students of color. Many of these teachers spend time participating in programs designed to improve their knowledge of the needs of students of color. Third, many White teachers begin teaching with some knowledge of the racial dynamics of schools—and their role as White people in those dynamics—because most are required to take at least one class on race and culture in schools during their teacher preparation programs.

In these courses, often called sociocultural or multicultural perspectives, teachers are asked to examine whiteness and their cultural backgrounds while learning about the racial and cultural identities of their students. The courses help teachers learn how race, class, language, and ethnicity influence our lived experiences, as well as how to examine racism within these contexts. Teachers learn to recognize and draw upon the rich cultural experiences of their students, their families, and communities to enhance the curriculum and student engagement.

A major goal of these courses is that teachers will use this knowledge as a foundation for understanding the policies, goals, assumptions, strategies, and practices of culturally relevant pedagogy. In addition, many of these courses attempt to teach teachers how to recognize instances of racism, bias, inequity, and discrimination within themselves, the wider school community, and school policies, and to be able to employ strategies to address such biases and advocate for social justice.

The ultimate goal of these courses is to enable teachers themselves, and in partnership with colleagues and families, to provide respectful, academically rigorous, inclusive, and culturally relevant learning environments for all students.

Many White teachers who have taken these courses report being transformed by them. They report having their eyes opened to experiences and perspectives that were foreign to many of them and feeling committed to supporting their students of color. The following quotes are from White teachers who have taken these types of courses:

> Activism is something that I've always been passionate about. Whether it was going to LGBTQA rallies with my friends in high school, decades ago, or going to Defund the Police rallies, and the last week of instruction reminded me how important activism is for creating equality in our public-school systems. It also helped remind me that high school students are smart, strong; they have a loud collective voice and should embrace their want to advocate for the rights of all. I should not keep my activist history secret, going to rallies one town over in fear of whatever consequences being seen strongly supporting a cause. I should be visible, active, and supportive within my community. I should support my students should they feel the need to take a stand for something they believe in.

An aspiring high school teacher said this:

I envisioned that the class would be about the "other," the minority, the marginalized, the underserved. Of course, it was, but the class was also about me, about what I need to know as a White male, what I need to keep learning and what conversations I need to initiate.

Another came away with this valuable realization:

I feel like I would not have been well-equipped in terms of knowledge and even my behavior to deal with students coming from diverse backgrounds. That is not to say that people coming from diverse backgrounds need special teachers. It means to be an effective educator, I need to learn where my students come from. I remember reading about the Iceberg concept of culture, and I really resonated with that. Later, in one of the breakout rooms, while discussing this concept, my group realized that this was so true.

When we think we know about a certain culture it is usually coming from a place of, "Oh yes. I know all about it. I know about the food they eat. The clothes they wear, the different holidays they celebrate . . ." But when we apply these aspects to our culture, we realize that these do not even make up a small part of our culture and all the core things lie much deeper. I would certainly not think that if someone knew about the food eaten, and clothes worn in my culture, that person would really "know" my culture.

Yet, it is habitual to say we "know" cultures based off this very limited information. I now understand the importance of not ignoring our differences, or arguing over them, but to celebrate them. As an educator, I look forward to designing culturally responsive lessons and also just being part of conversations where I get to learn about cultures and races first hand.

And finally, this teacher learned about the importance of recognizing implicit bias:

The one goal that I have for myself is that I need to actively work on learning more about where other people come from and also fight off any implicit biases that come from within me. Sure, I did not grow up in an environment that ever called for such goals, but now I feel like I am personally responsible for becoming more ethical, informed and accepting than the society I grew up in.

As a teacher, I am going to have major responsibility on my shoulders, and before I even begin to worry about my students' academic performance I need to make sure I am not a reason or a factor in their mental health issues. What I say and how I say something has so much power, and I am now fully aware of it. It is very important for me to create a safe learning environment for my students where they feel well accepted. Only then, they can better concentrate on academia. Being brought up in a society that lacks diversity, you tend to be a bit outspoken.

You know all the things that a person might find offensive because you share the same beliefs. However, now I have to be intentional with words because I am going to be dealing with different races and cultures, and what is acceptable in mine could very well be offensive in theirs. The only way forward is to learn more, and preferably from people who belong to that culture, and not the internet.

These statements demonstrate the conscious desires of some White teachers to be a force for racial healing and an advocate for Black, Brown, and immigrant children in their classrooms. However, despite being truly appreciative of the knowledge these courses have afforded them, and genuine in their determination to act for their students of color with this new knowledge in mind, many White teachers struggle to carry out their commitments around race and racism once they enter the classroom.

Several factors contribute to this. First, the new teacher has to be attentive to racial dynamics in the classroom and act on what she observes in anti-racist ways, while also learning to carry out the overwhelming number of tasks that a new teacher has to absorb. Second, the new teacher has to do all of this despite a lack of support structures in place to help them navigate all aspects of their new job, including the racial dynamics, which are seldom discussed in schools. Third, taking one course on sociocultural perspectives is not enough to overcome the angst that new, White teachers experience when confronted with racial dynamics in real time in the classroom.

For many White teachers, much of this angst around race is rooted in their desire to be a good person, which in this case means not being seen as racist. This causes them to take one of two stances in reaction to the students of color in their classrooms. First, they tend to deemphasize racial differences among their students, stressing the importance of taking a colorblind approach which allows them to not see or acknowledge their students' racial identities. White teachers who take this stance strongly believe that acknowledging a student's race is calling attention to a false marker.[2]

> I really don't see race or color. A student is a student as far as I am concerned. The fact that a student is African American, to me, would be immaterial. I got just a different upbringing . . . I went to a high school where we didn't look at people like that, race wasn't involved. But I think there are a lot of people out there who would be influenced by race. I think people preconceive, preconceive, preconceive!
>
> This is not me trying to be PC (politically correct) but I really can't say I have seen any difference between White students, Latino students, African American students, and Black students who are not African American.

White teachers who take this stance truly believe that it is "proper" not to see or acknowledge a student's race and that it is the *right* thing to do. This is because they equate seeing color with confirming differences, thereby creating inequalities that they fear might lead to conflict or discomfort in the classroom.

> Rather than emphasizing the Blackness of the content, I would rather emphasize the content, but not to the point where we don't acknowledge where it came from. We have to do that, but to put race right up at the top seems to me to set up confrontation possibilities, to set up difficulties, when really the goal in my classes is to get people, all of us, to work together rather than dividing. What great Black historical figures or artists can do for us is we're not viewing them as Black in particular, but as part of the big picture. They're, for most people, they're human beings and that's what is exciting about these people.[3]

White teachers who suppress or deflect classroom discussions about race in the name of creating a "safe" space for all students are really maintaining a safe space for themselves.

It is this fear of discussing race and racism that leads them to take a colorblind stance in the first place. Unfortunately, because these teachers "do not see race," they are unable to see racism and other factors that hurt their students. They end up suppressing any awareness they might have about how their students are hurt by racial dynamics in their classroom or the school.

These teachers must recognize that the "colorblind" approach to race is no longer acceptable. They must make the mental shift from believing what they may have been taught—that "race doesn't matter"—to understanding that race does matter and must be acknowledged. Finally, they must accept that the colorblind approach is damaging to the students that they care about.

Some white teachers do acknowledge their awareness of the racial differences among their students, but they are so apprehensive about acting on that awareness that they take a cautionary stance in acknowledging those differences. This causes them to become overly hesitant or even paralyzed with fear about discussing racial incidents that come up in the classroom, either during class discussions or as part of their interactions with individual students. One White teacher explained that she was hesitant to discuss racist events happening in society with her students because she was not sure how to facilitate the conversation.

> I think it carries risks. I think you have to ask yourself what are the costs of doing that. I mean something can explode. One of the things you always worry about is that you might say something racist. And for me, as a White person

trying to manage this, my first reaction is "no, I'm not"; second, "maybe I am"; third, "Where is this going?"

So, the instinct to keep it in the bottle is pretty substantial when you're dealing with something that can go off in lots of different directions, including inside yourself. My point is, it's got to be recognized as hard, not because somebody's a jerk; it doesn't have anything to do with whether you're a jerk. These are hard problems you can—people can—get hurt. The risks are real for all sides.[4]

This teacher poignantly describes the dilemma for White teachers, that acknowledging racial differences during classroom discussions can potentially open them up to charges of racism and conflict in the classroom. For them, this is personally risky and many White teachers do not know what to do in these situations.

Another White teacher described the same dilemma while working with a Black male student in her class who was having trouble understanding how to complete a lab assignment. The teacher was trying to explain it to him, but felt that her explanations were not getting through. She said,

Am I reinforcing a message of "you ain't smart"? Since I know that is out there. I know that's in their heads from any number of sources like their comparisons with other students in the class or any number of things. I'm very worried about playing into that, and that may inhibit me from pushing to hard. . . . You know that Claude Steele article?[5]

That article really revolutionized my thinking about trying to get students to identify with the academic enterprise, to get them to feel like they are part of schooling, that they aren't outsiders looking in. . . . I felt badly about the situation. He got the lowest grade in the class and I felt badly about it, but you know, it's hard.[6]

This White teacher's awareness of the social situation and the educational needs of Black students gets translated into worry and concern about protecting the student from a perceived lack of confidence rather than into an ability to motivate the student to meet the academic challenge. The realization that they can act in racist ways, despite their good intentions, can lead to emotions of personal disappointment and anxiety in White teachers, and cause them to feel sadness and guilt. These personal disappointments cause them to fear saying the wrong things about race and to resist examining their own racial belief systems.

In her article "Sincere Fictions," Lee Anne Bell points out that

Color blindness operates for many Whites as a way to avoid appearing to be racist. Seeing race means being racist, something [many White teachers] clearly wish to avoid, and naming White as a race is something only White supremacists do. The contortions required to deny what one sees also prevent Whites from unearthing and addressing racist assumptions and feelings they would prefer to avoid.[7]

What White teachers do not understand is that these beliefs, and the actions those beliefs lead to, ultimately hurt students of color. White teachers' inability to acknowledge their students' race leaves them with the belief that all of their students are the same, with the same backgrounds, upbringing, experiences, and values. This prevents them from thinking about how a different background might lead to different experiences which might require them to seek out alternative ways of motivating and engaging their students.

It prevents them from realizing that they may need to spend time learning more about their students' communities, families, and cultures to better connect the subject matter to student interests. Because they claim to "see no differences between their students" they are forced to attribute student difficulties to individual factors such as "they are not interested in learning" or "they can't learn," which might be one reason that White teachers refer students of color to special education programs more frequently than do teachers of color.

Not seeing color also prevents White teachers from seeing themselves as cultural beings. This leads them to assume that their own values, beliefs, and behaviors are the norm to which students of color should aspire.[8]

White teachers do, however, as demonstrated above, have some knowledge of the dynamics of race and culture in America, which unfortunately gives them a false sense of the depth of their racial understandings. Despite their learnings, they have no, or very little experience of how racism operates in schools and how they, as White teachers, reproduce racist outcomes. When they finally get their own classroom and can gain some actual experience, two things happen. First, they seldom see their colleagues practicing anti-racist teaching.

Second, without collegial support, all they have in their tool kit at this point is what they learned in their one sociocultural class and their desire to truly do right by their Black and Brown students. That desire is not enough! Third, as soon as they get in the classroom they are inundated with a tsunami of new learning. A recent literature review of nine articles supports the fact that new teachers "struggle to implement the understandings they built through coursework regarding sociocultural knowledge related to students, facing barriers of time, resources and knowledge."[9]

As we saw from Robin's[10] experiences, her cognitive capacities became so overloaded just trying to teach one lesson while managing classroom behaviors, that she was not even able to carry out her plan to target those students who needed specific help during her question and answer session, even though she knew who those students were ahead of time. This experience was so troubling for Robin because she was aware of what she did in terms of the racial dynamics, and *why* she did it.

She relied on the few White and Asian students to answer the questions when she knew that the Black and Latinx students would benefit more from having the practice because she just needed the lesson to move along. However, it would have been all but impossible for Robin to act on her awareness during the lesson because her working memory was at capacity, literally preventing her from thinking about anything else in that moment.

It was not until she went home for the evening that she was able to think about and process what happened. Unfortunately, her awareness led her to experience guilt and anxiety, which exacerbates the situation because anxiety also overloads cognitive capacity.

Research has shown that people tend to fall back on stereotypes when cognitive resources are depleted, making novice teachers' efforts in this regard even harder. "Stereotypes act as energy saving devices and are more likely to be used as a basis for responding when people are short on cognitive energy."[11] This explanation is not presented as an excuse for White teachers. Rather, it is an explanation for why White teachers who have expressed a heartfelt desire to be an antiracist educator might fall back on stereotypical behaviors that further racist outcomes.

"Many people lack the regulatory abilities to inhibit the effects of implicit racial bias, especially in situations that limit their opportunity to deliberate when making a response." Other research has shown that "when individuals have the time and cognitive capacity, they are able to bring their [standards for anti-racist responses] to mind,"[12] and to act on those standards.

It is clear that many White teachers who teach in high-poverty, high-needs schools have *both* a desire to implement antiracist teaching *and* a psychological resistance to doing so. As new teachers, they also have not had enough experience, and very few models, from which they can learn how to actually teach in antiracist ways in the classroom. Finally, it is important to acknowledge that there are White teachers, especially those who have more experience teaching students of color, who enter the classroom with an antiracist stance and who are ready and able to teach in culturally relevant ways.

These teachers can, and often do, act as allies who collaborate with and support teachers of color in providing an equitable education for Black and Brown students. However, these teachers are not free from the psychological and emotional challenges posed by race in the classroom. What they end up experiencing is similar to the sense of demoralization that teachers of color experience. Next we examine the challenges faced by teachers of color.

TEACHERS OF COLOR TEACHING STUDENTS OF COLOR

Many teachers of color, a majority of whom teach in high-poverty, urban, and rural schools, come to teaching with an expressed commitment to give back to the community by helping low-income and minority students succeed academically. This is most likely the reason why teachers of color are more likely than White teachers to work in schools that serve low-income, majority-minority student populations. This commitment grows not from knowledge gained while preparing to teach, but from lived experience, often both as a student and as a community member.

Teachers of color enact this responsibility in several ways. They tend to approach teaching as a "change agent," as someone who works to reduce social and structural inequalities, not only in their students' lives, but also within the school community. The commitment of many teachers of color does not stop at the schoolhouse door. Female teachers of color especially describe teaching as "community work," as work that allows them to stay anchored in, but also to give back to, the community through their work with children.

Many evoke the image of the mother, nurturing both children of color, their families, and their communities. For many teachers of color, the community figures prominently in their teaching. They often see themselves as providing cultural and linguistic resources to young people and their families. For these teachers, good teaching is "shared, culturally responsive mothering."[13]

These commitments highlight the deeply held internal motivation that teachers of color have to teach and support low-income students of color, including bilingual and immigrant students, and their families and communities. However, this desire is a double-edged sword for teachers of color because it keeps them in high-poverty, low-resourced, high-needs schools.

Over forty years of research have shown that teachers of color are more likely to teach in schools that have high percentages (70 to 100 percent) of low-income, racially and culturally diverse students. This is especially true for novice teachers of color, with some studies finding that nearly 54 percent of new teachers of color through their first three years of teaching are "concentrated in urban schools, as compared to just 27 percent of White novice teachers."[14]

This would not be a problem if high-needs schools that serve high concentrations of poor students of color received the full complement of resources needed to serve their students well. But we all know this is not the case. Rather, these schools tend to lack high-quality facilities and instructional materials, have lower levels of teacher decision-making about school policies, especially policies concerning instruction and how best to teach students, and have lower teacher retention rates. But guess what? "Teachers of color are more likely to remain in these schools than are their White colleagues."

In fact, studies of several large urban districts throughout the US have consistently shown that "teacher turnover tends to decrease for teachers of color as the number of students of color increase."[15] Finally, when teachers of color do leave these schools, they tend to move to schools with even higher proportions of students of color, this is especially true for African American teachers. This is the opposite of White teachers, who tend to move to schools with fewer students of color when they leave.

Unfortunately, staying in hard-to-staff, high-poverty, urban schools exacts a deep psychological toll on teachers that manifests in many ways. First, teachers of color have such deep commitment to serve students of color, that it threatens their self-concept when they struggle to engage and motivate students to learn the material they are teaching. This is especially a problem for novice teachers of color who are still learning how to engage students who may also be suffering from poverty, systemic racism, and other social traumas.

Unfortunately, these new teachers seldom get the support they need as novice teachers starting in a low-resourced school. Being unable to motivate students and engage them in one's lessons leads to cognitive dissonance, which threatens the teacher's sense of competence, calling into question her sense of certainty about why she wanted to teach in the first place. Teachers of color also experience these difficult psychological processes when they witness antagonistic relationships between the school and parents and other community organizations.

Again, this impacts novice teachers of color the most because they have not yet built up enough capital within their school or with parents or the community to counter these conflictual relationships and often feel "caught in the middle" when a parent has trouble with administration or with a colleague, or when a community organization cannot gain any traction within the school around school/community issues.

Experiences like these often motivate teachers of color to serve on committees and to work with parent, community, and partner organizations in an attempt to help improve their relationships within the school. These extra service activities can quickly become burdens for teachers of color, who can end up finding themselves in multiple roles, with multiple non-white students, and family and community members associated with the school. Being put in the role of advocate for students and parents of color can be exhausting and can threaten the cultural self-efficacy of teachers of color.

Darnell, a novice Black male math teacher illustrates this when he says,

> I get a lot of pressure as an African American male math teacher. Parents say things like, "my kid doesn't have a strong father figure, so I need you to be that man in his life and tell him what he needs to do because I can't do it." . . . When I was trying to find a job, there was an overwhelming, "We really need you here to help our boys." I heard it from so many people that for me, it was like, "What if I'm not good at this? What if I'm not good at teaching math?" I don't want to be just a Black teacher, I want to be a good teacher. It was a big burden for me because I feel like "I'm 25, I can't save all Black boys!" but I feel like I have that on me a lot and it's a lot of pressure.[16]

Deepa, a veteran South Asian teacher has had similar experiences,

> As a teacher of color, I have had to juggle many hats, aside from just my teaching—I am the faculty advisor to many student clubs, the teacher that . . . stays late to help students, the one who drives them places. I'm a personal advisor, a mentor, etc. Many students call me mom, something that is common for several women of color teachers at this school.[17]

Incidents like these are especially frustrating for teachers of color, because they often feel that they would be able to better engage students, parents, and the community if they had support from the school to do so. This was one of the major frustrations that Quay had during his first year of teaching. Quay wanted to teach using methods that emphasized hands-on learning. He believed that these methods worked better for urban kids, but his colleagues and the school, discouraged it, especially because he was teaching one of the "testing subjects."

Unfortunately, hard-to-staff schools tend to be constantly under pressure to implement state-mandated reform efforts. These efforts often prevent teachers of color from implementing instructional methods that they know work better for their students. This thwarts their need for autonomy, which might feel more crucial to teachers of color who may be more willing to fight for the ability to make decisions about instructional materials and methods.[18] This also hurts their sense of curricular competence if they do not feel successful using practices designed for teaching to the test.

Research has shown that teachers of color are more likely than White teachers to buck certain reform efforts because they tend not to agree that they will lead to authentic student learning.[19] It is these types of dilemmas that lead to demoralization among teachers of color. Knowing they can teach in ways that will engage and support students of color, but being prevented from doing so for reasons that just don't make sense given their professional expertise, can result in cognitive dissonance and even moral injury. Both of these psychological states are accompanied by emotional struggles that hurt teacher well-being.

In situations like these, teachers of color want to be able to turn to colleagues and administrators for emotional and social support, and they want that support to directly address the unique challenges they face as teachers of color. For example, new teachers of color tend to begin their careers expecting to teach in culturally relevant ways and they expect to be supported in their efforts through school-wide conversations about race and equity.

It is particularly demoralizing for these teachers when they discover that their school does not support dialogue around culturally relevant or socially just teaching, or worse, tolerates low expectations and negative attitudes about students and parents of color.[20] When this happens, these teachers seek out colleagues, mentors, or other support structures that can help them process these instances of discrimination and racial bias by providing resources and encouragement for their approach to teaching students of color.[21]

When those structures are not present, or worse, when teachers of color experience outright institutional and personal racism, they can feel isolated as their need for relatedness goes unfulfilled. In many school environments, teachers of color often experience two forms of biased interactions with their colleagues. First, they have to deal with color-blindness, which can feel to teachers of color like their colleagues are ignoring race and racial differences. This becomes especially evident in collegial discussions around the achievement gaps between student racial and ethnic populations within the school.

One Latinx teacher, working in a racially integrated school that had a large disparity in achievement between ethnic groups, expressed her frustration with her colleagues' hesitancy to directly acknowledge and attack the problem:

> Our students of color are not doing as well as they should be. Although this is recognized, there is still a silence that consumes the campus with regard to effective solutions. Only a few faculty members have ever engaged in a conversation about this with me. They insist that all students are the same and should be treated the same, but this does not reflect the social reality where our students of color and their respective communities are not treated the same.

Teachers of color want their colleagues to understand that "silencing discussions of race also denies the discussion of racism, stifling any movement toward justice."[22]

Second, they experience racial microaggressions which are "rooted in factors associated with race such as language and culture."[23] Chester Pierce, who first coined the term, described racial microaggressions as "racial offences or put downs that are done in automatic, *preconscious* or *unconscious* fashion."[24] Critical race scholars argue that racial microaggressions are "covert forms of systemic racism that exist in educational institutions."[25] Those who study racial microaggressions point out that "because of their elusiveness, it can be hard to pinpoint racial microaggressions as racism, though they have very real manifestations and consequences for teachers of color."[26]

For example, Quay experienced a form of racial microaggression when his colleagues discouraged and denigrated his approach to teaching. Quay wanted to use a more engaging teaching method so that he could create a bridge between the subject matter and his students' lives. Given Quay's relationships with his students and his proven ability to engage them, being questioned in this way is a racial slight, demonstrating a disrespect for both his cultural and pedagogical knowledge.

All teachers want to work with supportive colleagues. This is reflected in the National Education Association poll of teachers which asks in every survey about school factors that help teachers teach better. Consistently, the most important factor has been "cooperative/competent colleagues/mentors." Teachers of color are no different. They want to work with competent and cooperative colleagues because it helps them better teach their students of color. Yet colorblindness and microaggressions, no matter that both may be engaged in unconsciously, hurts collegial relations between teachers of color and their White colleagues.

In order for colleagues to support each other, they need to work in schools that are characterized by trust. They need school structures that encourage and support cooperation and dialogue, and a mission that is shared by all teachers. A key piece of this is that teachers do not only rely on their colleagues for professional support. They also rely on them to fulfill their relational needs for "social interaction, reassurance and psychological support."[27]

Another aspect that highlights the importance of colleagues is that teachers want to be able to count on each other. In fact, teachers are less willing to work together if they work "in schools where [they] doubt whether their colleagues are 'doing the right thing' for the right reasons."[28] Part of this for teachers of color is that they tend to care very deeply that their colleagues share a commitment to social justice.

These facts complicate things for teachers of color. In addition to experiencing cognitive dissonance and the frustrations of dealing with public perceptions of teaching, accountability systems, students' social-emotional struggles with poverty and trauma, the cognitive complexity of teaching, and the struggles to meet their basic psychological needs, teachers of color also have to deal with institutionalized racism and implicit bias toward themselves within their own schools.

Even though the challenges raised by race in the classroom for teachers of color and White teachers have very different roots and manifest in very different ways, the physical, psychological, and emotional outcomes that they suffer are similar and have similar detrimental impacts on their health and well-being. The impact that cognitive dissonance has on teachers in terms of the various emotions associated with it, and the physical outcomes caused by prolonged experience of those emotions has been outlined above. Racial dynamics in schools are also very emotionally fraught.

Difficult interactions involving race, from the perspective of a White teacher or a teacher of color, generate deeply personal beliefs and emotions about the self. This happens for White teachers when their part in school-based racial interactions causes them to question their values, their goodness as a person, and their commitment to supporting all children. It happens for teachers of color when their experience of school-based racial interactions renders them invisible, hurts their sense of teaching efficacy, and causes them to question their professional abilities and their commitments to children to whom they feel incredibly responsible.

The emotions and feelings described above as resulting from cognitive dissonance are similar to the emotions and feelings that grow out of racial conflicts and confusion. To summarize, these experiences lead to feelings of psychological discomfort, feelings of anxiety, frustration, doubt, uncertainty, regret, and guilt. These emotions interrupt cognitive functioning and diminish attentional capacity, while also focusing one's attention on immediate, problematic concerns. This hurts the teacher's ability to think broadly and to problem-solve in the moment.

These emotions impact the types of attributions teachers make and lower their levels of intrinsic motivation, which ends up diminishing their teaching efficacy. These emotions lead to feelings of both hopelessness and helplessness because they diminish the teacher's sense of control over personal and professional outcomes. The most difficult emotions generated by school-based conflicts are psychological discomfort and stress.

Taken together, these emotions and feelings can lead to debilitating physical outcomes such as exhaustion, sleeplessness, chest pain, headaches, and stomach and digestive problems. They can make teachers more susceptible to heart attacks, heart disease, high blood pressure, diabetes, obesity, and chronic depression.

The emotional struggles discussed above, the ones that teachers are already experiencing within the school context, are heightened when race is added to the equation. Racial conflict and confusion magnify the feelings, the personal relevance, and the stakes of the challenges that teachers are already dealing with in poorly resourced urban and rural schools. This is because "stressors deriving from systems of inequality may provoke a more severe psychological and physiological response because they are inherently personal and humiliating."[29]

Also, when the stress one experiences threatens a person's self-concept that stress is more likely to impact one's physical health.[30] Stress created through racial conflict harms a teacher's self-concept in pernicious ways, especially for teachers of color because racial conflict in schools tends to be aimed at their professional standards and approach. This is especially difficult for novice teachers whose self-concept is just developing.

Race is a key factor in the challenges plaguing public schools in this country. This is true for BIPOC teachers, for White teachers, and students. We need to acknowledge this and provide teachers with the necessary supports to address these challenges across racial lines.

NOTES

1. National Center for Education Statistics (NCES), "Race and Ethnicity of Public School Teachers and Their Students," *Data Point* (September 2020), https://nces.ed.gov/pubs2020/2020103/index.asp.

2. Lisa Gonsalves, "The Dance of Safety: Examining the Stances Taken by White Faculty in Relation to Black Males," in *English Studies: Learning Climates that Cultivate Racial and Ethnic Diversity,* ed. V. Villanueva and S. Fowler (Washington, DC: American Association of Higher Education, 2002), 10.

3. Lisa Gonsalves, "The Dance of Safety," 10–11.

4. Lisa Gonsalves, "The Dance of Safety," 13.

5. Claude Steele, "Stereotype Threat and the Intellectual Test Performance of African-Americans," *Journal of Personality and Social Psychology,* 69, no. 5 (1995).

6. Lisa Gonsalves, "The Dance of Safety," 13.

7. Lee Anne Bell, "Sincere Fictions: The Pedagogical Challenges of Preparing White Teachers for Multicultural Classrooms," *Equity and Excellence in Education,* 35, no. 3 (2002), 4, doi: 10.1080/713845317.

8. Christine Sleeter, "Preparing White Teachers for Diverse Students," *Handbook of Research on Teacher Education,* 3rd ed., ed. Marilyn Cochran-Smith et al. (New York: Routledge and the Association of Teacher Educators, 2008).

9. Melissa Mosley Wetzel, "Preparing Teachers with Sociocultural Knowledge in Literacy: A Literature Review," *Journal of Literacy Research,* 51, no. 2 (2019), 145, doi: 10.1177/1086296X19833575.

10. Robin was a new White teacher in her first year of teaching.

11. Margo Monteith and Corrine Voils, "Prone to Prejudice Responses: Toward Understanding the Authenticity of Self-Reported Discrepancies," *Journal of Personality and Social Psychology*, 75, no. 4 (1998), 903.

12. Margo Monteith and Corrine Voils, "Prone to Prejudice," 903.

13. A. McGray et al., "African-American Women's Decisions to Become Teachers: Sociocultural Perspectives," 15, no. 3 (2002), as quoted in Betty Achinstein et al., "Retaining Teachers of Color: A Pressing Problem and a Potential Strategy for 'Hard to Staff' Schools," *Review of Educational Research*, 80, no. 1 (March 2010), 85, doi: 10.3102/0034654309355994.

14. Betty Achinstein et al., "Retaining Teachers of Color," 91.

15. Betty Achinstein et al., "Retaining Teachers of Color," 90.

16. Rita Kohli, "Behind School Doors: The Impact of Hostile Racial Climates on Urban Teachers of Color," *Urban Education*, 53, no. 3 (2018), 322.

17. Rita Kohli, "Behind School Doors," 323.

18. Marilyn Cochran Smith and Ana Maria Villegas, "Preparing Teachers for Diversity and High Poverty Schools: A Research-Based Perspective" in *Teacher Education for High Poverty Schools*, ed. Jo Lampert and Bruce Burnett (New York, Spring 2015).

19. Betty Achinstein et al., "Retaining Teachers of Color."

20. Betty Achinstein et al., "Retaining Teachers of Color."

21. Kam Lau, Evelyn Dandy, and Lorrie Hoffman, "The Pathways Program: A Model for Increasing the Number of Teachers of Color," *Teacher Education Quarterly*, 24, no. 4 (Fall 2007).

22. Rita Kohli, "Behind School Doors," 316.

23. Rita Kohli, "Behind School Doors," 318.

24. Rita Kohli, "Behind School Doors," 318, quoting C. Pierce, in Psychiatric "Problems of the Black Community," in ed. S. Arieti, *American Handbook of Psychiatry* (New York, NY: Basic Books, 1974) 515.

25. Rita Kohli, "Behind School Doors," 318.

26. Rita Kohli, "Behind School Doors," 319, quoting Juan Carrillo, "Teaching That Breaks Your Heart: Reflections on the Soul Wounds of a First-Year Latina Teacher," *Harvard Educational Review*, 80, no. 1 (Spring 2010).

27. Nicole Simon and Susan Moore Johnson, "Teacher Turnover in High-Poverty Schools: What We Know and Can Do," *Teachers College Record*, 117 (March 2015), 20.

28. Nicole Simon and Susan Moore Johnson, "Teacher Turnover in High-Poverty Schools," 20.

29. Ilan Meyer, "Prejudice, Social Stress, and Mental Health in Lesbian, Gay, and Bisexual Populations: Conceptual Issues and Research Evidence," *Psychological Bulletin*, 129, no. 5 (September 2003), doi: 10.1037/033-2909.129.5.674.

30. Ilan Meyer, "Prejudice, Social Stress, and Mental Health."

Part III

Reforming Urban Schools for Teacher and Student Well-Being

As we have seen, teaching in low-resourced, high-poverty schools is damaging to teacher health and well-being. Teacher health is compromised by negative portrayals in the media, by the impact of accountability systems, and by an extreme lack of support around student social, emotional, and learning challenges. These factors exacerbate the cognitive and social complexities of teaching. Teaching in these conditions prevents teachers from fulfilling their basic psychological needs, leaving them to deal, on their own, with the negative mental and physical impacts on their overall health.

Then, on top of all of this came the pandemic. Teachers probably have some nostalgia for those first weeks of the pandemic when parents all over the country sang their praises. Those early days in 2020 gave many Americans a truer sense of all that teachers do for their children day in and day out. Many discovered that teachers actually do things that they could not, nor wanted, to do for their own children. Many discovered that they did not know everything that teachers teach. As one parent said in a video that went viral on Facebook just two weeks after the pandemic started:

> I wanted to do this video to apologize. This apology is coming from my heart. I have been the parent who has complained every now and then about some decisions that teachers have made. I've complained about some of the things that my children have learned. . . . This is the second day of homeschooling and my brain cells—I actually feel them popping, one by one. I want to say to teachers I am sorry if I took you for granted. I am sorry for complaining. . . I don't know what an improper fraction is. I don't know the difference between an improper fraction and a mixed number.
>
> My kids now realize that I don't know everything, but you know they say, "my teacher knows" and so, I want to apologize to all the teachers, and I want to ask them to forgive us, forgive me, and any other parent out there who took you

for granted. I have spent just one hour teaching my children and I want to run away. Teachers forgive us and come back, wear what you want, wear gloves, wear face masks, do whatever you need to do—but please come back.[1]

That same week, the *New York Times*'s published an Op-Ed arguing that "teachers deserve more respect."[2] The Op-Ed started with a chronicle of one teacher's outrageously busy day, describing how after teaching for a full day, he coached football after school, then reported to his part-time job (to supplement his $40,000 salary), then came home to grade papers and prepare the next day's lessons. He had high blood pressure and his doctor warned him that he might have a stroke if he didn't give something up.

After this, the stay-at-home order was announced and many districts wanted teachers to show up anyway, so that parents could keep working. This is even though teachers "were among the groups most at risk of exposure to the coronavirus."

The Op-Ed points out that "Many Americans are not aware of how bleak the education landscape in this country has become," and goes on to document much of what is discussed above. When teachers were asked what they wanted most from our political establishment, the answer was "restoring respect for teaching as a profession." As one teacher said, "when I started teaching in the late 1990s, teachers were not seen as idiots who couldn't be trusted. We weren't viewed as evil and lazy like we are now."

It is no coincidence that the 90s was the start of the accountability era. These words are harsh, but they capture the feelings of countless teachers. The article ends with a plea for teachers, stating that they are "among the most vital, hardest-working, passionate and selfless members of the workforce—yet they are also among the most disrespected, underappreciated, overworked and underpaid."

As a country, we should be ashamed of this fact. Teachers work so hard because they are called to serve children. They are professionally committed to the welfare of children. But as the Op-Ed points out, one of the largest sources of teachers' "workplace stress and anxiety" is a lack of resources, both "human and financial" for their work with students. Despite the fact that teachers need these financial and human resources for themselves, in order to do their jobs better, they are still focused on the needs of the children.

One teacher explained that without resources, "my hands are tied. I watch kids I know could be saved drop out, commit petty crimes, use drugs, and make bad choices. We could fundamentally change the lives of millions of children, but we're simply too overwhelmed to meet their needs in the way we know we should."

Most recently, the pandemic has been blamed for triggering a mass exodus from teaching. In reality, teachers are leaving teaching in droves because of the issues laid out in the first two sections of this book. The pandemic only exacerbated the situation by adding more stress, more anxiety, more criticism, and more emotions with which teachers had to deal. Educational administrators and policymakers have added insult to injury by adding professional development workshops on mindfulness, meditation, emotional regulation, and other wellness practices in an attempt to help teachers cope with what has become an "emotionally draining, bottomless workload."[3]

These techniques can be helpful, but they are no substitute for fixing the intractable systemic and structural problems facing today's schools. They end up taking up more time, while nothing else changes in the teacher's day-to-day working lives. As one teacher said, "I feel like I am drowning, and they throw you a rubber ducky. Rubber duckies are cute and all, but I'm not in a position to take it because I am literally drowning."

Another thirty-year veteran pointed out, "When people in charge recommend wellness to teachers instead of fixing the situation, it comes off as being insincere, patronizing, or even just shortsighted, wanting to put a band-aid on a problem." Once again, those in leadership positions have left teachers out of the conversation about what they need to make their jobs sustainable.

All of this has pushed teachers to leave the profession in droves. The Bureau of Labor Statistics reports that America's teaching force has dropped by 567,000 teachers since before the pandemic. According to the most recent National Education Association (NEA) Poll, which was conducted in January of 2022, 43 percent of posted teacher openings have not been filled.

Every job that is not filled in a school, leads to more work for other teachers, who are often expected to cover classes during their own break or planning time. "Our morning emails every day start with the vacancies in the building . . . and tell us where we have staffing shortages and ask us to step in in any way or any time that we can."[4]

What can be done about this? As the first part of this book shows, we, literally, have been trying to "fix" schools ever since their inception. The problem is huge and feels intractable. This book does not claim to have the answers to fix this problem, but it does present some ideas I have gained after working with and preparing teachers throughout my career in education. These ideas involve justice, community, and professionalism. The way we treat teachers is unjust, period. Schools do not do enough to care for *all* members of their community, and teachers need to be treated as the professionals that they are.

Other professions, such as nursing, can provide us with models that translate to the field of education. Education can learn a lot from the field of nursing, which has worked hard to restore a sense of professionalism and justice to the practice of medical healing in communities.

NOTES

1. Adaeze Chiwoko, Facebook, https://www.facebook.com/adaezec/videos/10159069450324796.

2. Alexandra Robbins, "Teachers Deserve More Respect," *The New York Times*, March 2020, https://www.nytimes.com/2020/03/20/opinion/sunday/teachers-coronavirus.html?.

3. Alyson Klein, "Superficial Self-Care? Stressed Out Teachers Say No Thanks," *EducationWeek* (March 2022).

4. Anya Kamenetz, "More Than Half of Teachers are Looking for the Exits, A Poll Says," NPR (February 2022), https://www.npr.org/2022/02/01/1076943883/teachers-quitting-burnout.

Chapter 10

Teacher Preparation

What Education Can Learn from the Field of Nursing

There are many similarities between the work of nurses and the work of teachers. Both are professions that are dominated by women who feel they have been called to serve their respective populations of patients or students. Both professions also suffer from some of the same pitfalls. Nurses and teachers, especially those working in high-needs institutions, face very similar psychological and cognitive challenges.

These include working conditions that force them to constantly assess a situation and alter their approach, deal with a high number of interruptions, and work in an atmosphere of controlled chaos. Nursing also tends to evoke the same types of emotions in nurses that teachers experience in the classroom.

However, unlike the field of education, the field of nursing has implemented specific processes and practices to help nurses cope with the difficult and complex psychological aspects of their profession. These processes and practices start when a nurse begins her training and continue throughout her first job in the field. For example, nursing preparation programs are more likely to address the psychological aspects of nursing in the curriculum, and many hospitals offer programs designed to deal directly with the stressful demands of the workplace.

These personal processes and practices are embedded in professional development throughout a nurse's career. Not only that, the processes and practices that help nurses cope with the psychological demands of the job are also taught to, and *practiced* by, other professionals who work in the hospital, from the doctors to the aides to the janitors. This happens because nursing knows something that education does not. Nursing knows how important the emotional, mental, and physical well-being of each nurse is to the success of the hospital's mission. They have elevated this fact, along with scholarship, professionalism, and leadership in their preparation programs and their professional development agendas.

Let's start by comparing the preparation of novice nurses to that of novice teachers. Both education and nursing are driven by committed professionals, mostly women, who feel called to the field out of a deep desire to care for others. Nursing has put this ethic of care at the center of everything they do in a way that education has not. Of course, this makes sense given that a nurse's main responsibility is to care for children and adults who are sick and suffering.

The main point here is that in nursing, this ethic of care goes beyond the patients. It is equally applied to themselves because nurses know that they cannot properly care for others if they are not caring for themselves. Nurses know that their own well-being is key to their ability to do the best job for their patients.

Not only do nurses understand this fact, but they have also been able to incorporate this understanding into policy and practice, both at the national and local levels. There are several examples of this in the policy statements of the American Nurses Association (ANA) and the American Association of Colleges of Nursing (AACN). These organizations play both an advocacy and an advisory role, advocating for nurses at the state and federal levels, and promoting standards and policies that ensure a common knowledge base, promote specific values, and identify best practices, that guide the profession.

Colleges and universities that prepare nurses echo these policies and standards in their own mission and value statements. Thus, the overall field of nursing is governed by a common, clear, and well-articulated set of guidelines that runs throughout the profession. Education has similar organizations such as the National Education Association (NEA), the American Federation of Teachers (AFT), and the American Association of Colleges of Teacher Education (AACTE).

These organizations have strong connections to teacher preparation programs nationwide, and they advocate for teachers through the research, reports, resolutions, and policy statements that they produce and promote. These organizations do impact the pedagogical and content-based knowledge and practices that govern teaching at a national level; however, the commitments and values of these educational organizations are not as clearly reflected in the statements and standards of individual teacher preparation programs, nor are teacher education candidates consistently taught about these standards as they are in nursing.

Both nursing and education promote similar concepts and practices, and have similar values concerning how patients, students, and families should be treated and how nurses and teachers should communicate and collaborate in the workplace and the community. The main concepts they have in common are communication, collaboration, ethics, equity, diversity, inclusion, professionalism, leadership, justice, and partnerships. These concepts are embedded throughout the standards that guide policy and practice in each field.

However, when one compares the education and nursing standards and mission and value statements to each other, there is one major difference between them. This difference is perfectly captured by a quote that is highlighted in the InTASC/CCSSO[1] "Model Core Teaching Standards and Learning Progressions for Teachers."[2] The quote, highlighted in blue so that it stands out in the document declares, "It's about the teaching practice and not about the individual teacher."

Herein lies the biggest difference between nursing and education. Nursing focuses equally on the needs of the nurse and the patient, whereas education focuses almost exclusively on the needs of the learner and what the teacher can, and must do, to meet those needs, without mentioning what the teacher can and must do to care for the self. Research has overwhelmingly demonstrated that the teacher is the single most important factor in learner success, yet the standards developed by most educational organizations, including by the top teacher preparation programs, consistently neglect to mention what the teacher needs in order to foster student success.

The following examples taken from documents outlining the standards and competencies from both professions demonstrate the extent of this difference.

In 2021, the American Association for Colleges of Nursing (AACN) published an updated version of a document called "The Essentials: Core Competencies for Professional Nursing Education." This document lays out the domains, concepts, and competencies that make up the AACN's "framework for the practice of nursing." The examples below compare this seventy-six-page document to the fifty-four-page InTASC document on education standards referred to above. Along the way, similar documents prepared by other key organizations from both fields are also examined.

The "Essentials" document from nursing is organized according to the domains, concepts, and competencies of nursing practice. Domains represent the areas of competence that are considered "essential" to nursing practice. The concepts represent "core components" of the knowledge and skills that nurses must have to be successful in the "multiple situations and contexts within nursing practice." Finally, the competencies represent the knowledge and skills a nurse needs to be successful in the domains of nursing.

The "Models" document from education is organized according to categories, which are similar to domains, and standards, which are similar to competencies. The standards are separated into performance, knowledge, and dispositions. These three are like the concepts in the nursing document, in that they represent, for education, the components of each standard. It is important to note that in describing the aspect of performance, the "Models" document states, we put "performance first, as the aspect that can be observed and assessed in teaching practice." The implication is that knowledge and dispositions cannot be observed or assessed.

The first major difference between the two professions can be seen in what each field prioritizes. For example, the first two domains in nursing are *knowledge* and *person-centered care*, whereas the first two categories in education are the *learner* and *content*. Focusing on and prioritizing knowledge is putting the nurse first. Knowledge is something that the nurse possesses. As the nursing document explains, it is a nurse's knowledge that allows the nurse "to function as independent, intellectually curious, socially responsible and a competent practitioner."[3]

These characteristics are about the nurse; they focus on the qualities the field values in nurses. First and foremost, the field encourages nurses to be independent. Knowledge, for nursing, also includes the liberal arts, as they point out, it is a liberal education that allows the nurse to "understand self and others, contribute to safe and quality care and informs the development of clinical judgment."[4] In other words, a nurse's knowledge includes self-understanding, which involves understanding one's needs in relation to the work of nursing.

The mention of clinical judgment demonstrates the importance of a liberal education to the work of nursing because it is the depth and breadth of a nurse's knowledge that aids in making those judgments. The competencies under this domain stress what nurses do with their knowledge. They identify, apply, understand, translate, analyze, synthesize, demonstrate, and integrate that knowledge in the service of good nursing. By emphasizing the full extent of a nurse's knowledge and skills, the field is putting the nurse at the forefront, because the knowledgeable nurse is what leads to success and excellence in patient care.

Once the document establishes what the nurse brings to the field, it then turns to the patients, but the document does not refer to the patients; rather it emphasizes what the nurses do in regard to the patients. The nurses provide *person-centered care*. It describes this care as contextual and as "individualized, just, respectful, compassionate, coordinated, evidenced-based, and developmentally appropriate."[5] Thus, person-centered care is guided by the nurse's knowledge interpreted within the context and experience of the patient.

The education categories flip this order by putting the *learner* first, followed by *content*.

The "*learner and learning*" category states that "teaching begins with the learner," not with the overall knowledge that the teacher brings. It outlines what teachers need to know about learners to teach them well; they need to understand all aspects of development, individual differences and abilities, personal and cultural backgrounds, and personality and skill differences. Finally, it states that teachers need to collaborate with families, colleagues, and communities in order to teach students well.

Yes, teachers need to know the things listed above; however, it is important to highlight the differences in priorities.

Only after outlining the learner's needs, does the document turn to the *content*. Significantly, the document talks about teaching *content* rather than teacher *knowledge*. Content can be thought of as specific information that has specific applications whereas knowledge is broad and broadly applicable. Content is often described as something contained, as in a box or a brain. One popular image of this definition of content, popularized by Paulo Freire, is the banking metaphor where educational content is deposited into students' brains; content is passive.

Knowledge, on the other hand, is thought of as awareness or understanding that is gained through experience and/or study. Knowledge can lead to effective action; acting upon one's knowledge helps in the achievement of one's goals. Of course, it is important for teachers to have a "deep and flexible understanding of their content area" as the category states. This allows teachers to make the content accessible, integrative, and relevant for students. But teachers, and teaching, are more than the content.

This category demonstrates this by listing everything teachers need to "know" in order to teach students well. They must know about "development, individual differences and abilities, personal and cultural backgrounds, and personality and skill differences."[6] This list demonstrates how teacher *knowledge* goes way beyond content. Nursing values the liberal arts enough to stress their importance in creating "the foundation for the development of intellectual and practical abilities."[7]

Nursing goes further by stating that a "liberal education is the key to understanding self and others: contributes to safe, quality care; and informs the development of clinical judgment."[8] Thus, it is their liberal education that allows teachers to integrate their knowledge about the psychological elements of student development in ways that aid student learning. Sadly, none of this is emphasized in the education document.

This tight focus on the content goes hand in hand with the push for accountability. Teachers deposit the content into students' brains and then students withdraw that content for the standardized assessments that determine the teacher's success or failure. This is what education has become, a message that has unfortunately been reinforced by think tanks like the Rand Corporation. A recent report from Rand states that "a better way to assess teachers' effectiveness is to look at what they do in the classroom [performance] and how much progress their students make on achievement tests."[9] The education standards echo this approach.

Talking about teaching in these ways is limiting. It does not encourage the kind of "independent, intellectually curious, socially responsible and competent" professionals advocated for in the field of nursing. It is a fact that teachers are the most important factor in student achievement. Teachers have the greatest impact of all school-based factors on student success in school."[10] As most teachers know, successful schooling is not only about standardized test scores.

It is also measured by the graduate's ability to be a successful adult. This often includes graduating from college and the ability to economically support oneself and one's family. Test scores are a pitifully small part of this success. A more significant predictor of adult success is a student's ability to self-regulate, be adaptable, and be motivated to try new things. Research has shown that the students of teachers who foster these types of "non-cognitive" skills have better attendance and higher grades and are more likely to graduate from high school than teachers who foster improved test scores.[11]

Teachers know that test scores reflect a very small part of how they impact students' lives. For example, recent research using a "benefit-cost analysis framework" has been able to quantify the impact that teachers have on the overall health of their students.[12] The study found that the students of teachers who foster their social and emotional well-being had better long-term outcomes in terms of their health, education, and employment.

This is no surprise given what we know about the brain, that it requires a safe and positive environment to learn and to function optimally. This research shows that having teachers who are anxious and stressed out for the reasons outlined in this book hurts student learning.

This brings us back to the frameworks. As pointed out above, the biggest difference between nursing and education is that the nursing framework and competencies are written to emphasize the experience and needs of the nurse. The nurse is the central figure in these documents. We can imagine what the writers of the education categories and standards might say in response to this point. They may claim that they agree with what is said in the nursing documents but consider this information to be so obvious that they do not need to state it directly.

But it is *crucial* to state these things directly. It is *urgent* to highlight the centrality of the teacher to the enterprise of teaching. This is what builds an ethic of teaching. This is how the values of the profession are instilled in new entrants. This is what fosters a strong commitment to the profession. Emphasizing the values and responsibilities of nursing in their standards documents is how nursing, as a profession, builds and instills an ethic of nursing.

By making their values, beliefs, and actions explicit, nursing is articulating a set of principles for practice in the nursing profession that both guides and governs nursing behavior, which serves to cement a nurse's identity. It is these ideas that foster a nurse's commitment to nursing. Education needs to do the same!

There are six principles emphasized in the nursing frameworks document that are either missing or not fully developed in equivalent documents in education. The first principle is a commitment to *"evidence-based practice."* The idea of using evidence to support one's practices runs throughout the nursing frameworks and shows up in several of the domains and competencies. Nursing expects those in the profession to understand the research process and to then translate, apply, and implement the "best evidence into their clinical decision making" processes.

Nurses are also encouraged to evaluate research-based evidence in the context of their patient's experiences and to react when they see inconsistencies between "practice policies and the evidence." Finally, experienced nurses are also encouraged to be "innovative" when good evidence is not available.

Because of the push for accountability-based systems, collecting and analyzing student data has become a major component of teaching over the last several years. However, the focus on data analysis for accountability purposes is very different from the use of evidence-based practice. The idea of evidence-based practice is mentioned only once in the education documents as a part of "professional responsibility." It falls under the standard focused on "professional learning and ethical practice."

But the evidence in these documents is mentioned only in relation to the teacher's own practice. For example, the standard states that teachers are expected to "use evidence to continually evaluate his/her practice, particularly the effects of his/her choices and actions on others (learners, families, other professionals, and the community)."[13] Here evidence becomes an evaluation tool for how well the teacher is teaching, working with parents and colleagues, and interacting with the community.

It is not clear from this standard where the evidence comes from, but we can assume that it comes from student outcomes data from both the teacher's own assessments and from standardized assessments. We can assume this because research is not mentioned in this standard. The nursing standard ties evidence to what they call "nursing scholarship," and states that this scholarship "informs science, enhances clinical practice, influences policy and impacts best practices for educating nurses as clinicians *and* scholars."

Even though there are no specifics in the education standards as to how teachers are supposed to use the evidence beyond self-evaluation, we know that teachers do this all the time, especially in relation to standardized testing. How many times have teachers explained that their students are not ready for standardized tests because of gaps in past learning or social/emotional issues? How many times have teachers explained that the readings from packaged curriculum programs such as pre-AP are not relevant to their students' lives?

These charges by teachers *are* based upon evidence, both researched and experiential. Perhaps the evidence is not widely included in the education standards because federal and state education policymakers do not want teachers to question their policies and practices.

Evidence is mentioned again in the Instructional practice category in the standard focused on "planning for instruction." This is the one place where education's use of evidence comes closest to how it is used in nursing. The standard states that teachers should "know a range of evidence-based instructional strategies."[14]

Even though the standard states that teachers teach using researched-based instructional practices, we all know of instances where teachers have pointed out, again and again, that teaching to the test is not best practice, only to be ignored like Stephanie was. Stephanie was doing exactly what the nursing standards call for, using research and community engagement practices to better instruct her students, and we saw what happened to her.

The second principle is the importance of having an understanding of, and an ability to work within, *systems*. In nursing, the domain states that an "understanding of systems-based practice is foundational to the delivery of quality care and incorporates key concepts of organizational structure, including relationships among macro-, meso-, and microsystems across health care settings."[15] This standard refers to nurses as "change agents and leaders" and points out that "cognitive shifting from focused to big picture is a crucial skill set" for nurses in relation to the various systems within which they work.

There is nothing that calls for a systems-based approach in the education standards. In fact, the education standards often read as if the teacher is the sole actor, responsible for all educational outcomes. Yes, the education standards point out that the teachers must collaborate with families, colleagues, and communities to "better understand their students and maximize their learning." But collaboration is not the same as understanding and knowing how to work within systems. More importantly, collaboration does not teach teachers how to work within those systems to the best effect for student success.

Like nurses, a teacher's work with her students is impacted by the healthcare, prison, youth services, law enforcement, government, social service, and federal and state educational policy systems. If a teacher does not understand how these systems impact her, and her students, and more importantly, how to interact within these systems, then her efforts in the classroom can be easily thwarted. As the nursing standard states, "integrated systems are highly complex, and gaps or failures in service and delivery can cause ineffective, harmful outcomes. System awareness . . . is also needed to address such issues as structural racism and systemic inequity."[16]

This quote points to the change agent role that nurses are expected to play for their patients and communities. Many teachers also see themselves as change agents and advocates for their students, but what kinds of change can teachers effect if they are not even having conversations about their impact beyond the classroom? The next chapter discusses how an understanding of systems can be integrated into the work of teachers.

The third principle emphasizes the *ability to work in teams*. The education categories highlight the importance of collaboration with families, colleagues, and community organizations, but they do not explain what this looks like on the job, nor do they describe the skills one needs to collaborate well. For example, the two education categories that explicitly refer to collaboration state that "the teacher seeks opportunities to collaborate" and "the teacher works with others two create supportive learning environments."[17]

This is the extent of how they talk about collaboration. The nursing domains explain that

> Partnerships require a coordinated, integrated, and collaborative implementation of the unique knowledge, beliefs, and skills of the full team for the end purpose of optimized care delivery. Effective collaboration requires an understanding of team dynamics and an ability to work effectively in care-oriented teams.[18]

The knowledge that nurses bring to the team is equally valued. "Nursing knowledge and expertise uniquely contribute to the intentional work within teams and in concert with family and community preferences and goals."

Unfortunately, this was not Stephanie's experience. Neither her nor her colleagues' knowledge as the teachers, nor the knowledge of the parents and community members they worked with, was enough to stop the directives that came from the district about how teaching would be approached once the standards were implemented. Productive teamwork does not just happen. It must be valued by the profession. As the nursing standard points out, this requires that

> professional partnerships build on a consistent demonstration of core professional values (altruism, excellence, caring, ethics, respect, communication, and *shared accountability*), in the provision of team-based, person-centered care.

Sadly, the word accountability is not used in the InTASC standards. The word respect is only used to emphasize that teachers must respect students and families, whereas the language in the nursing standard makes clear that respect is required by all, and for all, in order for teams to be successful in providing for the needs of one's clients.

The fourth principle is *professionalism*. Both nursing and education have a domain and several standards focused on professional responsibility. The InTASC document states that teachers have four main professional responsibilities:

> to engage in ongoing professional learning, to use evidence to evaluate their practice, to seek leadership roles and other opportunities to take responsibility for student learning and to collaborate broadly to ensure learner growth and advance the profession.[19]

The education standards do encourage "self-renewal and self-reflection," but they do not address professional ethics, values, and actions that teachers should demonstrate, nor does education address the professional responsibilities that a teacher has to *herself*. It is on these aspects of professional responsibility that the nursing standards focus. The most important thing for nursing is that the nurse develops a professional identity.

> Professionalism encompasses the development of a nursing identity embracing the values of integrity, altruism, inclusivity, compassion, courage, humility, advocacy, caring, autonomy, humanity, and social justice. Professional identity formation necessitates the development of emotional intelligence to promote social good, engage in social justice, and demonstrate ethical comportment, moral courage, and assertiveness in decision making and actions.[20]

This identity requires the nurse to act ethically, to take a participatory approach to her work, to be accountable, and to be an advocate for social justice and equity. Finally, as a professional, the nurse should "demonstrate an awareness of personal and professional values and conscious and unconscious biases"[21] by modeling respect for diversity, equity, and inclusion.

The differences between education and nursing are obvious. Nursing approaches professionalism by emphasizing the values and principles that underlie nursing practice. It stresses those attributes that help the nurse become a caring and competent professional, such as emotional intelligence, courage, advocacy, and so forth. Education approaches professionalism by stressing the instrumental tasks that teachers need to perform: they must keep learning and reflecting, they have to use evidence, and they have to collaborate, among a host of other skills and abilities.

Finally, the fifth and sixth principles, *quality and safety*, and the idea of personal, professional, and leadership *development*, are related. These two principles address what this book is all about, how to maintain the well-being of teachers. For nursing, the quality and safety domain acknowledges that it is the nurse's responsibility to promote a safe environment and quality care. The domain states:

Safety is inclusive of attending to work environment hazards, such as violence, burnout, and so forth. There is a synergistic relationship between employee safety and patient safety. A safe and just environment minimizes risk to both recipients and providers of care. It requires a shared commitment to create and maintain a physically, psychologically, secure and just environment.

It is important to point out that nursing includes three aspects of safety in the work environment that are also crucial for teachers. First, they include violence and burnout as environmental hazards. Second, they emphasize safety for both nurses and patients and acknowledge that quality care is not possible without a sense of safety, and third, they stress *psychological safety*.

In its standards and domains, nursing separates the introspective and personal growth aspects of professional development from the idea of professional responsibility. The *development* domain stresses "participation in activities and self-reflection that foster personal health, resilience, and well-being."[22] It goes further by stating that "the aim is to promote diversity and retention in the profession, self-awareness, avoidance of stress-induced emotional and mental exhaustion, and re-direction of energy from negative perceptions to positive influence through leadership opportunities." Here, nursing directly addresses the impact of workplace stress and how it affects a nurse's emotional and mental health.

Unfortunately, none of the education categories or standards address the well-being of teachers or even mentions stress, burnout, or emotional and mental health. One education standard that hints at this is focused on learning environments which states "the teacher works with others to create environments that support individual and collaborative learning and that encourage positive social interaction."[23] This standard is one place where the educational organizations that helped to create these standards could have addressed the issue of teacher well-being.

For example, we all know that violence is an issue in public schools. In the 2017–2018 school year, at least 71 percent of schools reported at least one violent incident, and 3600 schools reported incidents with a handgun or explosive device. These are extreme examples of how the psychological safety of teachers is compromised, yet this standard on school environments does not mention the impact these incidents have on teachers. This also raises a crucial issue that schools are not talking about, which is how teachers should deal with the systemic nature of many issues that plague schools.

The systemic nature of many workplace challenges is something that nursing names. For example, nursing assigns more responsibility to the systems than it does to individual nurses. This is as it should be, as we all know that 90 percent of the most extreme challenges faced in both hospitals and schools are systemic. The nursing domain states, "quality and safety challenges are viewed primarily as the result of system failures, as opposed to errors of an individual . . . Addressing contributors and barriers to quality and safety, at both individual and system levels, is necessary."[24]

The need to attend to systemic issues in nursing is also reinforced in the American Nurses Association's (ANA) Nursing Code of Ethics which states that nurses are expected to call out questionable practices, the majority of which stem from systemic problems. The code also makes it clear that nurses cannot always act because of institutional policies and systems and calls on nurses to be advocates for patients when this happens.

In these situations, the ANA offers resources that help nurses do this. Most importantly, the nursing code of ethics urges nurses to attend to their own health and safety because only then can they truly care for patients. There is nothing in education that calls on teachers to call out questionable practices by administrators and other school leaders or that encourages them to care for themselves as well as their students.

Finally, the National Education Association (NEA), which is like the ANA, offers resources for teachers. In fact, at the top of their website, under "student success," the NEA has a statement about student and educator health and safety and then a set of resources for teachers that are focused on mental health, gun violence, COVID, facilities, and school crises. The website states, "A child who is sick cannot learn, and a sick educator cannot teach—our elected officials owe it to every parent and family in America to ensure the health and safety of future generations and those who foster them."[25]

However, none of these documents talk about the psychological, day-to-day well-being of teachers. There is no direct discussion of how the school itself, or school policies, contribute to ill health among teachers and what they can do about this. The website also has a statement on teacher quality which focuses on PD and leadership, but nothing on how teacher health impacts quality.

Finally, there is a section on just and equitable schools. Again, the focus is on students and what teachers can do to make schools more just for students. This is a necessary and worthy effort. Teachers are in the best position to make schools more just. But schools also need to be more just for teachers and this needs to be explicitly stated in this and similar documents.

Documents like the InTASC "Model Core Teaching Standards," the AACN's "Core Competencies for Nursing Education," and other standards documents, are important because many are adopted by colleges and universities responsible for preparing these professionals, and instilling the lifelong values espoused by them in new recruits. An analysis of the mission and value statements of the top ten schools of nursing and education in the country shows that there were only two areas of overlap between education and nursing programs. First, they both name their goals of achieving social justice and equity for all patients and students and their focus on diversity and inclusion.

The second area of overlap is their emphasis on instilling strong communication and collaborative skills in candidates. But the similarities end there. Only the nursing programs name the values that guide the profession and emphasize an ethical approach to nursing. A majority of the programs also mentioned the importance of attending to the mental and physical health of nurses, as well as the political and psychological aspects of the profession. None of the top education programs mentioned these things in their mission and vision statements. The next chapter demonstrates how nursing is able to prioritize these aspects of the nurse's working life.

NOTES

1. InTASC is the Interstate Teacher Assessment and Support Consortium and CCSSO is the Council of Chief State School Officers.

2. This research was developed by a committee of representatives from the best known "education organizations" in the nation. It is important to name the most well known: AACTE, NCATE, AFT, NEA, Associate of Teacher Educators (ATE), Learning Forward, National Associations for Elementary and Secondary School Principals, National Board of Professional Teaching Standards (NBPTS), Teacher Ed Accreditation Council (TEAC), National Assoc. of State Boards of Ed. plus eight more organizations.

3. The American Association of Colleges of Nursing (AACN), "The Essentials: Core Competencies for Professional Nursing Education," *The American Association of Colleges of Nursing* (April 2021), 27.

4. The American Association of Colleges of Nursing (AACN), "The Essentials," 27.

5. The American Association of Colleges of Nursing (AACN), "The Essentials," 29.

6. The American Association of Colleges of Nursing (AACN), "The Essentials," 27–28.

7. The American Association of Colleges of Nursing (AACN), "The Essentials," 27–28.

8. The American Association of Colleges of Nursing (AACN), "The Essentials," 27–28.

9. Isaac Opper, "Teachers Matter: Understanding Teacher's Impact on Student Achievement," The Rand Corporation (2019).

10. Se Woong Lee, "Pulling Back the Curtain: Revealing the Cumulative Importance of High-Performing, Highly Qualified Teachers on Students' Educational Outcome," *Educational Evaluation and Policy Analysis*, 40, no. 3 (April 2018).

11. Kirabo Jackson, "What Do Test Scores Miss: The Importance of Teacher Effects on Non-Test Score Outcomes," *Journal of Political Economy*, 126, no. 5 (October 2018).

12. Clive Belfield et al., "The Economic Value of Social and Emotional Learning," *Scholarly Journal*, 6, no. 3 (Fall 2015).

13. Interstate Teacher Assessment and Support Consortium, (InTASC), "Model Core Teaching Standards and Learning Progressions for Teachers," Council of Chief State School Officers (CCSSO) (April 2013), 9.

14. InTASC, "Model Core Teaching Standards," 41.

15. AACN, "The Essentials," 44.

16. AACN, "The Essentials," 44.

17. InTASC, "Model Core Teaching Standards," 8–9.

18. AACN, "The Essentials," 42.

19. InTASC, "Model Core Teaching Standards," 9.

20. AACN, "The Essentials," 49.

21. AACN, "The Essentials," 51.

22. AACN, "The Essentials," 53.

23. InTASC, "Model Core Teaching Standards," 8.

24. AACN, "The Essentials," 53.

25. National Education Association, "School Health and Safety," 2002, https://www.nea.org/healthy-schools.

Chapter 11

School Culture and Environment
More Lessons from the Field of Nursing

Clearly, the field of nursing, from its professional organizations to its preparation programs, has a more uniform approach to how they talk about, and protect, the values and needs of nurses. Why is that? One reason is that nursing, as a profession, is committed to the idea of fostering psychologically safe workplace environments. Psychological safety is defined as an employee's ability to take interpersonal risks at work without feeling that they will be criticized, ostracized, or punished.[1]

PSYCHOLOGICAL SAFETY IN NURSING

For nursing, working in a psychologically safe environment means that they are not afraid to speak up about medical mistakes, for example, whether those mistakes are made by the nurse or the doctor. The nursing profession knows that patient safety is paramount, and a psychologically safe environment encourages the discussion of mistakes, near misses, and other errors that can compromise patient care. Unfortunately, the types of school environments described in chapter 8 are not psychologically safe for teachers.

It does not help that psychological safety is not something that is discussed in the education reform literature. Since the purpose here is to show how education can benefit from the practices of the nursing profession, the notion of psychological safety is discussed from the perspective of nurses and teachers who work in hospitals and schools.

Psychologically safe environments are crucial for workplaces that have the following characteristics: they are interpersonally challenging; the work takes place within a system of high-stakes accountability; the work involves complex human interactions and intense relationships that must be developed as part of the struggle to provide essential services; the work takes place within contexts that require continual employee learning and change. Most significant, the work involves immense uncertainty and interdependence.[2]

These characteristics very closely resemble the public school environment, especially those in under-resourced, urban, and rural schools where teachers struggle to close achievement gaps and to differentiate their instruction so they can effectively teach students with different abilities and from diverse cultural, racial, and economic backgrounds. Teachers do this within a system of high-stakes accountability for student outcomes while being required to continually change their practices "amid scarce resources and intense scrutiny."[3] To work most effectively under these uncertain and ever-evolving conditions teachers must be interdependent and collaborative.

Many features of struggling schools inhibit the school's ability to form a psychologically safe environment. Some of these features are cultural. For example, the schools that Payne studied, as described in chapter 8, had cultures of blame that prevented the teachers from forming healthy relationships with each other. Rigid hierarchical structures contribute to a culture of blame. School cultures that overemphasize the difference in status between a principal, teacher, and paraprofessional, for example, are often perceived by staff as having a heavy emphasis on evaluation.

This perception can lead to a lack of communication across levels, hurting an employee's ability to meet his or her needs for professional success. This can lead to uninspiring teamwork because cultures of blame tend to foster negative emotions, which can infect teacher groups through emotional contagion as discussed in chapter 8. This prevents teams from tackling their professional challenges.

Teachers who work in schools with negative cultures lack a sense of safety in general, causing them to affiliate according to their groups (novice teachers, third floor, etc.) and grievances, isolating themselves within their classrooms. As the second section of this book illustrated, all of this takes a huge toll on teacher well-being. A school's systems and support policies play a big role here as well. Psychologically unsafe schools tend not to have systems that support open communication or structures for dealing with problems of practice.

Finally, the workload is another school feature that hurts psychological safety. Unmanageable workloads cause teachers to experience stress and anxiety that inhibits relationship building and engagement. Psychological safety cannot thrive in a culture of individualism. Individual factors also prevent the formation of psychological safety. For example, novice teachers, who do not have enough experience to have developed a strong sense of teaching efficacy tend to have lower levels of confidence in their teaching ability.

This lack of experience contributes to a new teacher's fear of asking for help or resources. This is one of the many reasons why schools with high turnover, which must rely on novice teachers to fill their ranks year after year, have trouble establishing healthy cultures.

Psychological safety is focused on creating work environments that encourage learning and change in challenging contexts. This is crucial for organizations like hospitals and schools where professionals must continue learning and changing to keep up with the latest research about learning and social/emotional development, and where they must maintain relationships with myriad students, families, and communities. This is what teachers are expected to do in addition to considering the many educational reforms that are introduced on an almost yearly basis.

Teachers need to have a sense of psychological safety to deal with the need to adjust their practice on a daily basis. Yet, many school environments make it all but impossible to enact this kind of change. This reality leads to conditions that make it very hard for adult learning. A very large part of psychological safety is the ability to take risks. Adults who cannot take risks on the job cannot learn on the job.

Psychological safety within schools requires open communication about common goals that are shared across professional levels. Expectations for each role in the school should be clear and collaboratively established. Strong collegial relationships, across levels, are also crucial for psychological safety. Strong relationships lead to a psychologically safe environment because they foster trust and help people to feel cared for on the job. Schools that have a healthy number of teachers with more experience and a stronger sense of self-efficacy promote psychological safety.

This is partly because there are more professionals who have higher levels of expertise, making them feel more confident about taking interpersonal risks and giving others feedback. Finally, schools that have specific systems in place to help employees reach out when they have questions or concerns, or when they need advice about practice, promote psychological safety. These features make it much easier for all professionals in the organization to engage in interpersonal risky behaviors. Being able to engage in these ways at work impacts the professional's ability to adapt and grow on the job. They give employees a voice within the organization by making it easier for them to engage in the following activities:

- Speaking up if there is a problem
- Asking for help
- Engaging in open communication
- Voicing concerns about a particular student or practice or colleague
- Seeking feedback on their own practice or interactions

- Sharing information with each other
- Pointing out errors or mistakes
- Making suggestions for improvement or ways to do things better
- Collaborating and sharing materials

Professionals need a psychologically safe environment in order to engage in the activities on this list, and these practices are required for both individual and organizational growth. Being able to engage in these practices helps workers manage the challenging conditions within which they work. Those challenges include being able to keep up with constant changes in knowledge and practice, learning from mistakes and failures, and facilitating constructive conflict.

In fact, psychological safety is essential in order to have productive conflicts with colleagues about approaches to practice. Professionals can learn a lot when they have different ideas, viewpoints, and opinions about practice, but that learning can only happen if they can discuss their differences in productive ways. Professionals are better able to engage in these behaviors if they feel psychologically safe at work.

Education reformers, school leaders, and teachers need to start talking about psychological safety and ways to implement it in our nation's schools. Among other changes, this will require a very different approach to professional development. First, schools need to do more to consciously help teachers build trusting relationships with each other. This would entail having professional development workshops that focus on inclusive behavior and understanding individual differences that teach teachers how to have open and respectful communication in department and team meetings, and how to resolve conflict when it arises.

These types of professional development workshops, often called "improvisation training," are known to improve psychological safety because they can "increase feelings of equality and encourage team members to be present and listen to one another, [and also, how to] celebrate failure."[4] Teachers also need PD on how to deal with complex and sensitive issues that impact their work and relationships with each other and their students.

Finally, teachers and school leaders need workshops that help them understand how each staff member's roles and responsibilities contribute to student and staff success. This type of information helps teachers and other staff value each other's contributions and foster respect and trust among all school personnel.

Psychological safety in the work environment is one feature that allows nurses to feel safe exercising their voice at work. This is critically important in the field because when nurses make a mistake, patients can die. The finality of death requires this approach. However, the damage done to students when their teachers are overworked and stressed is also a type of death. It is the death of achievement, the death of opportunity, and the death of a shot at living a productive and satisfying life. We should be equally concerned about the social, emotional, and psychological deaths that happen in the classroom for students and teachers every day.

A JUST CULTURE FOR TEACHERS AND TEACHING

Psychological safety is one feature of organizations that have adopted what is called a "just culture."

> Just culture refers to a values-supportive model of shared accountability. It's a culture that holds organizations accountable for the systems they design and for how they respond to staff fairly and justly. In turn, staff members are accountable for the quality of their choices . . . and for the ways they communicate their struggles within the system.[5]

A just culture gives nurses more autonomy over their work. It prevents nurses from being continually held accountable for issues that have systemic causes. The same is not true for teachers, who are continually blamed for problems caused by systemic issues that are completely out of their control. Of course, a comparison between nurses and teachers can only go so far, but education can learn a great deal from how nursing has implemented the just culture framework, especially when it comes to psychological need satisfaction and support for dealing with the more challenging aspects of the professional workplace.

Five major components need to be in place for an organization to implement and follow the tenets of a just culture. The first is a focus on systems. In terms of education, school-based systems are designed to coordinate the work of teachers, counselors, administrators, students, and other staff for optimal learning. Each group within the system has specific roles to fill, which, if fulfilled according to design, lead to the desired outcomes of the school.

Working within a just culture framework is to acknowledge that when things go wrong, 99 percent of the time, it is the systems that are to blame. A hospital or school cannot simply change the people, without also changing the systems if they want to meet their goals. However, we all know that this happens countless times in schools. In fact, removing the people is the main mechanism for reforming "turnaround" schools in this country. We will never truly "reform" our schools if we continue this futile practice.

School-based systems need to be thoroughly interrogated and made transparent. Transparency is the second component of a just culture. The first step toward transparency is the articulation of the commitments and values that professional employees make to themselves, to their colleagues, to the work itself, and to the organization. Hospitals call these Commitment Statements or Credos. For example, Massachusetts General Hospital's Credo[6] states the following:

As a member of the MGH community and in service of our mission, I believe that:

- The first priority at MGH is the well-being of our patients, and all our work, including research, teaching, and improving the health of the community, should contribute to that goal.
- Our primary focus is to give the highest quality of care to each patient delivered in a culturally sensitive, compassionate, and respectful manner.
- My colleagues and I are MGH's greatest assets.
- Teamwork and clear communication are essential to providing exceptional care.

As a member of the MGH community and in service of our mission, I will:

- Listen and respond to patients, patients' families, my colleagues, and community members.
- Ensure that MGH is safe, accessible, clean, and welcoming to everyone.
- Share my successes and errors with my colleagues so we can all learn from one another.
- Waste no one's time.
- Make wise use of the hospital's human, financial, and environmental resources.
- Be accountable for my actions.
- Uphold professional and ethical standards.

Schools also need to develop commitment statements that all professionals can endorse. Based on the MGH model, a school's Commitment Statement might look something like this:

As a member of "Equity" school community and in service of our mission, I believe that:

- The first priority of "Equity" school is the academic, social, and emotional development of our students, and all our work, including teaching, counseling, and coaching, should contribute to that goal.
- Our primary focus is to teach and support each student at the highest quality delivered in a culturally sensitive, compassionate, and respectful manner.
- My colleagues and I are "Equity" school's greatest assets.

- Teamwork and clear communication are essential to providing exceptional instruction and student support.

As a member of "Equity" school community and in service of our mission, I will:

- Listen and respond to students, their families, my colleagues, and community members.
- Ensure that "Equity" school is safe, accessible, clean, and welcoming to everyone.
- Share my successes and lapses with my colleagues so we can all learn from one another.
- Collaborate, communicate, and problem solve with my colleagues so the whole school can ensure success at all levels.
- Be accountable for my actions.
- Uphold professional and ethical standards and values.

Commitment statements like these, articulated and signed by all employees, set the stage for organizational and personal expectations. Once the standards, responsibilities, and values of the organization are articulated, it becomes easier for people to act according to those standards and uphold those values. Individuals are not expected to sustain these actions alone, however. The third component of a just culture, collaboration, which involves communication, trust, and teamwork, is what leads to system monitoring and change. Transparency goes hand in hand with communication and teamwork. A just culture is a learning culture.

Professionals in an organization with a just culture are transparent about areas for improvement. They "openly identify and examine their own weaknesses."[7] They can do this because they feel supported and safe when voicing concerns. They feel comfortable talking about their weaknesses and the types of assistance they need to be successful. This is possible because these employees know that they will not be blamed for systemic problems, rather, they are expected to speak out about system failures when those failures impact the quality of care, or for teachers, of instruction.

One example of how this might work in an educational environment is that it would encourage discussion about why students in the school performed poorly on the latest standardized assessment. The teachers would lead these discussions. Counselors, social workers, paraprofessionals, tutors, and those responsible for school discipline would also be part of the discussion. The teachers would talk about their teaching, including the aspects of the content that they covered to prepare students for the assessment.

They would describe levels of student engagement, as well as the areas that students struggled with during both the preparation and the actual assessment. They would talk about their own struggles when teaching the unit and what contributed to those struggles. Other teachers from the same content area would share their approaches and successes and struggles as well.

The counselors, paras, social workers, and discipline staff would share their strategies for working with the students who struggled. Together, this "team" would examine school-wide factors, classroom factors, student factors, and instructional factors that contributed to student performance on the assessment. They would then use this information to revise their instructional approach, building in more of what worked and changing what did not.

Of course, for these discussions to be successful, schools would need to employ other professionals whose job would be to support the teachers and the student support personnel. There would be a team of data analysts who would be responsible for gathering, analyzing, and sharing student data on all dimensions, not just on standardized assessments. Yes, it is vital that teachers understand and work with student data, but given the amount of data, they cannot be responsible for collecting, organizing, analyzing, and sharing that data themselves. It is just too much given all the other day-to-day responsibilities that teachers have.

Schools need to start hiring full-time data teams. Data gathering and analysis play a large role in a just culture because collecting and understanding the data can uncover systemic issues and lead to system change. However, just cultures do not only prioritize one type of data; they examine all data, student data, teacher data, community data, partner data, administrative data, and support staff data. They focus on data about every aspect that contributes to an organization's main goals. For a school, that would mean collecting data on all aspects that contribute to student learning and development.

Schools would also need to hire a team of professional network coordinators. These positions would be similar to the parent or community liaison positions that many high-needs schools already employ, but their work would go beyond the work of a liaison. These "network coordinators" would be responsible for tracking, contacting, and communicating with the main adults in their students' lives. For some students, this would be the parents, but for others, it could be social workers, courts, coaches, employers, and those in the juvenile justice system.

Yes, teachers need to develop and maintain relationships with their student's parents, but today's students have significant relationships with other adults outside of school. It is vital that schools have an awareness of what those adult connections are and how they are impacting the student's performance in school. As we will see in the next chapter, students benefit tremendously when there are connections between the important adults in their lives. Teachers and student support personnel need help understanding the significance of each student's outside-of-school connections so that they can use those connections to enhance student learning and development.

Accountability, the fourth component, is central to the need for a just culture. The number one goal of organizations that follow just culture principles is their commitment to evaluate and assess individuals justly. In nursing, a just culture acknowledges that most serious errors result from systemic issues. However, the language of "error" does not really work in the educational context. In education, when things go wrong in terms of student learning and development, it is usually because of a problem of practice.

Following the tenets of a just culture laid out above would help educational teams identify the problems of practice that prevent the students in the school from achieving at the expected levels. Those problems of practice could rest with the teacher or the team, or they could result from systemic issues within the school, the family, the community, or the society.

Getting at the cause of these problems is only possible through open communication, collaboration, and transparency. Everyone who works with students needs to be involved to truly unpack the factors that lead to student failure. For example, as we all know, teachers are held accountable for student results on standardized assessments. We also know that in many cases, the students are not learning because of factors completely outside of the teacher's control.

However, unlike in nursing, teachers are blamed and held accountable for those factors, with serious consequences that impact their compensation and even employment. This would not be tolerable within a just cCulture. Of course, one of the issues in education is that many of the systemic aspects of problems that prevent student learning and development are not within the control of the teacher or the school but are a result of forces outside of the schoolhouse.

This is no secret; it is something that educators at the national, state, and local levels know. Yet they persist in holding teachers accountable for local and national social problems. This is not acceptable, and it must stop. Adopting a just culture, with dedicated staff to collect real data and to work with families and communities, is one way that schools, and teachers, can begin to get out of this trap that society has created. Systemic issues cannot be remediated by individual employees, no matter how knowledgeable or "trained" they are.

Hospitals that have adopted a just culture use what is called the "Unsafe Acts Algorithm"[8] to assess individual versus system accountability. The algorithm asks four questions,

- Did the employee intend to cause harm?

- Did the employee come to work drunk or impaired?
- Did the employee knowingly and unreasonably increase risk?
- Would another similarly trained and skilled employee in the same situation act in a similar manner?

If the answers to the first three questions are "no," and to the last question is "yes," then the unsafe act is determined to be organizational or systemic rather than individual.

What might this look like in an educational context? Since education is all about student learning and development, and since teachers are the ones directly responsible for student learning, education might use something called the "preparation for teaching performance algorithm." This algorithm might ask the following questions in relation to the outcomes of a standardized assessment, or any key assessments that the school relies upon to gauge student progress:

- Was the teacher fully prepared to teach the lessons necessary for success on this assessment?
- Did she have unit and lesson plans that she was following?
- Did she have activities ready for the students to engage in?
- Did she differentiate her instruction for students with moderate disabilities, for ESL students?

If the answer to these first four questions is yes, then the team would ask the following four questions:

- What percentage of the teacher's students need special accommodations for academic challenges, for social challenges, for emotional challenges, and for behavioral challenges?
- Are these needed accommodations documented?
- Did the student(s) receive the needed accommodations?
- Has the teacher ever informed other teachers and staff of students' needs?
- Has the teacher discussed her experiences with teaching these students with others?

This last set of questions is about the student's needs and the extent to which the teacher worked to help the student(s) meet their needs. If the teacher has a high percentage of students who need special accommodations, but many of these are not documented or the students do not receive those accommodations, then the teacher knows that it is her responsibility to inform others about the student's needs and to talk about her own experiences in attempting to teach the students who have unmet needs.

These questions hold the teacher accountable for her responsibilities as a teacher while also providing information that the team can use to improve their practice. For example, each teacher in the department can share their unit and lesson plans with each other; they can study and compare their lessons and methods to see which were more or less effective, allowing them all to grow and learn about which methods, content, and practices lead to higher achievement for their students. Finally, these questions clearly reveal where systemic issues play a role in student achievement.

Working within a just culture—one that has a high level of psychological safety—will allow the teacher to feel comfortable and safe in discussing these aspects of her practice because she will know that she will not be ridiculed or criticized for her methods, or held accountable for aspects that are out of her control. She will also feel comfortable talking about any struggles she has had in teaching her students because she knows that she will get support for those struggles.

Finally, the teacher will be held accountable for the aspects of her teaching that do fall under her control such as the need to discuss her struggles with teaching her students, and to be prepared to teach all her lessons.

If the teacher has not fulfilled her main roles and responsibilities, then the school can provide support and training. For those problems that are systemic, then the school, not the teacher, can set about doing whatever it needs to do to fix those systemic problems, at least for the students who attend their school. This will require additional staff with specific professional skills, but it is the only way for high-needs schools to save teachers from the psychological stresses plaguing them in today's educational environment.

This brings us to the last component of a just culture; it must be patient or student-centered. However, one cannot talk about patient or student-centric practices without also discussing the culture of an organization and the structures necessary to ensure that organizational practices and goals are focused on those the organization serves. These aspects of a just culture are discussed in the next chapter.

Once in place, these five components combine to create a sense of psychological safety and trust at work. Feeling safe means that teachers are able to talk about and report problems without the fear of being blamed for those problems, but it also goes beyond problems and reporting. A just culture gives teachers a voice to share their knowledge, their concerns, and their vulnerabilities about certain outcomes or task performances while on the job. This openness, communication, and collaboration is what leads to a learning culture, which is what schools should be, not only for students but for teachers as well! The next chapter examines what this might look like in public schools.

NOTES

1. K. Grailey, E. Murray and T. Reader, "The Presence and Potential Impact of Psychological Safety in the Healthcare Setting: An Evidence Synthesis," *BMC Health Services Research* (2021), doi: 10.1186/s12913-021-06740-6; Roisin O'Donovan, Aolfe Brun and Ellish McAuliffe, "Healthcare Professionals Experience of Psychological Safety, Voice, and Silence," *Frontiers in Psychology* (2021), doi: 10.3389/fpsyg.2021.626689; Amy Edmondson et al., "Understanding Psychological Safety in Health Care and Education Organizations: A Comparative Perspective," *Research in Human Development* (2016), doi: 10.1080/15427609.2016.1141280.

2. Edmondson et al., "Understanding Psychological Safety."

3. Edmondson et al., "Understanding Psychological Safety," 68.

4. Roisin O'Donovan, Aolfe Brun, and Ellish McAuliffe, "Healthcare Professionals Experience," 12.

5. Barbara Brunt, "Developing a Just Culture," *HealthLeaders* (2022) https://www.healthleadersmedia.com/ nursing/developing-just-culture?page=0%2C1.

6. Gregg Meyer and Edward Lawrence, "Just Culture: The Key to Quality and Safety," *Outcome Engineering* (2009), slides 12–13.

7. Allen Frankel, Michael Leonard, and Charles Denham, "Fair and Just Culture, Team Behavior and Leadership Engagement: The Tools to Achieve High Reliability," *Health Research and Educational Trust* (2006), doi: 10.1111/j.1475-6773.2006.00572.x.

8. Allen Frankel, Michael Leonard, and Charles Denham, "Fair and Just Culture," 1697–1698.

Chapter 12

Nurses, Teachers, and Clinical Microsystems

It has become apparent over the last few years that the current struggles plaguing public schools in this country are hurting both students and teachers. Students suffer from low achievement and diminished educational outcomes. Teachers' emotional and physical health has worsened to the point where many are leaving the field. If ever we needed to take a different approach to schooling, the time is now.

Clearly, our reform efforts over the last sixty years have not worked to truly make a difference in schooling. Rather than coming up with more reforms that attempt to work within our increasingly dysfunctional educational system, we need to create new systems. Systems that take a radically new and different approach to how we educate children in our most troubled school districts.

CLINICAL MICROSYSTEMS IN NURSING

But what would this look like? Once again, we can look to the field of nursing for an answer. In nursing, patient care happens in what they call "clinical microsystems," which the field defines as "a small group of people who work together on a regular basis to provide care to discrete subpopulations of patients.... [The clinical microsystem] has linked processes and a shared information environment and it produces performance outcomes."

They are "complex adaptive systems and as such, they must do the primary work associated with the core aims"[1] of the organization. Three overarching principles underscore the work that happens in clinical microsystems, "will, ideas and execution."[2] Everyone who works within a clinical microsystem has the will to provide the best care and services for patients, access to the latest ideas on how to improve care and services, and the ability to execute change quickly when needed.

All adults who work as a team within a clinical microsystem are expected to be actively engaged in achieving the three key goals of the system, "better patient outcomes, better system performance, and better professional development." The team achieves these goals through the focused use of data and the amount of knowledge they have about the patient. However, having knowledge about individual patients is not enough. The team also needs to have information about the entire population of patients served through the microsystem, so that they can better understand trends and anomalies.

The team also needs to be connected to, and have knowledge about, the other clinical microsystems their patients might be part of, both within, and outside of, the hospital. Finally, all staff who work within a particular microsystem must understand that they have two responsibilities. One, they must be responsible for their own work, and two, they must be responsible for continually *improving* their work.

The efforts of the clinical microsystem are reinforced and supported by the larger organization in several ways. First, each microsystem is provided with the knowledge and skills they need to do the best job possible. Second, all staff are given the time and space to learn new knowledge and skills, and the opportunities to put their new knowledge and skills to work by being asked to work on special projects for example. Last, the staff is rewarded for their efforts in these areas with recognition, awards, and opportunities to participate in varied and strategic work roles.

CLINICAL MICROSYSTEMS IN SCHOOLS: AN ECOLOGICAL SYSTEMS APPROACH

We must take a similar approach in schools. This requires that we think about the main components of a school—the classroom, the counseling office, student support offices, athletics, school clubs—as microsystems. Within an educational context, these microsystems would be comprised of small groups of adults and students who work together on a regular basis to aid the learning and development of discrete subpopulations of students.

The classroom would be the most important microsystem. Within each classroom, we would identify the needs of each student on every dimension: academic, social, emotional, and behavioral. We would also identify the needs of the teacher. We would determine, for example, her level of teaching experience and her comfort and knowledge in working with particular groups of students. Most important, the teacher would not be the only professional in the classroom's microsystem.

Depending upon the needs of her students, she would be joined by a social worker, by a teacher specializing in working with students who have moderate disabilities, and also, if necessary, by a teacher who specializes in working with students who speak English as a second language. There might also be one or two paraprofessionals in the classroom. The lead teacher, as a trained professional, would be the one to guide the team, in consultation with the other members, about the best educational practices for that particular class of students given their particular needs.

In the educational context, this is an ecological systems approach. This approach to education would require schools to focus on the relational conditions necessary to create and maintain a healthy school culture while also keeping the need for optimal growth and development of each school constituent—students, teachers, support personnel, and school leaders—at the forefront of their work.

This cultural/developmental approach allows us to focus on two essential aspects of schooling. It is developmental because it acknowledges that part of the work of schools is to foster the continued growth and development of all school constituents, including teachers. For example, we see this in nursing through the constant opportunities nurses have to engage in professional development focused on knowledge, skills, and personal and emotional health and well-being.

It is cultural because it depends upon a transparent and collaborative school culture. This is reflected in the just culture principles of transparency, communication, and collaboration. To change a school's culture, we must first make transparent the relationships, beliefs, behaviors, and expectations of all school stakeholders.

If culture is defined as the unstated values, norms, assumptions, and expectations that shape beliefs and guide behavior over time, then our work in schools must entail *explicitly* helping all school constituents uncover and transform the values, norms, and expectations that guide adult behavior and shape relationships both within and outside of the schoolhouse walls.[3] This cultural/developmental approach provides us with a blueprint for how we can build a just culture framework for schools.

Developmental psychologist Urie Bronfenbrenner's ecology of human development focuses on optimal human development *at all age* levels. This means that in the context of the school, optimal growth and development would be the ultimate goal for all constituents. All other reform efforts, the tightening of educational standards, the strengthening of school partnerships, the overhaul of curriculum, and the restructuring of school communities, would be in service to this goal.

We can think of this as a spotlight that shines on various school constituents at various times. Bronfrenbrenner explains that humans develop within overlapping contexts, or sets, of ecological systems. Changes in one system impact what happens in the other systems. Thus, the ways in which humans develop are a function of the individual, the environment, and the interaction between the two.

First, there is the microsystem. The microsystem is made up of all the settings where the individual has face-to-face relationships. These are the primary settings within an individual's life. Microsystems can be connected like a network. Those connections make up the mesosystem. The third layer is called the exosystem.

The exosystem includes settings within which the individual has no direct contact, but that impact the individual indirectly through interactions with some aspects of the individual's microsystem. For example, a parent's employer can have a great impact on a child, even though the child does not have direct contact with that employer. The fourth layer is the macrosystem. The macrosystem represents the cultural values, laws, policies, structures, and beliefs of a society that impact individuals through their various systems.

As explained in the previous chapter, a key component of a just culture is being student-centered. This chapter focuses on what this might look like in schools. This is a necessary focus in a book about teacher well-being because we cannot improve teachers' emotional and physical health in schools without giving students everything they need to succeed. It is the struggle to properly serve students while fighting against the many political and social barriers that thwart teachers' efforts, that hurts teacher well-being the most.

Ecological systems put new emphasis on the student's total environment or network. This network consists of all a student's microsystems. The face-to-face settings closest to the student include the home, school, neighborhood, friend groups, tutors, and jobs, as well as any social affiliations the student has, such as with the church, sports or social clubs, after-school programs, health care centers, or the courts.

Students who have more connections between their face-to-face settings have a stronger mesosystem and are more likely to develop in healthy ways. One reason for this is that students will have more adults in their lives who understand the student's whole context and who can work with each other to better serve the student's needs. Those settings in which the student has only indirect contact include the parent's workplace, school-based departments, the school committee, some school partners (Figure 12.1).

Working within the context of the school then, an ecological systems model encourages us to ask, with whom does the student have face-to-face contact? In this model, all the student's face-to-face relationships and primary settings become potential contexts for development. These are contexts that teachers and other adults in a student's life must exploit for the well-being of the student. A critical component for optimal student development is relationships.

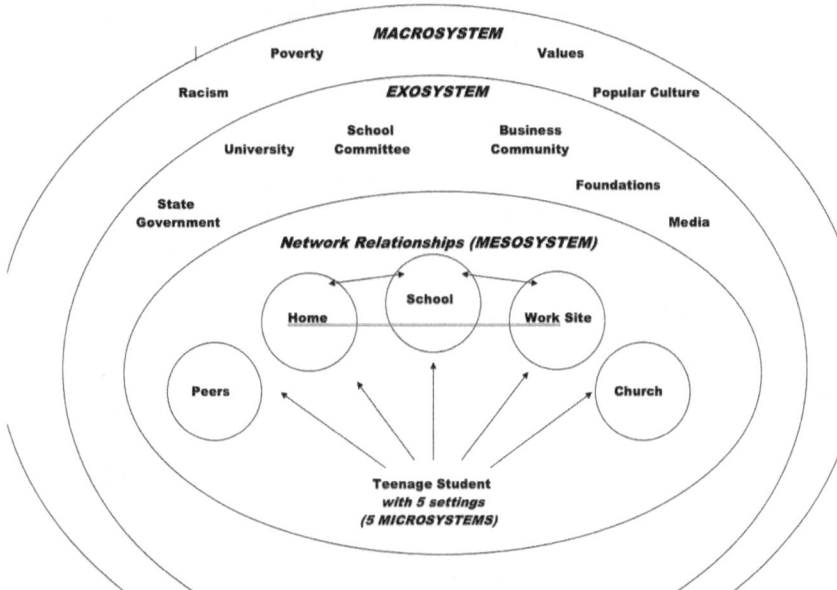

Figure 12.1. One Student's Social, Bioecological Systems. *Source:* Urie Bronfenbrenner, *The Ecology of Human Development*, Harvard University Press, 1979

The capacity of each one of the student's face-to-face relationships for fostering optimal development is enhanced by three things: strong interconnections within and between each setting, effective communication between the adults in each setting, and accurate and up-to-date knowledge about the other settings. In other words, when the adults within and across settings who are responsible for the student's well-being engage in informed, open, face-to-face interactions with each other, the better the student's chances for well-rounded, healthy development.

These social relationships form a network around the student. This network can be tightly woven, with few gaps and strong threads that support and promote the student, or it can be loosely woven, with wide gaps and broken threads that allow the student to fall through. Strong links between the student's primary settings—home and school, school and neighborhood, workplace and school—enhance development; weak, unsupportive links delay development.

We want student networks to be strong, supportive vehicles for student learning and development. Therefore, in struggling schools, and in those schools that have two or more classrooms of students who need extra support, the classroom has to be run like a clinical microsystem. This classroom would be led by a teacher who is responsible for students' academic learning.

This teacher would lead a team of other teachers specializing in moderate disabilities and/or students who speak English as a second language, as well as paraprofessionals and social workers or counselors. The classroom would have a network coordinator and a data specialist attached to it who would be at the ready with information needed by the other adults in their quest to serve the students.

This system would work well at the early childhood and elementary levels, where students spend the whole day with one teacher, leaving occasionally for "specials" or being "pulled out" for extra support in various subjects. In this new model, students would spend the whole day with their team. The team would also have ample time built into the day to discuss each student's progress, needs, and special services. Not all classrooms in the school would need a full team of adults present, only those that had a certain percentage of struggling students.

The system would work a little differently at the high school level. In many low-resourced high schools, about 30 percent or less of the classes are attended by students who struggle with behavioral and social/emotional issues that make teaching more challenging. Other classrooms in the high school may do well with only one or two adults present. The challenging classrooms would have a team of several adults present, again a lead teacher, a social worker, learning specialist, and paraprofessionals. But this team would not manage the services.

These high schools would create a new department or support center that would be responsible for managing the data and maintaining the networks of all the high school students who need special services. This department would be responsible for meeting with the classroom teams and providing them with information about the struggling students in their classrooms. They would also be responsible for meeting with the students and representatives from all of their microsystems. Basically, this department would regularly bring all the adults involved in these students' lives together, so they could all focus on what each student needs.

Sadly, some students do not have many microsystems with which they interact. In addition to their teachers and school support professionals, they may have only a parent or guardian, an employer, and maybe someone from child services, and that is it. In cases like these, the school would work to strengthen the networks the student does have and perhaps help the student expand their networks by helping them to pursue other interests. In these cases, the school would provide the strongest network of adults for each student. This alone would go a long way toward improving student behavior and learning outcomes.

The quality of direct relationships in the student's primary settings is only part of the story, however. Students are also impacted by decisions made in settings outside of their networks. Thus, when the state legislature passes educational reform laws or when an employer changes a parent's working hours, these decisions directly impact the quality of the relationships between students and adults within some of their face-to-face settings. Even though the student is not involved in these settings as a direct participant, events and decisions made in these settings influence and affect what happens in other primary settings.

Thus, the forces that impact the adults who interact with a particular child influence that child as well. This is especially true of the forces that impact the students' teachers. As we have seen in previous chapters, teachers who are not well will have a harder time contributing to the optimal development of their students. Also, teachers cannot navigate each student's network on their own. This is why it is crucially important to have school staff who are explicitly responsible for managing and maintaining student networks, making sure that all school personnel have relevant information about each student.

Today's high schools are also surrounded by networks of people whose members most likely do not have direct, face-to-face contact with students. For example, school administrators, district personnel, business and university partners, school boards, and unions do have direct relations with teachers, school leaders, tutors, and guidance counselors, but not with students.

In most cases, the individuals and organizations that make up this second-level network are once removed from students. But this network is important for teachers. The strength of the interconnections between the teachers and the members of this network either enhances or inhibits the ability of the teachers, tutors, and guidance counselors to do their job in the service of students.

For example, unions need to have information about the needs of the students their teachers teach, and then they need to advocate on behalf of those students. Students are a key part of a teacher's life in schools. What happens with students, impacts teachers. Therefore, unions cannot only advocate for teachers but must also work to make sure that student issues are resolved. If students are suffering or not getting needed services, then teachers will suffer. This must become a union issue.

The same is true for businesses and universities that partner with schools. These organizations most likely work with either student or teacher groups, but seldom work across both groups. These organizations, especially the business community, often have more power than teachers and other school personnel. They need to use that power in service to any issues that prevent the teachers from teaching and the students from learning.

One example of how business and university partnerships used their power to make sure students got what they needed in terms of academic support took place in Boston. The principal at Dorchester High School[4] (DHS) wanted his teachers to be more involved in planning systemic, school-wide reform efforts. The school's business partner at the time, New England Telephone (NET) sponsored a day-long retreat that NET used for management training called "Investment in Excellence."

The workshops emphasized enhanced self-esteem, motivation, and personal goal setting; those who attended the workshops were so enthusiastic that they held another for more staff. It is important to note that these first workshops for teachers focused on personal change. In addition to NET, faculty from DHS's university partner, the University of Massachusetts/Boston, worked with the department heads to improve their own planning and self-evaluation strategies so that they could in turn improve their curriculum planning and their supervision skills. UMass Boston also worked directly with DHS teachers to establish think tanks and run summer institutes that focused on curricular issues of interest to the teachers.

New England Telephone was powerful in Boston business circles and a leader of the Private Industry Council (PIC). The company played a key role in helping PIC to understand the true needs of the school. For example, PIC had been working with DHS to place students in summer jobs. PIC believed that providing jobs in area businesses would motivate the students to improve their attendance and academic performance at school.

PIC worked with a few teachers to get referrals, but after the students were placed for the summer, their contact with the teachers was minimal. PIC maintained contact with the students, but the students lost sustained contact with the teachers in their school microsystem. Yes, they were able to work and earn money over the summer, but their academic and school performance did not improve because the students did not get help in connecting the two experiences.

Once New England Telephone started working with PIC, thus connecting two entities from the students' exosystem, real systemic change came to DHS. Specifically, PIC partnered with teachers to create a program called Compact Ventures which provided academic and social support to at-risk ninth graders at the school. Compact Ventures operated like a clinical microsystem. Each teacher in the program was a member of a cluster of four teachers who met daily to discuss student progress. The teachers developed close relationships with the students because the students moved through their classes as a cohort, taking English, reading, math, and science with the same teachers.

This allowed the teachers to catch problems early, whether personal, social, or academic. The cluster also employed a youth worker and three teaching assistants to work in the classrooms. Tutors were available to work with the students in all subject areas. The principal gave the Compact teachers a lot of autonomy to run the program as they saw fit. Common planning time was a key feature of Compact Ventures; the teachers held daily meetings to discuss student needs and curriculum planning.

The program succeeded in improving the academic outcomes for students. In September, half of the students in the cluster were reading at a fifth-grade level. By June, their reading level had jumped to mid-year seventh grade. The most telling sign of success was revealed in the 11 percent drop-out rate for Compact Venture freshmen, as compared to DHS's 22 percent drop-out rate for ninth graders the previous year.

This is an example of what can happen with business and university partners working with both teachers and students to effect change in high-needs schools. In this case, the partners used their power and resources to create a small community (a clinical microsystem) that gave teachers the resources and connections to successfully improve academic outcomes for their high-needs students.

Finally, in addition to this second-level network, there is a third level, outside network operating in the service of schools. This network involves the local and state government, school funders, and the media. The individuals in this network most likely have direct relations with the district and business and university partners working with the school, but not with the teachers or school administrators.

Strong interconnections between this third-level network and members of the second-level network also enhance or inhibit the ability of the second-level network to do their job in service to the school. These examples show how an ecological systems approach to educational reform allows us to highlight the relationships across levels so that we can shine the spotlight on any set of individuals, organizations, or networks, from multiple contexts or settings so that we can pinpoint exactly what services are needed and by which constituents.

This leads to what we believe is the most important question for those leading school reform efforts—on whom is the spotlight focused? For optimal growth and development, the students and those that they have direct relationships with, must be the ultimate focus; however, in order to realize optimal student development, sometimes the spotlight must be on teachers and other school staff.

When business, university and community partners, school districts, and state and federal governments work with schools, it is important to view school personnel as developing persons and to view schools as developing institutions. For example, we know that teachers are developing in many ways in their role as teachers. We also know that teachers benefit greatly when their roles are expanded and when they gain more responsibility and autonomy over their working lives. This is especially true for teachers who are developing their capacity to teach diverse individuals in challenging contexts.

When we focus the spotlight on a particular constituent within the context of the school, we end up working with a different network of individuals, and within different settings. For example, when the student is in the reformer's spotlight, it becomes necessary to focus also on the settings and individuals with whom the student has direct relationships, like her teachers, parents, employers, peers, tutors, coaches, and friends. These individuals make up the student's primary network.

Therefore, when outside partners want to work directly with students, they must also work within, and become a part of, the students' other networks. Other educational reformers may choose to work closely with teachers, thus putting those teachers in the spotlight. In this case, it becomes necessary to also focus on those settings and individuals with whom the teacher has direct relationships, such as her students, other teachers, school leaders, paraprofessionals, union representatives, student support personnel, and school counselors or social workers.

This framework not only helps us understand and create optimal environments for all school constituents as developing people, but it also helps us understand and create optimal environments for developing institutions. High-needs schools, by virtue of the intense focus and effort by many sectors in society to reform them, are developing institutions. It follows then that educational reformers, and business, university, and community partners, can enhance the overall growth and development of the school as an institution if they approach the school from an ecological perspective.

Relationships between the school and its partners ought to be as reciprocal as possible, with a "mutuality of positive feeling and a gradual shift of the balance of power in favor of the developing" institution.[5] Those who work with schools must be mindful of the developmental needs of school personnel and the developmental needs of the school as a developing institution.

Finally, development is impacted by the ideological and cultural belief systems that shape the behaviors and actions of those who occupy particular settings. Every environment or setting operates within a sea of unstated values, norms, assumptions, and expectations. For example, the various environments that urban and rural students have to navigate, such as the school, the neighborhood, and their homes and workplaces, are often shaped by different or even conflicting cultures.

Those who have strong interconnections between their primary settings—between their home and school or school and workplace—can more successfully navigate the transitions between settings that operate according to different cultural rules.[6]

CULTURAL REFORM AND THE ECOLOGICAL SYSTEMS MODEL

Some high-needs schools also need help transforming their school cultures. Creating and maintaining school cultures that provide optimal opportunities for growth and development of all constituents is a very complex task. It's complex because it involves reflection, introspection, and change on the part of all stakeholders both within and outside of the schoolhouse walls. We can't forget that culture is always local. For example, in each setting in which the student participates, there is a prevailing culture—a culture which can be supportive or encouraging or achievement-oriented or neglectful or toxic.

When there is cultural consistency across the student's primary settings, when the cultures are complementary, students will prosper; when the cultures across settings are contradictory, healthy development is undermined. Furthermore, the world of the student is embedded in a larger sea of cultural forces, cultures that predominate in central administration, the school committee, or community partners, for example.

Each of these, in turn, operates in the sphere of American values and belief systems that predominate in society and are heralded in the media. What is important for the student's welfare is that the clash or complement of cultures has an impact on development. For these reasons, it is important for anyone working with schools, especially policy makers, to be cognizant of the networks that surround teachers and students, as well as the cultural environments in which those individuals operate in order to know if the proposed reforms will help or hinder learning and development.

In other words, understanding only the internal culture of one school is not sufficient to explain the failure of effective school reforms. We must also understand the many cultural settings that influence the student, directly and indirectly, and consider the relationship between these cultural settings. As Bronfenbrenner says, the "key to the enhanced effectiveness of public education lies not within the school itself but in its interconnections with other settings in the society."[7]

This is why we must adopt an ecological approach to educational reform, for ecology focuses on the big picture of relationships between organisms and their various environments. An ecologist, for example, may study a field, noting the ecological niches where various birds, mammals, and reptiles live and how the niches are arranged and interact with one another. We need to understand schools in the same way. An ecological approach delivers us from fixating on one local culture and helps us capture the relationships between cultures.

An ecological systems approach to educational reform, with its additional emphasis on human development and cultural cohesion, can be distinguished from many other known approaches to school reform. However, many of these approaches to reform do not focus on student and teacher needs (although they may claim to). Current efforts also tend not to distinguish between direct relationships, indirect relationships, and the various networks of stakeholders described above.

The ecological model posited here stresses two points about school reform. First, we can't focus solely on the tasks and practices in which schools, and teachers, engage. We must also focus on the health, well-being, and development of teachers and students, the key stakeholders of the educational enterprise. Second, reforms need to extend outward to build relationships with all the settings that impact students, and thus pave the way for teachers to focus on creating educational experiences that foster student learning and development.

JUST CULTURE AND RELATIONAL TRUST

This is one reason why schools need to adopt a just culture framework. The focus on transparency, communication, and collaboration builds trust between all the stakeholders in a school. The concept of relational trust helps us begin to think about the dynamics of forming relationships both within schools, between colleagues, and between schools and other parent and community settings. Schools function better for students and adults when there are strong relationships among and between all stakeholders.

However, the work of schools is dependent upon various sets of interpersonal exchanges between individuals who are "mutually dependent" upon each other. For example, teachers depend upon parents to ensure that students will complete homework and be prepared to participate in school each day. Parents depend upon teachers to properly educate and care for their children. Teachers depend upon other teachers to share practices, provide feedback, and offer support. Finally, teachers depend upon administrators and school leaders to enact and maintain school policies that enable them to successfully fulfill their roles as teachers.

"These structural dependencies create feelings of vulnerability for the individuals involved. This vulnerability is especially salient in the context of asymmetric power relations." As discussed in previous chapters, there are many asymmetric power relations in schools, between novice and veteran teachers, between administrators and teachers, between teachers and paraprofessionals, and between teachers and parents. "A recognition of this vulnerability by the superordinate party and a conscious commitment on their part to relieve the uncertainty and unease of the other can create a . . . meaningful social bond among the parties."[8] Just cultures foster trust through psychological safety.

THE IMPACT OF ROLE EXPECTATIONS ON RELATIONSHIPS

A sense of relational trust is needed in order for the stakeholders in a school community to successfully overcome the vulnerabilities set up by their "mutual dependencies." In the ecology of a school each of the stakeholder groups—teachers, students, parents, support personnel, and school leaders—have their own understanding of the roles that others are supposed to play. These understandings are accompanied by expectations about how those who hold a particular role are supposed to behave, and how others are supposed to act toward them.

Roles themselves, especially those as established as "teacher," "principal," and "parent," are imbued with societal, cultural, and historical meaning.[9] These larger contextual meanings also influence the activities engaged in and the relationships established with other stakeholders while the role is enacted. A sense of relational trust is cultivated when the role expectancies each party has of the other are reciprocated.

Therefore, cultivating relational trust is the first step toward establishing quality relationships among all school stakeholders. All too often, in the most challenging high-needs schools, students and teachers have expectations about each other's roles that differ from actual behavior. Parents and teachers also get caught in this same trap. If too many teachers and parents experience role deviation in their relations with each other, this contributes to the stream of negative knowledge exchanged between the two systems.

This in turn sours communication and weakens the connections between home and school. Unfulfilled role expectations also hurt teacher-to-teacher and teacher-to-para relations, causing division and dissension among the school staff. Eventually, too much deviation from role expectations breeds anger among all stakeholders, poisoning the school culture.

Frustration, disappointment, and outright anger over unfulfilled role expectations are, unfortunately, a very common occurrence in many under-resourced schools. As we saw in previous chapters, it is nearly impossible for curricular reforms to tackle this problem. Structural reforms can help, but without explicit support in untangling these frustrations, it is very difficult for school stakeholders to see their way out of this kind of relational trouble. Focused cultural reform—reform that explicitly targets the norms, beliefs, and expectations embedded within the school community—is the only way to help schools combat this kind of difficulty.

Unfortunately, high-needs schools face many obstacles to achieving the kind of role reciprocity that cultivates relational trust. Bryk and Schneider studied the conditions that either foster or inhibit relational trust between various stakeholders in schools. They found that it was more difficult to establish relational trust between teachers and parents in schools that had a high rate of mobility. When school populations are stable, parents and teachers have more opportunities to interact over time. It is also more difficult to establish relational trust between teachers and parents in schools that have a history of academic failure.

Parents are more likely to see teachers as professionals when there are outside indicators of school-wide achievement. Schools with racial and ethnic tension have more difficulty establishing relational trust between all stakeholders, with schools that serve predominantly African American students reporting the lowest levels of relational trust. This contributes to the toxic school cultures we saw through Payne's work in the first part of this book. Last, Bryk and Schneider found that it is easier to establish relational trust in smaller schools where there are fewer people and more opportunities to communicate.

DEVELOPING INDIVIDUALS AND DEVELOPING INSTITUTIONS

At the most fundamental level, an ecological approach to school reform allows educational reformers to shine the spotlight on any of the networks operating within, or in service to, the school. Ultimately, the spotlight must shine on both students and teachers, lighting the way toward optimal learning and development for both. Toward this end, however, it is crucial to examine and highlight the interconnections and relationships at all levels, meaning the networks that comprise the student's primary settings, the networks that support teachers, and the networks at the upper echelons that support school districts and set school policy.

What the spotlight does is enable school reformers to understand who has face-to-face relations with whom; this in turn allows us to understand what types of networks are operating to serve the student and the teachers, what is missing from the networks, and most importantly, whether those networks have relationships with each other.

We have seen that mandated reforms coming from on high do not work. Schools need relationships, connections, and a cohesive, just culture. Teachers need psychological safety and autonomy. It can be said that as a country, despite all of our efforts to reform high-needs, low-achieving schools; despite knowing more about what's needed; we have not learned a lot from our mistakes, and we have not grown more reflective about our limited successes. True system-wide improved achievement in our nation's most challenging schools has eluded us. This is because we have shied away from a focus on teacher well-being, building relationships, maintaining connections, and on creating healthy cultures for teachers and students within schools. Worst of all, we have forgotten that without the teacher there can be no learning or development. Teachers need support, psychological safety, and autonomy to translate their knowledge into practice. We have forgotten how central the teacher is to the optimal learning and development of all students. However, there is hope for a better education system—and, in turn, a better world—but only if we remember that teachers are an integral part of the future, one that we must build together!

NOTES

1. Eugene Nelson et al., "Microsystems in Health Care: Part 1. Learning from High Performing Front-Line Clinical Units," *The Joint Commission on Accreditation of Healthcare Organizations* (September 2002), 474.

2. Eugene Nelson et al., "Clinical Microsystems, Part 1. The Building Blocks of Health Systems," *The Joint Commission Journal on Quality and Patient* Safety (July 2008).

3. Urie Bronfrenbrenner, *The Ecology of Human Development: Experiments by Nature and Design* (Cambridge, MA: Harvard University Press, 1979), 22.

4. Dorchester High School was closed in 2003.

5. Urie Bronfrenbrenner, *The Ecology of Human Development*, 59.

6. Terrence Deal and Kent Peterson, *Shaping School Culture: The Heart of Leadership* (San Francisco, CA: Jossey-Bass, 2003), 3.

7. Urie Bronfrenbrenner, *The Ecology of Human Development*, 226.

8. Anthony Byrk and Barbara Schneider, *Trust in Schools: A Core Resource for Improvement* (New York, NY: Russell Sage Foundation, 2002), 20.

9. Urie Bronfrenbrenner, *The Ecology of Human Development*, 59.

Bibliography

Allen, Scott, and Maria Cramer. "Crime Consumed a Family, and an 8-year-old Is Lost." *The Boston Globe*, August, 2007.
The American Association of Colleges of Nursing, (AACN). "The Essentials: Core Competencies for Professional Nursing Education." *The American Association of Colleges of Nursing* (AACN) (April 2021).
Anne E. Casey Foundation. "Children Living in High-Poverty, Low-Opportunity Neighborhoods." *The Anne E. Casey Foundation www.aecf.org*, 2017.
Anne E. Casey Foundation. "Children in Poverty by Race and Ethnicity in the US." Kids CountData Center. https://datacenter.kidscount.org/data/tables/44-children-in-poverty-by-race-and-ethnicity#detailed/1/any/false/37,871,870,573,869,36,868,867,133,38/10,11,9,12,1,185,13/324,323.
Arnsten, Amy. "Stress Signaling Pathways that Impair Prefrontal Cortex Structure and Function." *Natural Review Neuroscience* 10, no. 6 (2009): 410–422. doi: 10.1038/nrn2648.
Arvidsdotter, Tina. "Understanding Persons with Psychological Distress in Health Care." *Scandinavian Journal of Caring Science*s (2015): 687–94. doi: 10.1111/scs.12289.
Barksdale-Ladd, Mary Alice, and Karen Thomas. "What's at Stake in High Stakes Testing: Teachers and Parents Speak Out." *Journal of Teacher Education* 51, no. 5 (2000): 384–97. doi:10.1177/0022487100051005006.
Barsade, Sigal, Constantinos Coutifaris, and Julianna Pellemer. "Emotional Contagion in Organizational Life." *Research in Organizational Behavior* 38 (December, 2018): 137–51. doi:10.1016/jriob.2018.11.005.
Belfield, Clive, et al. "The Economic Value of Social and Emotional Learning." *Scholarly Journal* 6, no. 3 (Fall 2015): 508–44.
Bell, Lee Anne. "Sincere Fictions: The Pedagogical Challenges of Preparing White Teachers for Multicultural Classrooms." *Equity and Excellence in Education* 35, no. 3 (2002): 263–44. doi:10.1080/713845317.

Blackwell, D. "Family Structure and Children's Health in the US: Findings from the National Health Interview Survey, 2001–2007." *National Center for Health Statistics*. (2010).

Bradley, G. "Self-Serving Bias in the Attribution Process: A Reexamination of the Fact or Fiction Question." *Journal of Personality and Social Psychology* 36, no. 1 (1978): 56–71.

Broeck, Anja V., et al. "A Review of Self-Determination Theory's Basic Psychological Needs at Work." *Journal of Management* 42, no. 5 (July 2016): 1195–1229. doi: 10.1177/0149206316632058.

Bronfrenbrenner, Urie. *The Ecology of Human Development: Experiments by Nature and Design*. Cambridge, MA: Harvard University Press, 1979.

Brooks-Gunn, Jeanne, and Greg J. Duncan. "The Effects of Poverty on Children." *The Future of Children* 7, no. 2 (Summer/Autumn, 1997): 55–71.

Brunt, Barbara. "Developing a Just Culture." *HealthLeaders Media* (May, 2010): 13.

Brunt, Barbara. "Developing A Just Culture." *HealthLeaders* (2022): https://www.healthleadersmedia.com/nursing/developing-just-culture?page=0%2C1.

Bushaw, William J., and Shane J. Lopez. "A Time for Change." *Phi Delta Kappa*, 2010.

Byrk, Anthony, and Barbara Schneider. *Trust in Schools: A Core Resource for Improvement*. New York, NY: Russell Sage Foundation, 2002.

Centers for Disease Control and Prevention. *CDC.gov*. (2006–2017). https://www.cdc.gov/drugoverdose/deaths/index.html.

Chang, Mei-Lin. "An Appraisal Perspective of Teacher Burnout: Examining the Emotional Work of Teachers." *Education Psychology Review* 21 (2009): 193–218. doi: 10.1007/s10648-009-9106-y.

Chiwoko, Adaeze. Facebook. https://www.facebook.com/adaezec/videos/10159069450324796.

Cochran Smith, Marilyn, and Ana Maria Villegas. "Preparing Teachers for Diversity and High Poverty Schools: A Research-Based Perspective." In *Teacher Education for High Poverty Schools*, edited by Jo Lampert and Bruce Burnett, 932. New York, Spring 2015.

Coggshall, Jane, et al. "Retaining Teacher Talent: The View from Generation Y." *Learning Point Associates & Public Agenda* (2010): 716.

Coggshall, Jane, Amber Ott, and Molly Lasagna. "Retaining Teacher Talent: Convergence and Contradictions in Teacher Perceptions of Policy Reform Ideas." *Learning Point Associates and Public Agenda* (2010): 119.

Cohen, Jennifer L. "Teachers in the News: A Critical Analysis of one US Newspaper's Discourse on Education." *Discourse: Studies in the Cultural Politics of Education* 31, no. 1 (February 2010): 105–19.

Damasio, Antonio. *The Feeling of What Happens: Body and Emotion in the Making of Consciousness*. New York, NY: Harcourt, Inc., 1999.

Deal, Terrence, and Kent Peterson. *Shaping School Culture: The Heart of Leadership*. San Francisco, CA: Jossey-Bass, 2003.

Desi, Edward, L. Koestner, and Richard Ryan. "A Meta-Analytic Review of Experiments Examining the Effects of Extrinsic Rewards on Intrinsic Motivation." *Psychological Bulletin* 125 (1999): 627–68.

Duffy, Ryan, et al. "Calling and Life Satisfaction: It's Not About Having It, It's About Living It." *Journal of Counseling Psychology* 60, no. 1 (2013): 42–52. doi: 10.1037/a0030635.

Edmondson, Amy, et al. "Understanding Psychological Safety in Health Care and Education Organizations: A Comparative Perspective." *Research in Human Development* (2016): 65–83. doi: 10.1080/15427609.2016.1141280.

Elliot, Richard. "A Model of Emotion Driven Choice." *Journal of Marketing Management* 14 (1998): 95–108.

Erb, C. "The Emotional Whirlpool of Beginning Teachers' Work." In annual meeting of the *Canadian Society of Studies in Education*, Toronto, Canada. (2002).

Farkas, Steve, Jean Johnson, and Tony Foleno. *A Sense of Calling: Who Teaches and Why: A Report from Public Agenda*. Public Agenda, 2000.

Felitti, V., et al. "Relationship of Childhood Abuse and the Household Dysfunction to Many of the Leading Cause of Death in Adults, The Adverse Childhood Experiences (ACE) Study." *Journal of Preventive Medicine* 14, no. 4 (May 1998): 245–58. doi: 10.1016/s0749-3797(98)00017-8.

Fenstermacher, G. "Some More Considerations on Teaching as a Profession." (1990) p. 133 as quoted by Erin Sugrue in "Moral Injury Among Professionals in K–12 Education." *American Educational Research Journal* 57, no. 1 (February 2022): 43–68.

Fikri, Kenan, and John Lettieri. "From Great Recession to Great Reshuffling: Charting a Decade of Change Across American Communities." *Economic Innovation Group* (2018): 1–29.

Frankel, Allen, Michael Leonard, and Charles Denham. "Fair and Just Culture, Team Behavior and Leadership Engagement: The Tools to Achieve High Reliability." *Health Research and Educational Trust* (2006): 1690–709. doi: 10.1111/j.1475-6773.2006.00572.x.

Froese-Germain, Bernie. "Educational Accountability with a Human Face." *Canadian Teachers' Federation* (2004).

Gallup. "State of America's Schools: The Path to Winning Again in Education." *Gallup, Inc.* (2014). http://www.gallup.com/services/178709/state-america-schools-report.aspx.

Glaser, Danya. "The Effects of Maltreatment on the Developing Brain." *Medico-Legal Journal* 82, no. 3 (2014): 97–111. doi: 10.1177/0025817214540395.

Goldstein, Dana. *The Teacher Wars: A History of America's Most Embattled Profession*. New York: Penguin Random House, 2014.

Gonsalves, Lisa. "The Dance of Safety: Examining the Stances Taken by White Faculty in Relation to Black Males." In *English Studies: Learning Climates that Cultivate Racial and Ethnic Diversity*, edited by V. Villanueva and S. Fowler, 7–21, Washington, DC: American Association of Higher Education, 2002.

Gonsalves, Lisa, and Jack Leonard. *New Hope for Urban Schools: Cultural Reform, Moral Leadership and Community Partnership*. Westport, CT: Praeger, 2007.

Graham, Sandra. "An Attributional Theory of Motivation." *Contemporary Educational Psychology* 61 (April 2020): 1–11. doi: 10.1016/j.cedpsych.2020.101861.

Grailey, K., et al. "The Presence and Potential Impact of Psychological Safety in the Healthcare Setting: An Evidence Synthesis." *BMC Health Services Research* (2021): 733. doi: 10.1186/s12913-021-06740-6.

Greenberg, M., T. Brown, and R. Abenavoli. "Teacher Stress and Health Effects on Teachers, Students and Schools." *Edna Bennett Pierce Prevention Research Center, Pennsylvania State University* (2017).

Griffith, K. "Column: The Growth of a Just Culture." *The Joint Commission Perspectives on Patient Safety* 9, no. 12 (2009): 8–9.

Hannibal, Kara E., and Mark D. Bishop. "Chronic Stress, Cortisol Dysfunction, and Pain: A Psychoneuroendocrine Rationale for Stress Management in Pain Rehabilitation." *Physical Therapy* 94, no. 12 (2014). 1816–25. doi: 10.2522/ptj.20130597.

Hargreaves, Andy. *Changing Teachers, Changing Times: Teachers' Work and Culture in the Postmodern Age.* New York: Continuum, January 2001.

Harris, Deborah L., and Helene M. Anthony. "Collegiality and Its Role in Teacher Development: Perspectives from Veteran and Novice Teachers." *Teacher Development* 5, no. 3 (2001): 127–28. doi: 10.1080/13664530100200150.

Heine, Steven J., Travis Proulx, and Kathleen D. Vohs. "The Meaning Maintenance Model: On the Coherence of Social Motivations." *Personality and Social Psychology Review* 10, no. 2 (2006): 88–110.

Hiatt, Diana. "Parent Involvement in American Public Schools: A Historical Perspective." *School Community Journal* 4, no. 2, (Fall/Winter, 2000): 247–58.

Hirsch, E., and S. Emerick. "Teacher Working Conditions are Student Learning Conditions." *A Report on the 2006 North Carolina Teacher Working Conditions Survey* (2007).

Hogg, Michael. "Subjective Uncertainty Reduction through Self-Categorization: A Motivational Theory of Social Identity Processes." *European Review of Social Psychology* 11, no. 1 (2000): 223–55. doi: 10.1080/14792772043000040.

Howes, Loene M., and Jane Goodman-Delahunty. "Teacher's Career Decisions: Perspectives on Choosing Teaching Careers, and on Staying or Leaving." *Issues in Educational Research* 25, no. 1 (2015): 18–35.

Isen, A., and P. Lavin. "The Effect of Feeling Good on Helping: Cookies and Kindness." *Journal of Personality and Social Psychology* 21 (1972): 38–48.

Jackson, Kirabo. "What Do Test Scores Miss: The Importance of Teacher Effects on Non-Test Score Outcomes." *Journal of Political Economy* 126, no. 5 (October 2018): 2072–107.

Jarzabkowsli, Lucy. "The Social Dimensions of Teacher Collegiality." *Journal of Educational Enquiry* 3, no. 2 (2002): 1–20.

Johnson, Jean. "Will it be on the Test?: A Closer Look at How Leaders and Parents Think about Accountability in the Public Schools." *The Public Agenda & The Kettering Foundation* (2013).

Johnson, Jean, Ana Marian Arumi, and Amber Ott. "Reality Check 2006: Issue No. 3: Is Support for Standards and Testing Fading?" *Education Insights at Public Agenda* (2006): 1–25.

Johnson, Jean, Jonathan Rochkind, and Samantha Dupont. "Don't Count us Out: How an Overreliance on Accountability Could Undermine the Public's Confidence in

Schools, Business, Government and More." *The Public Agenda & The Kettering Foundation* (2011).

Johnson, Susan Moore. *Where Teachers Thrive: Organizing Schools for Success.* Cambridge, MA: Harvard Education Press, 2019.

Johnson, Susan M., Matthew A. Kraft, and John P. Papay. "How Context Matters in High Needs Schools: The Effects of Teachers' Working Conditions on Their Professional Satisfaction and Their Student's Achievement." *Teachers College Record* 114 (2012): 1–39.

Jones, Mark, et al. "A Brief History of the Opioid Epidemic and Strategies for Pain Medicine." *Pain and Therapy*, 7, no. 1 (April, 2018): 13–21.

Jorgensen, Margaret A., and Jenny Hoffman. "History of No Child Left Behind Act of 2001 (NCLB)." *Pearson* (August 2003): 1–8.

Kaiser Family Foundation. "Opioid Overdose Death Rates." *KFF.org*, 20062017. https://www.kff.org/other/state-indicator/opioid-overdose-death-rates/?currentTimeframe=0&sortModel=%7B%22colId%22:%22 Location%22,%22sort%22:%22asc%22%7D.

Kamenetz, Anya. "More Than Half of Teachers are Looking for the Exits, A Poll Says." *NPR*, February, 2022. https://www.npr.org/2022/02/01/1076943883/teachers-quitting-burnoutFieldCodeChanged.

Kardos, Susan M., et al. "Counting on Colleagues: New Teachers Encounter the Professional Cultures of Their Schools." *Educational Administration Quarterly* 37, no. 2 (April 2001): 250–90.

Keefe-Perry, Callid. "Called into the Crucible: Vocation and Moral Injury in US Public School Teachers." *Religious Education* (2018): 489–500. doi: 10.1080/00344087.2017.1403789.

Kenworthy, Jared, et al. "A Trans-paradigm Theoretical Synthesis of Cognitive Dissonance Theory: Illuminating the Nature of Discomfort." *European Review of Social Psychology* 22, no. 1 (2011): 36–113. doi: 10.1080/10463283.2011.580155.

Klein, Alyson. "Superficial Self-Care? Stressed Out Teachers Say No Thanks." *Education Week* (March 2022).

Kohli, Rita. "Behind School Doors: The Impact of Hostile Racial Climates on Urban Teachers of Color." *Urban Education* 53, no. 3 (2018).

Lampert, Magdalene. *Teaching Problems and the Problems of Teaching.* Yale University Press, 2003.

Lau, Kim, Evelyn Dandy, and Lorrie Hoffman. "The Pathways Program: A Model for Increasing the Number of Teachers of Color." *Teacher Education Quarterly* 24, no. 4 (Fall 2007).

Lavergne, Karine, and Luc Pelletier. "Predicting Individual Differences in the Choice or Strategy to Compensate for Attitude-Behavior Inconsistencies in the Environmental Domain." *Journal of Environmental Psychology* 44 (2015): 135–48. doi: 10.1016/j.jenvp.2015.10.001.

Learner, Jennifer S., and Philip E. Tetlock. "Accounting for the Effects of Accountability." *Psychological Bulletin* 125, no. 2 (1999): 255–75.

Lee, Se Woong. "Pulling Back the Curtain: Revealing the Cumulative Importance of High-Performing, Highly Qualified Teachers on Students' Educational

Outcome." *Educational Evaluation and Policy Analysis* 40, no. 3 (April 2018): 359–81.

Levison, M. "Moral Injury and the Ethics of Educational Injustice." *Harvard Educational Review* 85 (2015).

Lortie, Dan. *Schoolteacher: A Sociological Study*. London: University of Chicago Press, 1975.

Marcus, R. "The Role of Affect in Children's Cooperation." *Child Study Journal* 17 (1987).

Maslach, C., W. Schaufeli, and M. Leiter. "Job Burnout." *Annual Review of Psychology* 52, no.1 (2001): 397–422.

McGrath, April. "Dealing with Dissonance: A Review of Cognitive Dissonance Reduction." *Social Personal Psychology Compass* (2017): 123–62. doi: 10.1111/spc3.12362.

McGray, A., et al. "African-American Women's Decisions to Become Teachers: Sociocultural Perspectives." 15, no. 3, (2002) as quoted in Betty Achinstein, et al., "Retaining Teachers of Color: A Pressing Problem and a Potential Strategy for 'Hard to Staff' Schools." *Review of Educational Research* 80, no.1 (March 2010). doi: 10.3102/0034654309355994.

Meyer, Gregg, and Edward Lawrence. "Just Culture: The Key to Quality and Safety." *Outcome Engineering* (2009).

Meyer, Ilan. "Prejudice, Social Stress, and Mental Health in Lesbian, Gay, and Bisexual Populations: Conceptual Issues and Research Evidence." *Psychological Bulletin* 129, no. 5 (September 2003): 674–97. doi: 10.1037/033-2909.129.5.674.

Mishra, Raja. "Gauging Toll of Abuse on a Child's Brain." *The Boston Globe*, December 15, 2000.

Monteith, Margo, and Corrine Voils. "Prone to Prejudice Responses: Toward Understanding the Authenticity of Self-Reported Discrepancies." *Journal of Personality and Social Psychology* 75, no. 4 (1998).

National Center for Education Statistics (NCES) "Race and Ethnicity of Public School Teachers and Their Students." *Data Point* (September 2020). https://nces.ed.gov/pubs2020/2020103/index.asp.

National Commission on Excellence in Education. "A Nation at Risk: The Imperative for Educational Reform." *The Elementary School Journal* 84, no. 2 (November, 1983): 113–30.

National Education Association. "School Health and Safety." 2002 https://www.nea.org/healthy-schools.

Nelson, Eugene, et al. "Clinical Microsystems, Part 1. The Building Blocks of Health Systems." *The Joint Commission Journal on Quality and Patient Safety* (July 2008): 367–78.

Nelson, Eugene, et al. "Microsystems in Health Care: Part 1. Learning from High-Performing Front-Line Clinical Units." *The Joint Commission* 28, no. 9 (September 2002): 472–93.

Nichols, Sharon L., and David C. Berliner. *Collateral Damage: How High-Stakes Testing Corrupts America's Schools*. Cambridge, MA: Harvard University Press, 2007.

O'Donovan, Roisin, Aolfe Brun, and Ellish McAuliffe. "Healthcare Professionals Experience of Psychological Safety, Voice, and Silence." *Frontiers in Psychology* (2021): doi:10.3389/fpsyg.2021.626689.

Opper, Isaac. "Teachers Matter: Understanding Teacher's Impact on Student Achievement." *The Rand Corporation*, 2019.

Palmer, Parker J. *The Courage To Teach: Exploring the Inner Landscape of a Teacher's Life*. San Francisco, CA: Jossey-Bass, 2007.

Pascoe, John, et al. "Mediators and Adverse Effects of Child Poverty in the US." *American Academy of Pediatrics Technical Report* (2016).

Payne, Charles. *So Much Reform, So Little Change: The Persistence of Failure in Urban Schools*. Harvard Education Press, 2008.

Perry, Bruce. "The Neurodevelopmental Impact of Violence in Childhood." In *The Textbook of Child and Adolescent Forensic Psychiatry*, edited by D. Schetky and E. Benedek, 221–238. Washington, DC: American Psychiatric Press, 2001.

Peterson, Anne, Joshua Joseph, and Monica Feit. "New Directions in Child Abuse and Neglect." *The National Academies Press* (2013). http://www.nap.edu/catalog.php?record_id=18331.

Robbins, Alexandra. "Teachers Deserve More Respect." *The New York Times*, March, 2020. https://www/nytimes.com/2020/03/20/opinion/sunday/teachers-coronavirus.html?.

Rochkind, J., et al. "Lessons Learned: New Teachers Talk about Their Jobs, Challenges and Long-Range Plans." *Issue No. 3, Teaching in Changing Times* (2010).

Ryan, Richard M., and Edward L. Desi. "Self-Determination Theory and the Facilitation of Intrinsic Motivation, Social Development and Well-Being." *American Psychologist* 55, no. 1 (2000): 68–78. doi: 10.1037//0003-066X55.1.68.

Santoro, Doris. "Good Teaching in Difficult Times: Demoralization in the Pursuit of Good Work." *American Journal of Education* 118, no. 1 (November 2011): 1–23. doi: 10.1086/662010.

Sauter, Steven. "Stress . . . at Work." *National Institute for Occupational Safety and Health* Publication number 99–101 (1999). https://www.cdc.gov/niosh/docs/99-101/default.html#print.

Shephard, Lorrie A. "A Brief History of Accountability Testing." In *The Future of Test-Based Educational Accountability* edited by Katherine E. Ryan and Lorrie A. Shephard, 25–46. New York, NY: Routledge, 2008.

Shonkoff, Jack P., and Andrew S. Garner. "The Lifelong Effects of Early Childhood Adversity and Toxic Stress." *American Academy of Pediatrics* 129, no. 1 (2012): 232–46. doi:10.1542/peds.2011-2663.

Silliman, Rebecca, and David Schleifer. "Our Next Assignment: Where Americans Stand on Public K–12 Education." *Public Agenda*, 2018.

Simon, Nicole, and Susan Moore Johnson. "Teacher Turnover in High-Poverty Schools: What We Know and Can Do." *Teachers College Record* 117 (March 2015): 1–36.

Sleeter, Christine. "Preparing White Teachers for Diverse Students." In *Handbook of Research on Teacher Education*, 3rd ed., edited by Marilyn Cochran-Smith, et al., 559–582. New York: Routledge and the Association of Teacher Educators, 2008.

Snyder, C., and Raymond Higgins. "Excuses: Their Effective Role in the Negotiation of Reality." *Psychological Bulletin* 104, no. 1 (1988): 23–35.

Statista. "Poverty Rate in the United States from 19902021." *Statista*. https://www.statista.com/statistics/200463/us-poverty-rate-since-1990/.

Steele, Claude M. "The Psychology of Self-Affirmation: Sustaining the Integrity of the Self." *Advances in Experimental Social Psychology* 21 (1988): 261–302.

Steele, Claude. "Stereotype Threat and the Intellectual Test Performance of African-Americans." *Journal of Personality and Social Psychology* 69, no. 5 (1995): 797–811.

Stephens, Mary Ann, and Gary Wand. "Stress and the HPA Axis: Role of Glucocorticoids in Alcohol Dependence." *Alcohol Research: Current Reviews* 34, no. 4 (2012): 468–83. doi: 2013-28231-001.

Stevens, Jane Ellen. "The Adverse Childhood Experiences Study: The Largest, Most Important Public Health Study You Never Heard of Began in an Obesity Clinic." *ACES Too High Blog*, October, 2012.

Stodder, Sarah. "A Heartwrenching Story about why Teachers are Leaving DC in Droves." *Washingtonian*, November, 2018. http://www.washingtonian.com/2018/11/04/a-heartwrenching-story-about-why-teachers-are-leaving-dc-in-droves.

Sutton, Rosemary E., and Karl F. Wheatley. "Teachers' Emotions and Teaching: A Review of the Literature and Directions for Future Research." *Educational Psychology Review* 14, no. 4 (December 2003): 327–58.

US Dept of Health and Human Services. "Poverty Guidelines 2020." ASPE Office of the Assistant Secretary for Planning and Evaluation (2020). https://aspe.hhs.gov/poverty-guidelines.

U.S. Department of Education. "Every Student Succeeds Act: Summary of Final Regulations," https://www2.ed.gov/policy/elsec/leg/essa/essaassessmentfactsheet1207.pdf, 15.

Watson, Angela. "Why I Quit My Teaching Job Mid-Year (No, it Wasn't the Testing)." *Truth for Teachers*, November 22, 2012. https://truthforteachers.com/why-i-quit-my-teaching-job-mid-year/.

We Are Teachers. "These 2022 Teacher Shortage Statistics Prove We Need to Fix This Profession." Newsletter, June 15, 2022. https://www.weareteachers.com/teacher-shortage-statistics.

Wetzel, Melissa Mosley. "Preparing Teachers with Sociocultural Knowledge in Literacy: A Literature Review." *Journal of Literacy Research* 51, no. 2 (2019): 138–57. doi:10.1177/1086296X19833575.

Will, Madeline. "How Teacher Strikes are Changing." *Education Week*, March, 6, 2019. https://www.edweek.org/steaching-learning/how-teacher-strikes-are-changing/2019/03.

www.ingramcontent.com/pod-product-compliance
Lightning Source LLC
Chambersburg PA
CBHW032023230426
43671CB00005B/177